PATTERNS OF BRITISH LIFE

PATTERNS OF BRITISH LIFE

A study of certain aspects of the British people

at home, at work and at play,

and a compilation of some relevant statistics

With a foreword by

EDWARD HULTON

HULTON PRESS

Published in 1950 by

HULTON PRESS LIMITED

Shoe Lane, London, E.C.4

produced by

Colman, Prentis and Varley Ltd.

printed by

Tapp & Toothill Ltd.

Leeds and London, and Johannesburg

Typography by Peter Ray, F.S.I.A.

A NOTE ON COPYRIGHT

CONTENTS

The text which forms the first part of this book was written by

GEOFFREY BROWNE

The statistical tables at the end of the book

and the seventeen diagrams based upon them, were edited and compiled by

J. W. Hobson and Harry Henry

with the assistance of the staff of Market Information Services Limited

FOREWORD

This is a new kind of book and at first glance it may raise in the reader's mind a number of questions which he would like to ask the editor. For example, "What do you mean by *patterns* of British life—what makes you assume that the British people conform to any patterns—and what use will it be to me to know what they are?" And there will be some readers who reject in advance the idea that people can be arranged in patterns. "We are individuals, we have separate lives, free wills, different outlooks," they say, "and any other concept reduces us to the level of an ant-heap."

They look at their lives and those of their friends and they note that each person has a different character and each life has its particular problems and interests. As they walk in a crowd to a Saturday afternoon football match their minds are filled with anticipation of the game— not with a vision of 50,000 other men streaming through the turnstiles at the same moment. Father and mother sitting on the crowded seafront trying to find something to keep a fretful youngster happy, or wondering where in the world they can hope to buy lunch in this crowd, are absorbed in their own problems and oblivious to the fact that hundreds of thousands of other fathers and mothers all round the British coast are facing the same problems, discussing them with the same words and solving them with the same expedients.

Though we may not always recognize these patterns, they arise nonetheless. They do not arise because men and women have no individuality, no free-will, but because individuality and will must operate in a framework of economic and social circumstances.

Subject to certain local or social variations we must all reach our places of work between 8 a.m. and 9.30 a.m. and therefore we must have our breakfasts at certain times to catch certain trains or buses. Ask the gas and electricity undertakings. They know all about the peak loads throughout the day as the population with one accord makes its breakfast, boils the kettle for elevenses, cooks the midday meal, or has its evening snack or nightcap; does its washing on Mondays, or roasts the Christmas turkey.

It is a sobering and perhaps distasteful reflection on our society that our limited incomes and routine-dominated lives offer few opportunities for us to be "different"; our uniform sources of information, education and entertainment leave us little scope for individual excursions of taste or interest. Whether it is Government control or the mass-production methods of private enterprise which will eventually regulate our lives is not, in this connection, relevant. In either case, when we grasp the consequences of 49 million people living on this small island, many of them in communities of millions or hundreds of thousands, the conclusions are inescapable. If the maximum numbers of people are to be guaranteed as many as possible of the material advantages of modern production or streamlined distribution, those advantages must come to us in uniform presentation—our water supply and newspapers, our cigarettes and groceries, our entertainment and hobbies.

This book depicts a large number of patterns as they emerge in relation to various separate activities. With each activity is associated several commonly-accepted courses of behaviour and the population as a whole (with exceptions based on genius or eccentricity) will follow one or other of these courses, so creating the patterns.

Take holidays as an example. Either a man will or will not take a holiday away from his home. If he does, he will go to the country or the seaside or another town or abroad. To get there he will travel by some form of transport or another—car, train, bus, bicycle or aeroplane. Because custom and the requirement of his job arrange these matters, the duration of the holiday will be one week or two weeks or a long Bank Holiday weekend. Because the summer is the best time for holiday-making in Britain, the holiday will normally take place between June and September, with a peak at the August Bank holiday, and during the school holidays.

When these facts are set out they appear obvious enough. They comprise a sequence of factors affecting 49 million people, which means that very large groups of people must be doing the same things at the same time.

But what is the use of this knowledge? First it is interesting and perhaps salutary to forget our own mode of living and take a view of the rest of the community—to observe the trend of social habits and the regional differences of custom. But the main value, the value that justifies so many firms in spending large sums of money in market research every year, is the view of the market which these figures offer. To know the character of this market a manufacturer must be in possession of a great deal of quantitative data about the habits of the buying public, and it is exactly such hard factual information which this book supplies. It includes, for example, the total number of families, analysed by social class and age of housewife; the average number of children per family in each social class and age-group; the type of accommodation in which they live; whether it has a gas or electricity supply; the number of persons planning to set up new homes. These factors influence the demand for practically every commodity, just as press and periodical readership (figures for which are also given) influence the success of the advertising which sells it, and the statistics on such specific products as cars, bicycles, domestic electrical equipment, beer, spirits and wines, tobacco, cosmetics; on leisure-time activities such as gardening and cinema going, and on holidays, are not only of value to those directly connected with these things, but also to every manufacturer, wholesaler or retailer whose market is to any extent dependent upon them.

In present conditions it is valuable both to the manufacturer and his customers if the production and distribution of his products can be arranged so as to satisfy the maximum number of people—a mass market on a national scale. Goods or services produced on such a scale can be produced much more cheaply and so can be within the reach of much larger numbers of people.

It might be thought that in the highly organized and controlled world in which we live, sufficient information should already be available. In fact this is not the case. There are curious omissions in the statistics published by the authorities, whilst those which are available are not always in a form which permits their combination with other statistics. For example the authorities know how much tobacco is consumed as cigarettes or pipe tobacco and the individual tobacco companies know how many cigarettes they make. But no one can know, except by researches such as are recorded in this book, how many people smoke, to what extent women and young people have taken up smoking, or how many cigarettes or how much tobacco the average smoker consumes. Yet, whether for the purpose of satisfying or modifying future demand, this information is a necessary starting point.

The method of research used in eliciting this kind of statistical data was that of sample survey—that is, 13,000 people were selected as being typical of the entire adult civilian population of Great Britain, it being mathematically demonstrable that such a sample, properly selected, will not differ significantly from the total population in its characteristics or attributes. The sample was so chosen that in respect of such factors as age, social class, town size, type of locality (rural and urban), region, etc., it was a true cross-section of the British people.

Whilst the technique of sampling is too widely used by Governments, industry and commerce throughout the world to need further comment here, it is as well, perhaps, to stress that all the findings given in this book are based on past facts or behaviour carefully and methodically ascertained. In no case are they founded on generalizations, opinions, or estimates of behaviour in hypothetical circumstances.

"Patterns of British Life" shows how, on a number of subjects of social and commercial interest, British behaviour follows certain patterns. Sometimes the general outline of these patterns was known beforehand; this Research records in fine detail what was previously only seen as a silhouette. In other cases the findings deal with subjects on which information of any kind has hitherto been lacking. As a whole it is believed that this book will be interesting and useful to a large number of people whose interests or jobs cause them to concern themselves with the collective behaviour of their fellow men and the community at large.

EDWARD HULTON

WHAT KIND OF PEOPLE?

A visitor to Britain could be bewildered by what he saw and heard during a short stay. When he left he might wonder whether he was lucky to be escaping from a huge concentration camp or whether he had been the privileged witness of a proud people at the dawn of a great new era of social progress.

During his visit he would listen to talk in pubs, trains and other places where ordinary people meet and eat and drink. And he could get almost any impression from this talk. He would hear of a nation tyrannized and in shackles; of resentment crystallizing in an underground movement with the war cry "Set the people free". But he would also hear about people who were wealthier and better fed than before the war. He would hear of the awful hardships of needless rationing, yet most people he saw would appear reasonably well fed, and instead of the emaciated infants he had expected, he would see broods of children who were better looking and healthier than those he could remember in any other country. He would hear of the sorry state of England—no fast bowler, and batting only to number five. There would be talk about apathy and indifference to work which would be difficult to reconcile with what he read about record achievements of production and exports. And these achievements would be nothing short of miraculous in a country where business men seemed always to be growling about crippled initiative, fettering restrictions, and ruinous taxation which stifled all enterprise. But there would be plenty of compromise. The sturdy individualist enjoys his newspaper in a corner seat provided by a state monopoly; the trade unionist reads his while sweetening his tea with lumps from a private monopoly.

Very confusing. Yet our visitor might be forgiven if he took with him one clear impression, that the British were usually preoccupied with inessentials. Export drive? But we're all going to enjoy the match on Wednesday. Our American representative coming on Friday? Pity, I must play off my round for the President's Putter. Tell him to see Jones; Jones was once in Brazil.

It doesn't make sense. Indeed, for a nation which does not care to fill the churches, which were built for a much smaller population, there is an unreasonable confidence that the Almighty will disperse the armada of troubles when it really becomes dangerous. So the games go on, and millions of people watch them. Test matches, County cricket, Wimbledon, Henley, Ascot and other high spots of the summer parade attract record crowds; every few miles in the English countryside the road opens to lovely village greens where, every Saturday, cricketers beget a thirst, and spectators recount with advantages the deeds they once did in these places. Conversation in the darker winter evenings is about the merits of some four-legged beast, or on the wisdom of financially supporting views about the results of next Saturday's football matches, or the advantages of sowing broad beans in the autumn.

All very trivial this must seem to the visitor, for surely Britain is fighting for its economic life. Are the British at all aware of the serious dangers which threaten them? Obviously they must be. Every day the newspapers headline some crisis or another; the government posters point out that the nation must work harder— or else; Ministers of the Crown speak eloquently of a nation which must go forward with its back to the wall; economists point to inflationary spirals, inelastic demands, hard currencies and the dollar gap. There is no lack of exhortation from those in power and of advice from those who know.

And the ordinary people respond by accepting

rationing as necessary and by paying huge taxes. Our friendly foreigner can mark these two things well. Britain is the only country where rationing really works; where the housewife can take her shopping basket and get each week the food she is entitled to have, at prices which she knows, and can budget for, before she sets out. The British, too, are the most highly taxed people in the world, but almost certainly there is less tax evasion here than in any other country. This is not just because of a dumb submission to the law; to pay all these taxes, and put up with all the rationing, form filling and restrictions needs not only patience and respect for the law but also a sense of responsibility and a high standard of integrity. And anyway they have got into the habit of doing these things and putting up with a lot of others.

Perhaps that is the danger; perhaps a lot of the things that were necessary in wartime were done so long that they now remain as habits. These include habits of mind as well as habits of action. In war the needs of the country can be clearly set out for all to know—maximum production of food and other necessary things; every available man and woman in the right job; full production at all costs. And in war, especially if it is accompanied by enough noisy reminders of imminent danger, we all work with a will and give that bit extra. If it all costs a huge amount, that is quite unimportant compared with the need for winning the war.

In peace it is not so simple. The problems are not as vivid as they are in war. When tankers are sunk and men killed it is easy to remember to save petrol. When a bomb blows up £5 million worth of food you realize what must be done about it; it is not the same when someone says that we are that amount short of dollars to buy food. A ship sunk obviously means less goods carried and less money earned; a railway handed over to foreigners to pay for war materials stops earning money to pay for part of Britain's food in peacetime, but the loss is not as easy to understand. In war Britain was fighting for her life. Fear, and the exhilaration of the common cause, united the whole nation in a war effort in which burdens, hardships, effort and finally victory were shared by everyone. Now Britain is fighting for a standard of living. There are

no trumpets and uniforms, and when one has become used to things being short, and when there always seems to be a loan or aid from America round the corner, there is little sense of urgency. Something may turn up; it may never happen; we are not doing too badly anyway.

Of course, the British have shown themselves on many occasions well able to cope with crises. They are individualists, but they can discipline themselves and work co-operatively. But the crisis has to be a fairly personal affair. It has to be something they can see or hear or smell; something that can be understood and related to individual lives. It is no good telling them the drains are bad. Nobody will do anything until there is a bad stench or a flood. General exhortations have no effect. High-minded words like the famous "Your courage, your resolution, your cheerfulness, will bring us victory", did not produce a single extra nut or bolt or potato in 1940; they only amused or irritated people. Yet nearly ten years later they were asked to respond to "Work or Want", which meant no more to the man in the street than that if he were fool enough to throw up his job he would get no wages. At the worst of times the ordinary citizen is slogan-proof; but when vague generalizations about impending doom are put around when everyone seems to be doing quite nicely, when wages are high, employment is secure and seems likely to remain so, when good prices are giving farmers and manufacturers good profits, when everything seems cosy with health services and state education, and there is little need to worry about quality of goods or work, those generalizations can even be dangerous. They seem so remote from the facts of the life of the individual that he is apt to suspect all official warnings.

And even when the newspapers tell of drains on the gold reserve, or suggest that Britain's salvation lies in multilateralism, or when they discuss the dollar gap and the troubles of the sterling area, it is difficult to get very horrified or very excited. The country's affairs seem just enmeshed in some celestial accountancy, and entries in a ledger are no inspiration for a fight.

Does this all mean, then, that the British machine will grind monotonously on until the country is faced with serious unemployment or starvation or some other calamity? It is a depressing thought. Yet that is what some people are saying. This planned economy in peacetime, they say, has no leadership, no impulse, no driving force, no inspiration really to work for the common good or even for one's own good. It is too soulless and cumbersome; it needs the stimulus of fear, the big stick; the nation is so gorged with carrots that it is suffering from the lethargy of overfeeding. This kind of talk does not fit the facts. It is nonsense to suggest that there is now no British way of life in which there is integrity, faith in the future, pride in craftsmanship, pride in giving value for money, and freedom to act on one's own initiative. No, all the traditional qualities are there, but it is true that Britain has still to make up her mind how she is going to use them in conditions which are part the legacy of war and part her own creation in an impatience for social progress.

This book tells something of how people in Britain were living in the midst of difficulties four years after the end of the war. It gives an idea of what work they do, what money they make, and how they spend it; what they are reading, and what holidays they take. It does not pretend to be an academic social study, and it certainly does not trespass into the realms of economic prophecy. But it tells something of the present life and habits of the ordinary man and woman,

the kind of life they like and things they value.

To tell this story we have drawn mainly on the material provided by surveys carried out for Hulton Press. How they were carried out is explained in the Preface to the Tables—and much more statistical detail is given in the Statistical Tables. But as reference is made in the text to people who are well-off, to the middle classes and to poorer people, and, in diagrams, people of different classes and of different income levels are shown as symbols AB, C, and DE, something must be said about this classification here.

The classes are defined in terms partly economic and partly sociological, i.e. the social and purchasing habits, as well as the purchasing power of an individual, are taken as classifying characteristics. The incomes quoted here are merely *typical* of those received by heads of families in the respective grades—they do not, of course, reflect total family income.

Briefly, AB is a combination of two distinct classes. A is the "well-to-do" (over £1,000 per year), B the middle class (£650–£1,000 per year). C is the lower-middle class (£400–£649 per year). DE is also a combination of two grades; D is the working class (£225–£399 per year) and E is the "poor" (under £225 per year). The classes are defined in greater detail on Page 87.

SECTION TWO

HOW MANY PEOPLE?

When *The Hulton Readership Survey* 1949 was carried out there were 49 million people in Britain. The population did not reach that total by a final bound or by any startling increase in recent years. Indeed, since the beginning of this century little has been added to the immense expansion of the previous hundred years.

For the nineteenth century was a period of economic and social transformation. At the speed of revolution a commercial and industrial Britain took shape, with factories, an enterprising middle class, powerful trade unions, and untidy new towns. Harnessing inventions and new techniques, the country was easily first in the industrial field;

by the second half of the century it was the world's manufacturer and banker, and was supreme as the world's carrier. The pound sterling was a world currency, and the world was becoming Britain's larder.

With the exuberant self-assurance of the Victorian era there was an astonishing growth of population. The first census was taken in 1801, and it showed a population of 10½ million in England and Wales; by the end of the century it was 37 million. This rate of growth is probably unparalleled in human history; even the speed of increase in Russia since 1917 seems sluggish by comparison.

Early in the century the rise in the number of people caused alarm. Wise men shook their heads and predicted famine and destitution for a population that would outstrip the means of feeding it, but their forebodings, and some mild propaganda for birth control, did not stem the torrent of babies. The birth rate remained high, the death rate decreased steadily, and the end of the century found the bigger population probably better fed, and certainly better clothed, than it had ever been. Total industrial production had increased continuously. Thanks to machinery, output per worker had raised the general standard of living, and there seemed to be no limit to the expansion of our markets and certainly population problems cast no lingering shadows on the scene. Population statistics were just a reflection of the vigour and vitality of Britain in this period. Indeed, without this great and rapid increase in numbers, her leadership in industry would have been

shortlived, and her influence on the economic development of the world would have been far less than it was.

The last few decades have been very different. Certainly there have been inventions as important as those of the nineteenth century, and there have been changes so big and fast that the Victorians would have been shocked, but the population has increased little. Even before the end of the nineteenth century the birth rate was falling, and since 1931, despite the low death rate, the population has crept slowly up and has increased by only 4 million. The confident abundance of the mid-Victorian family has given place to the caution or prudence, or selfishness or pessimism (it has been called all of those) of to-day. Britain to-day has 49 million people, but the changes that have taken place in our population are much more important than mere totals suggest. Alterations are occurring in the age structure of the

CHART 1

THE POPULATION OF GREAT BRITAIN, 1871-1949

Divided into three main age-groups

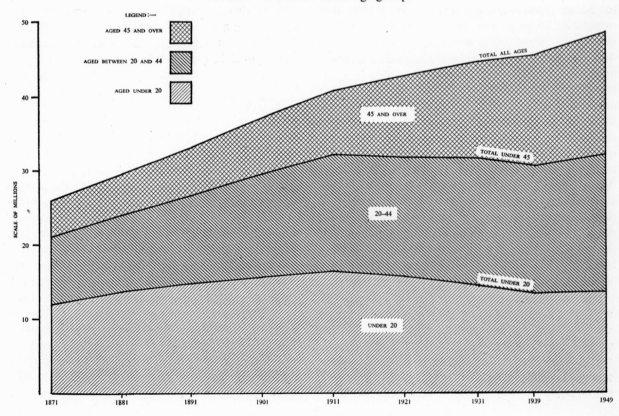

population that are of the utmost importance to the future of the nation. The average age of the population was under 27 in 1891: it is over 35 now. These changes are laying the foundation of the type of life our children will lead, and are making new problems for them and even bigger responsibilities.

Yet the significance of these changes is so often clouded by broad generalizations, half truths and scaremongering that it is not surprising that the ordinary citizen shrugs his shoulders in bewilderment and decides to take his family to another country, whose prospects may really be much worse than Britain's. Some expert paints for him a picture of Britain in the not-distant future, half-deserted, with disused factories and empty, decaying houses, but he still finds himself well down on the list for a new house. Then he reads that there are alarmingly few children and that it is his duty to produce more, yet the children he already has are crowded out of the local school. Very confusing.

But some facts are clear enough, and they tell us a great deal about the future course of events. At present it looks as if our population is likely to increase, but only for a time. How long the population will go on getting bigger before it goes down is not just a matter of excess of births over deaths this year or next. What it really depends on is the *net reproduction rate*, that is, the rate at which mothers are being replaced by other mothers. For a long time before the war the net reproduction rate in Britain as in many other European countries was less than 1·0, which means that mothers were not being replaced in equal numbers. If the rate remains at less than 1·0, and if people do not suddenly become able to live much longer than they do now, the population will eventually decline. Thanks to a post-war boom in babies the rate for the last three years has been above unity. So it was from 1920 to 1922, but it fell again and, in spite of the present family allowances and the national health service, it is unlikely that another fall will be avoided.

Statisticians have estimated what is likely to happen if recent trends return. They suggest that the total population will probably go on growing for at least one or two decades, but the increase will be small. In about thirty years numbers may begin to fall slowly. Perhaps that need not worry us. The resources of this country are already strained to maintain our present population in reasonable comfort, and smaller numbers might be a good thing. That is one school of thought.

But population is not just a matter of so many heads to count. What concerns us now, and will worry us a good deal more in the future, is how many little curly heads there are to pat, how many heads there are of breadwinning age, and how many grey heads are bent over the fire waiting for next Friday's pension. A glance at our own family album shows us something of what has been going on. In that picture taken forty years ago our grandparents are surrounded by a docile and self-conscious brood of children, but in last year's holiday snaps there we are with just our two children, who, we are glad to see, are bigger and fitter looking than those in the older picture. The nation's family album tells us much more. In 1901, one person in three was 14 or less and half the population was less than 25 years old. Now only one in five is under 15 and one in three is under 25. Near the other end of life the changes have been as big or bigger. At the beginning of the century less than 20 per cent were over 45; now one-third of our population is more than 45 years old. In this fast moving world perhaps 1901 seems just a year in ancient history, but more recent events are even more striking. In 1931 the population was less than 45 million, but there were nearly 7½ million school children aged 5–14; in 1948 when there were 49 million people there were only 6½ million children in that group.

Population figures like these are not just the dull raw material of unimaginative statisticians. They concern all of us whether we are industrialists, doctors, shopkeepers, school-teachers or merely pensioners with plenty of time to buy our rations. For instead of the expanding markets which we have become accustomed to, there will be shrinking markets at home for many varieties of goods and services, while people will want more of other things. Some industries, or parts of industries, will become redundant as the demand changes for different types of goods and services, while other industries will have to expand or adapt their production to altered conditions. The home market for children's toys is likely to diminish while manufacturers of ear-trumpets and cribbage sets may do well; baby foods will give place to the fancies of the aged, perambulators to armchairs. The boot and shoe manufacturer will gradually have to change his production plans to his changing clientele as the patter of small feet yields to the slouch of carpet slippers.

These are ready examples of the type of re-adjustments that may have to be made by the producer. But the effects of changing population are to extend much further; indeed, they will extend right through the economic and social life of the country. The pattern of the future market will evolve slowly, with the gradual change in the structure of the population. But consumers are at the very end of the production line. Population changes are already creating headaches further back on that line. Workers are getting older; their average age is already a good deal more than it was a generation ago. Whether we think of our major industry as coal mining or football, steel manufacture or playing test matches, the story is the same—higher average age of the people in those occupations, and workers as a whole will soon be fewer as well as older as the death rate rises, as eventually it must rise. Fortunately, people are living longer nowadays than they did even a few years ago. The boy of 5 can now expect to live about five years longer than his father was expected to live when he was 5. Women, too, are living longer.

This greater expectation of life, and the enormous drop in infant mortality—from 8·2 per cent of births in 1920–2 to 4·1 per cent in 1947—reflect the great improvement that has taken place in the nation's standard of health. Longer life and more chance of living do something to relieve the problem of manpower, and to postpone its worst

CHART 2
THE POPULATION OF GREAT BRITAIN, DECEMBER 1948
Divided by sex into ten-year age-groups

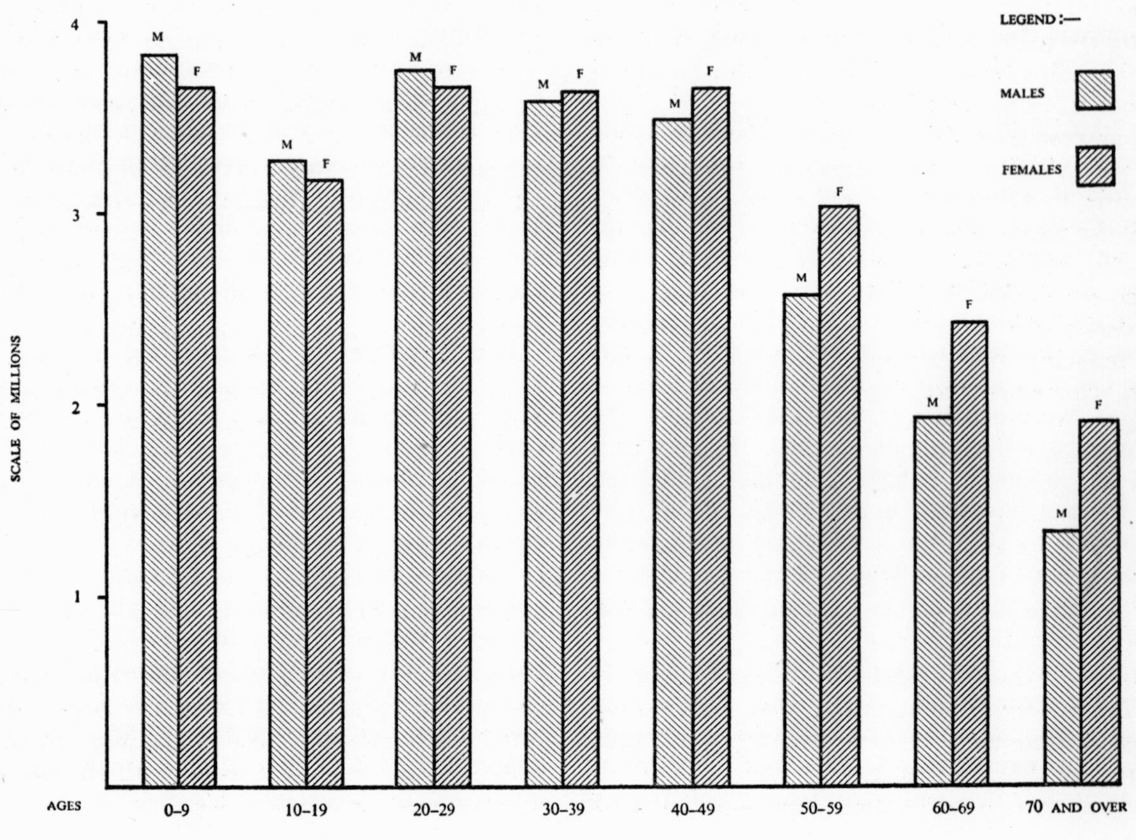

effects, but they do not remove the difficulties. Indeed, unless people (and this includes women employed outside the home) produce much more when they are at their jobs and, perhaps, spend more years of their life working, the increase in longevity could be an additional burden on the country. It would mean more non-producers to be supported by those doing the work, more pensions to be paid out of the national income. It is estimated that retirement pensions will cost the Exchequer £500 million in 1978 as compared with £238 million in 1948.

Obviously, things would be made worse if many young and active people emigrate without taking their aged or disabled relations with them. This does not mean that people should not be enterprising and take jobs in places away from their home town. On the contrary, necessity will make workers as well as industries go where they are most needed. It will be necessary, too, to guide young people into the right jobs. Already we see that the drift to London is arrested, that new industrial areas are being built, and new industries are replacing redundant ones in other areas.

But the main solution to this problem, as it is to our present one of balancing our overseas accounts, is more production per worker, and just as new power and resources and the greater use of machines confounded the pessimists a hundred-and-fifty years ago, so may new power and new means of using it enable an older population to maintain its standard of living. New machines and industries, and fresh technical processes can increase output per worker and, by reducing the amount of physical strength used, can enable an older population to work longer.

These are probabilities. We cannot foretell what inventions will come to our rescue, but it needs no crystal gazing to see that the demand for capital goods—power plants, machinery, tools and equipment of many kinds—which is already great, will be much greater for a long time, even though the population may soon start to decline.

In outline, without detail, this is the shape of things as they may be. Parents' caution, and the toll of two wars, has already drawn a new pattern of population. In a few decades we shall see whether present portents spell gloom and permanent decline, or whether numbers will be stabilized at a level more in keeping with the amount of food and other things at Britain's disposal. One thing is certain: parents nowadays have more power to control the number of children than they had in early Victorian times, and they are going to exercise that control. This is not because they are selfish; modern parents probably give more care and attention to their children than parents did years ago. Possibly their sense of values is wrong by some standards, but most people now are realists, for in periods of depression and instability such as the early 'thirties, the marriage rate went down and the birth rate was low. Obviously and rightly marriage and parenthood are influenced by moral and spiritual factors, but they are also determined by people's incomes, by how much taxation they pay, by the design of houses, availability of domestic help and labour-saving equipment, by the price of milk and the cost of education and perhaps the prospect of war. Other things, too, are the value they put on leisure and various forms of recreation, whether a wife and mother looks upon her work as a dutiful joy or a dreary drudgery, and how rosy the future seems to them.

Tables relating to the foregoing Section will be found on pages 89 to 92

SECTION THREE

THE BRITISH HOUSEHOLD

This is a crowded country. By the standards of all English-speaking countries, and most others, it is far too crowded. In Britain as a whole, there are 552 people to the square mile; in England and Wales alone, about 750. Just for comparison, Canada has no more than a quarter of our population, yet three or four Britains would go into a single Canadian province, say, Alberta, and there would still be plenty of room round the edges.

By far the greater part of our population lives in towns and cities—three-quarters of it, in fact. True, there are still about 9 million people in villages, hamlets and isolated farms and houses, but despite the foreigner's idea of the Englishman's lonely taciturnity and his own as a man of the wide open spaces, the English are a gregarious race. Inclination, the industrial revolution and sheer pressure of numbers has made them so. Like starlings they flock together, but there is this difference. Starlings congregate for a glorious natter after their day's work; the Englishman adventures in the great cities by day and returns to the impregnable bastions of his home and family by night.

For the great majority, the family is the focus of British life, and for most men and women over 24 years old, and for many less than that, this means married life. Of men of 16 and over, 67 per cent are married, and of all women of 16 onwards, 60 per cent are married; the smaller percentage of women married is because there are more women than men.

Not only is the proportion of adults who are already married very high, but the marriage rate in this country is well maintained. The rate is naturally influenced by the state of other things than of the hearts of the people concerned. For example the rate was low during the economic depression of the 'thirties and when many men were away in the forces; it was high at the very beginning of the war when, with unknown dangers ahead, young people sought this security. This is just what we should have expected. The marriage rate in Britain is also much the same as it is in most of the white nations, and, unless there are some fundamental changes in the moral or religious attitude to marriage, or unless economic or other circumstances are unfavourable, there is not likely to be much change in the rate.

Recently, however, there has been on average rather less chance of marriage continuing until death parts the couples. The divorce rate has been exceptionally high, and comparisons of the figures in the last fifty years or so are eloquent. In the 'eighties of last century the annual number of divorces was only about 300; in 1938 there were 7,800 and in 1947, 53,883. There are all kinds of reasons for this astonishing change. First, there are far more marriages to be dissolved. Then the

moral attitude to marriage has changed and divorce does not have the same social stigma as it did in Victorian days. The greater number of children in Victorian families made divorce a bigger family upheaval and economic dislocation than now. Family life then was for most people infused with the general atmosphere of assurance of that period. Most important of all, the Victorians were never subjected to the stresses and strains of ten years of war and the subsequent readjustment to new conditions. The very high marriage rate at the beginning of the war has obviously had a great influence on the number of recent divorces. But we shall leave examination of the causes of the current state of divorces to moralists, sociologists, anthropologists and cynics. We are mainly concerned with how people are living together in their communities; how many families, how many are living alone for one reason or another, and so on. So far the great increase in divorces has had little mathematical effect on the general marital status of the population. There is, however, one feature of the recent divorce figures which is more than just a statistical curiosity. Lately, more men than women have taken the initiative to get divorces. Before 1941 it was women who mostly filed the petitions; from that year more men have done so. If this goes on let us hope that at least it will reduce man's present ascendancy in homicide and suicide.

Returning to the figures about those who are still married, two facts stand out. One is that wives as a whole live longer than their husbands. The percentage of women who are on their own from the age of 65 is nearly twice that of the lonely men; in actual numbers the difference is even greater. There is nothing sinister in this, no drama of overwork or of nagging wives, just the physiological tendency of women to live longer than men.

Then the willingness or opportunity to marry is obviously influenced by financial position. Of the men in the more wealthy classes nearly three-quarters are married, but of the poorer ones the proportion is two-thirds. Similarly with the women.

But rich or poor, or somewhere between, most people in this country take on the responsibilities, joys and sorrows of marriage sometime in their lives. For the great majority of women this time

CHART 3

THE "ADULT" CIVILIAN POPULATION OF GREAT BRITAIN, SPRING 1949

Divided by sex, age and marital condition

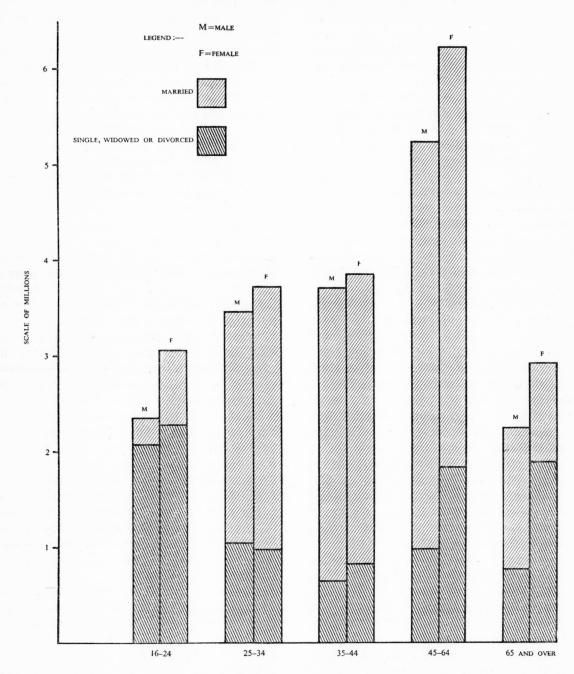

is before they are 30, and so, in their married lives, they usually have at least twenty years during which they can bear children.

In early Victorian days they not only could but did bear children and lots of them. Then, as now, it was woman's unique—many would still say their most important—function; but then, unlike now, it was their principal and, for some, almost their sole occupation. Women created a man's world. They had no vote; there was no Married Women's Property Act. They just ruled the home, and that only until the husband came home. *Punch* was able to picture her:

> I'm mother of seven and enduring my lot
> Without envying others the things I've not got.
> You may think me unhappy, I assure you I'm not—
> I'm a mother of Early Victorian days.

Enduring her lot, submission to the stronger or noisier sex, docility and gentility were the attributes most looked for by the male head of the household:

> My dearly-loved children, they quail at my nod.
> I bring up my brood in the fear of the rod,
> Thus discharging my duty to them, and to God—
> I'm a father of Early Victorian days.

Conditions have changed since those days. The brood of seven ruled by the despotic father and served by the apparently docile, and certainly prolific, mother have themselves begotten generations of children. If a strident Victorian dictator were to come down from his self-built and well-deserved heaven he would get a horrid shock. He would see his great-great-grandson aproned at the sink. First, he might admire the versatility of a descendant who was obviously coping unaided with the chores while the wife was ill or upstairs bearing another child. Such, he would say, is the result of war and of giving the lower orders opportunities of working above their station. When he learned that the wife was not a mother and was that evening addressing the local Labour Party on psychological incentives in industry he would say nothing, but return as soon as possible to his heaven where, at most, women could play second harp.

He would find plenty besides the fall of man to shock him. No longer the crocodile to church and evening prayers at home, and the Sunday ceremony of allocating to each of his many domestic responsibilities an area of the huge English sirloin of beef appropriate to their age and position. The catalogue of change and horror would be an unending one, but the most haunting memory of his visit would undoubtedly be the altered structure of the household, and man's changed status in it.

In his day the family of twelve might evoke a smile of admiration for the man and wife who were so conscientiously doing their duty to God and the British Empire. No more than that. Nowadays such a family is news, an oddity in a country where households with one or two children only are usual and with more than two becoming exceptional. Moreover, while there would still be occasional smiles of admiration for modern parents of this fecundity, there would be more murmurings or enquiry about their sanity, ignorance and intelligence quotient. The mother would be pitied and not envied by other women; men might think of her as a curiosity but not as an intellectual companion. We are very used to the small families, and most of us knows how to control the size of our own families, so we are apt to think of large numbers of children as a sign of ignorance or of passive submission to religious principles. Indeed, looking for a moment at the family structure of this country, we might think that there is something rather odd about having children at all. Of nearly 15 million households, there are just over three-fifths with no babies or other children. These households, of course, do not all consist of married couples. They include men and women living on their own, and friends living together, but just about a quarter of all the households consist of couples with no children.

We have already said something about the reasons for this. People know about birth control and are sensibly determined to use that knowledge. This does not mean that the English do not care for children. Certainly they do. More is lavished on children now than in any previous period. Perhaps it would be more accurate to be technical and say that each child gets a bigger proportion of a higher standard of living or material welfare than in days gone by. More pocket money—possibly too much—more toys, more books. And visits to cinemas and other entertainments often at an age so early, and to films so unsuitable, that again the Victorians would be horrified, unless they knew that it was only by taking the children that parents can go anywhere themselves. Then, children, especially those of the poorer parents, are better fed and clothed than they have ever been, as anyone who has lived for fifty or even thirty years in an industrial district could testify.

Nor are they forgotten by the State. Leaving aside direct financial benefits like income tax rebates and children's allowances, there are meals in schools, cheap milk and free milk for mothers and children and better equipment of schools. The nation has not forgotten her children. They have the tender regard of all political parties and the riches of an elastic purse. Thus, the fall in birth rate and the fewer children of school age does not mean that because where there were seven children there are now two or three, the market for children's things in that household has gone down to a half or less of what it was a few generations ago. Children have a higher status in the family. Instead of instilling meekness and obedience with the rod, parents are now encouraging their children to play a full part in the life of the household. A great part of that encouragement consists of material things. May-

be parents realise that they and their generation will one day depend on their children's efforts much more than did any previous generation of parents.

We have said a great deal about children, and in later Sections we shall say still more. A typical household then is one where there is a man and wife and a child or two. But there are many others, possibly a growing number, where people are living on their own or in twos or in groups of their own sex. More of these are women than men, partly because there are not enough men to go round, partly because women live longer than men. There are, too, a great many other reasons for this and as they also have a great deal to do with the present sizes of the family we shall look at some of them. These reasons mainly arise from the changed status of women.

A visitor returning to Britain after forty years

CHART 4

THE COMPOSITION OF THE AVERAGE FAMILY
In total and by social class

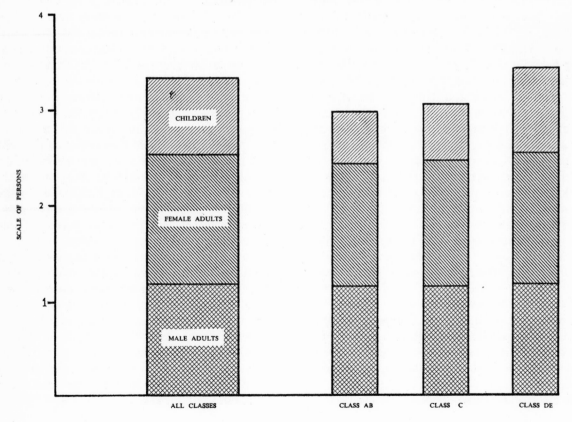

in Darkest Africa would certainly notice that there were fewer children than when he went away. He might or might not deplore the fact that the few were more audible than the many he left. But he would notice even more the great change in the status of women. He would enjoy noticing this and would pursue his researches with enthusiasm. For unless he had been driven to destroy lions by unrequited love for an Edwardian beauty, he would find the women nowadays better to look at than those he left behind in 1908. Possibly if he visited the West End of London first of all he would see little difference. Rather taller girls with rather shorter skirts and less bustle there would be, but, if he came just now, their styles might not seem greatly changed, though he would notice that these women would be parading with their neat umbrellas rather self-consciously as though with an unaccustomed dignity. Until he had settled down to the washing-up at the home of his married sister in Wimbledon he would deceive himself that Britain stood where it did. The rest of his disillusionment would be rapid.

But suppose he were an ex-M.o.H., an artist, or just a he-man from the jungle who liked looking at women, he would be impressed as he went around. Women of all classes, well-dressed, fewer hats but more lustrous hair, good complexions and finer teeth, figures pleasant to study, and limbs of length and symmetry he had not suspected. He would find, in fact, that women— and children too—reflected most remarkably and aesthetically the rise which had taken place in the general standard of living in the last few decades. They are better off, and they look it. Or perhaps we ought to be more cautious and say, most of them are better off and they all look better.

So much, at present, for appearances. Very pleasant they are, but when, in intervals of pegging out his other sister's washing, our visitor went around he would notice the great increase in the number of women about. Women bus conductors, women doctors, women soldiers, women clerks—millions of them—women with pitchforks, women company directors, women everywhere. That would interest him; it might not alarm him. He might reflect that in Africa the women did plenty besides rock cradles, but

here, unlike in Africa, a great deal of the really heavy work still seemed to be done by the men. On further investigation he would find that the country was ruled by women, for there were more than a million more women voters than men, and as far as he could see there was still a democratic system of government. That would shock him until he found that by far the greater number of M.P.s were men, just as he would find that most people in charge of almost anything except the Women's Institute, were men. That would restore his pride and his respect for woman's judgment.

Eventually he would see most of the evidence of women's emancipation. He would hear a good deal of it too, how the needs of two wars had established women's place as citizens: as workers side by side with men, and had stimulated, or confirmed, their intentions to make careers for themselves even when not coerced by wartime emergencies to do so. Nowadays, it is not less important for the daughter than for the son to be trained for a job. With an ageing population her efforts are needed. But even if they were not, few families would wish to support an idle daughter for long; and few daughters reconcile themselves to helping in the house, hoping for some young man to come to suggest that she contracts to do the same kind of thing for him on a long-term basis.

Nor are careers an alternative to marriage. With possible intervals for bearing children, it might be financially necessary for a married woman to carry on with her job and, probably, if she had no need to be kept at home by children and other duties she would want to go on working. There are still men whose masculine pride compels the woman of their choice to spin out two hours' work in a three-room flat for a whole day. But they are few. There are still some women who revel in an idle dependence on the man of their designs, but those who are temperamentally lazy generally prefer to idle in a more lucrative way.

Our friend from Africa would gradually learn all this and more, and in time would even have opinions on some outstanding problems like that of equal pay for equal work, whether cooking and baby bathing ought to be taught at Eton, who should do the housekeeping accounts and, indeed, who should provide the housekeeping money. He would also see the reason for a number of things that might have puzzled him when he first arrived. He would, of course, find in the changed status of women a great part of the explanation for the small number of children. That is obvious enough. It would explain why there were so many women in the morning trains, especially the earlier ones; why there were so many shopping baskets decorating business and government offices, why there were so many women students at the universities, in evening classes, at concerts and theatres and public lectures. Women have new responsibilities and new interests; perhaps most striking of all they have more money than ever before and more freedom to spend it. This last may or may not be the feature in their new lives most prized by women, but it is the one most in evidence. More will be said in a later Section about incomes and spending habits; at this point we need merely suggest that many women in employment have far more money to spend than they had before the war, and without a corresponding increase in the number and size of their commitments. This is a generalization and like most generalizations there are many exceptions to it, but it is none the less true as a whole. Indeed, employed women generally have a greater proportion of their incomes left to spend on clothes and non-essentials *for themselves* than can be afforded by most men in jobs.

Our susceptible visitor will probably think that appearances testify that the spending power is effectively used. Possibly he might think that while a pipe lends dignity and a hint of intelligence to a man, a cigarette does not do the same for a woman walking in a mink coat along Regent Street, but that would not affect his general opinion. He might wonder, though, whether what he had been told about equal rights by his unmarried sister in the Board of Trade was all quite true. There were still some disconcerting things he did not quite understand. One was that when he was cad enough to listen to conversations in buses, and while waiting to be noticed at the tobacconist's, the subjects of women's discussion seemed to have changed little since he was a boy. Now, as then, marriage in all its facets, clothes, parties and then more about men were the dominant topics. This seemed to be confirmed by a study of the women's magazines.

He might be pardoned if he came to the conclusions that, as he would immediately if he looked at our statistics, marriage was still the most important part of a woman's scheme of life and, that judging by the magazines, sex appeal mattered quite a lot to her working life, perhaps even to keeping her job.

He would notice also that although exceptions are sometimes made for those who were old, lame, or obviously pregnant, women were allowed to stand in buses and trains, but that they were usually accorded certain priorities and attentions. For example they were often encouraged to enter and leave lifts and trains first; this was always so when arrayed for an evening's entertainment and looking especially feminine. Also, despite the sometimes higher earnings of the girl friend, neither sex seems anxious to deprive the man of his traditional role of doing most of the paying. These things are just sidelights on the position of women of the present day. But they show that changed economic and political status has not altered the outlook of women quite as much as those who first fought for their emancipation might have wished. Chivalry is still apt to spread its protective cloak even in days when so much of the original reasons for chivalry have disappeared.

Nevertheless, in the structure of the family the womenfolk have an enormous influence on the amount and direction of spending, not just as the ultimate beneficiaries of man's whimsical generosity, but as spenders and budget planners in their own right, and with the encouragement of such men as may be around. They are dominant, too, in households where people are living not as families but on their own, because there are far more women doing this than men. Many have the dual role of breadwinner and housekeeper, usually with no help, and they have to plan their lives so that their housekeeping leaves them with energy, efficiency and comeliness for their paid jobs, and so that their jobs give them time and money enough for their housekeeping.

In the next Section we shall see a little more of how and where these people and groups of people are housed, and the problems that arise from their living. Meanwhile, we have noted something of the types of household which has to meet these problems. They are mostly married people, many without children, and only few with large families; many people living alone or with friends, and of these a large proportion are spinsters and widows, women fending for themselves. Throughout there is the greater and more direct influence of women in domestic finance and, indeed, in the whole buying of consumers' goods.

Postscript on pets

But this Section cannot end there. If it did it would show a shocking ignorance of the British household and, indeed, of one of the characteristics of the race: its love of animals. This affection is obvious to any foreigner, and it sometimes puzzles him. A Bill about animals can fill the House of Commons, while one aimed at relieving pain in childbirth, or at improving the welfare of children, may be ignored by all but a few. A father may go a long way out of his way to avoid meeting friends when he is pushing baby's pram. Babies embarrass him, but a dog will give him an air of virility and confidence, just as his pipe gives the impression of keen masculinity. A downtrodden housewife, too, assumes an unsuspected tone of authority when gentler persuasion ("he always comes when I call him") has failed to distract her fox-terrier from close study of forestry or from a cosy chat with an Airedale. A hulking brute of a man can even get sympathy for beating an erring wife, and a wife can go unscathed if she starves her husband, but any transgression against a pet dog or cat will bring the odium of the neighbours, enquiry by half-a-dozen societies and the attention of the police.

The reasons for his love of animals are deep-rooted. At least one foreigner has suggested that the Englishman's kinship with animals is because they are equally uncommunicative. Be that as it may, the affection takes a great variety of forms which reflect the character of all parties. One may choose for her companion the attentive, active and portable Pekinese; another the solemn, sultry St. Bernard; others shun the servility of dogs and prefer the graceful independence of cats. Then there are those whose instincts are to share the benefits of social security by keeping birds in cages, some for their song, others for their conversation. Others get joy enough from watching birds moving freely in fields and woods and by the sea.

There are also many people whose love of animals is altogether different. It does not really become manifest until the animal is killed and cooked, or has been deprived of its fur, or until its stuffed head glares from the billiard-room wall. Destruction for these ends is time-honoured, though some rituals of destruction can be bewildering to the observer. For example: if a fox were caught and tortured by dogs in a backyard the owner of the premises would get into serious trouble. His action would be cruel. But if he dresses up, digs up a fox, encourages a pack of hounds to chase it and finally tear it to pieces, he is just maintaining a respectable tradition. It is a tradition, moreover, that the Englishman knows the fox approves; otherwise it would not run so long or so fast.

Pets are certainly a part of British life. About one-half of all the families in the country keep at least a dog or a cat or a bird in a cage. To some householders one pet is the only constant companion; to others it is the friend of the family. Whatever may be their motives for keeping pets, the British look after them well. Possibly some visiting racehorses may run faster than ours, but no other country has so many handsome, contented and well-fed carthorses. Then one has only to contrast the healthy dogs, often of a recognized breed, in the British street with the mangy mongrels which slink around in France and Italy to understand why the British dog unconsciously adopts his master's sense of superiority.

Tables relating to the foregoing Section will be found on pages 92 to 100

THE ENGLISHMAN'S HOME

The word "home" has a different meaning for different people. To the New Zealander home means England, even although he has never been there. When an American refers to his several homes he is not alluding to the diversity of his affections, but to the fact that he owns several houses which he and his family can occupy. Similarly, other English-speaking people, outside this country, usually say homes or homesteads when talking about what we should call houses. If we said to a Canadian that someone was breaking up our neighbour's home, he would think it was the work of a demolition company unless we explained that the trouble was really a willowy brunette.

Even to people in this country, home has meanings varying according to the context in which the word is used. It can be the place a man returns to after struggling for a day at the factory or office; it is where a woman's work is never done; with suitable prefixes it may be a place for stray cats, or where children of richer parents are born; it has great significance when we are making our forecasts for football pools. There are plenty of other uses of the word, but in all of them we get the impression of a place where we live, where we are known, have security, possibly privacy and peace, or which is our sanctuary in this troublous world. Whether we are football stars or just ordinary citizens, to be at home gives us confidence. Usually we use the word in association with family life, but when we do so we are probably using it in narrower sense than was ever the custom in this country. According to historians, home, or the words from which it was derived, meant a settlement or the place of a group or tribe.

In Britain we like to think of ourselves as home-lovers, as a homely people, and by the standards of most nations we are probably right. When the man is not working he withdraws from the world to the company of his wife and children and busies himself with the affairs of the home. For him this busying may take a lot of forms, from really helping with the house and bathing the baby to just making encouraging noises to stir the wife to still greater efforts. For the woman the interpretation is less elastic; she just goes on working. Home, in a wider sense, is apt to dominate our lives at Christmas when other generations of the family are gathered together. We like to entertain our friends at home rather than take them elsewhere for their food and amusement. Certainly we do entertain more at home than, say, the Americans, but they might contend that this was due to lack of imagination, opportunity or money, or was just another form of exploitation of women. They might be right, too, in at least some of their suggestions, for with more facilities for travel, smaller families, and on average more money per person, the influence (some might say, the tyranny) of the home has diminished since Victorian days.

For with all our regard for hearth and home, there is sometimes a hint of second-best about them, a suggestion of something we settle down to when other and more exciting opportunities elude us or are past. We do not mean that there is a constant desire for boys to run away to sea or into the Government service to escape from the controls of home, or for girls to elope to escape restrictions—though, of course, there are always rebels. No, our disparagement is more general and gentler than that. The girl next door resents being called homely even although she aspires to be some day a wife and, later, a mother. She resents the term now just as if someone had said she was a good sort really, or meant well, or wore sensible shoes. It is because when applied to young people, whether married or not, homely implies comfortable, ordinary and well-scrubbed; in fact, just like the mouselike creature a few doors away, who has none of our glamour and only one boy friend. Perhaps it is just that way with the young. She will be far from offended if, when she is 60, she is called a nice, homely person. That is the real proof of the Englishman's belief in the home.

An etymological study of the word "home" is complex enough and leads us into prejudices and over national boundaries. There is infinitely more variety in the actual physical structure and conditions of the millions of homes in Britain. When Mr. Simpson, the manager, says to his secretary, "Miss Lightly, I am going home now. Please tell Mr. Simpkins, and don't wait yourself," where does he go? Then, what kind of a place does Miss Lightly go back to, and Mr. Simpkins? While we are about it, what about the other girls and clerks on the firm: the accountant and the chairman of the board of directors? Even when we have answered those questions we shall not have even touched the fringe of the pattern of British homes, the homes of the millions of industrial workers, the million or so people making a living on the land, and of those who are living on pensions, dividends or savings. Obviously it is impossible to draw a detailed picture of all those but from the information available we can get a rough idea of the main types of family accommodation and some of the problems arising from each.

Houses or flats?

In Britain there are rather more than 15 million families. Of these nearly 30 per cent own their own houses. As we should expect, the proportion of those owning houses is much greater for the wealthier sections of the populations than for those who are not so well off. Of the people who are classed in the Survey as well-to-do (though many of them would be irritated, flattered or at any rate surprised to be so called) about two-thirds own the houses they are living in. This, of course, does not necessarily imply affluence, since a very large proportion of these houseowners really own only a part of the houses they live in as they have obtained mortgages to purchase the properties. Nevertheless, they will one day be owners in their own right.

The proportion of houseowners in the lower income groups is much less. Of the lower middle classes, Simpkins and his fellow clerks of moderate seniority, about half own houses, while in the lowest groups—and the great majority of families come into them—just about one person in five owns his house. These differences in proportion as between the various classes are what one would expect, although with the great extension of mortgage facilities in the last few decades the

differences are almost certainly less than they were. Whether owned or not, the British like having a house to themselves rather than sharing them or living in flats. Taking all sections of the national household, over three-quarters of the families are living in houses, and about a third of these families own their houses. Living in self-contained flats comes a very bad second. Only about one family in six does this and the overwhelming part of these rent their flats as unfurnished; only about 140,000 families live in furnished flats compared with some 2,500,000 families in unfurnished ones. Rather less than a million families share houses, but as these figures were compiled from a survey carried out only four years after the end of the war, this number is likely to diminish as house building outpaces the increase in the number of families.

These figures tell us more about the British character than about the type of accommodation the people have. Most people like living in houses rather than flats, and they like having a house to themselves. They like their own private domain which can be locked against the outside world and, perhaps as much as anything, they are a nation of garden-lovers. They want space to grow flowers and vegetables and to sit on Sunday afternoons, and they want it to be private. This peculiarity is taken as a matter of course by the people themselves, but it used to irritate architects and town-planners until they realized that there are some deep-seated characteristics too stubborn to change by planning. The planners were of course right. This passion for houses and gardens is all very well in a country where there is plenty of space for each person, but in Britain where there are too many people for the available area, it must be exasperating. A block of flats accommodates the same number of people as does a number of houses and takes only a small fraction of the land area, even allowing for a communal garden. The advantages of flat-dwelling are obvious. When work and habit makes people live together in great cities, the case for flats seems unanswerable: the architectural tidiness of blocks of flats compares favourably with the sprawl of thousands of uniform villas. This very uniformity of so many of the houses provides still further argument against them. Maybe there is not much difference in the character and personality of the outside of

Flat 14 and Flat 414, but there is no more in any of the houses down the street.

The British have listened to all this, and to the sympathy and jibes of peoples from other countries, and they still want their house and garden. For some reason they spurn the neigh-bourliness of the handsome block of flats and ignore the blessings of central heating, rides in lifts and feeding in a handy restaurant, and even the view of the close-clipped lawn and privet hedge. Like the cat that has her kittens on a pile of newspapers under the stairs instead of in the

CHART 5

FAMILY ACCOMMODATION

Type of home, by social class

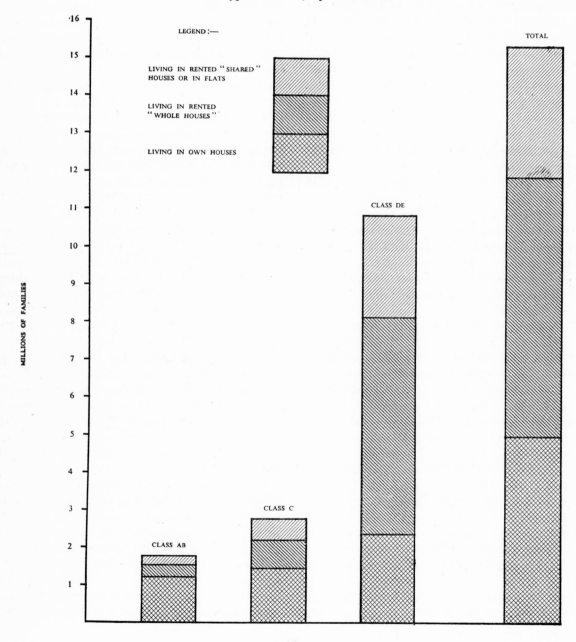

LEGEND :—

LIVING IN RENTED "SHARED" HOUSES OR IN FLATS

LIVING IN RENTED "WHOLE HOUSES"

LIVING IN OWN HOUSES

TOTAL

CLASS DE

CLASS C

CLASS AB

MILLIONS OF FAMILIES

lovely padded basket in the hall, they prefer it that way. Orderly minded people can be consoled by the knowledge that the dislike of flats is not as strong as it was, say, thirty years ago. Convenience, smaller families, lack of domestic help, and occasional outbursts of passion for America's idea of progress, made many people flat-minded between the wars. Now, with the added expedient of meeting shortage of accommodation generally, there are more of these people.

The proportions of people living in houses and flats are statistically neat, but we need to know much more before we can get a clue of the way the British live. We want to know what kind of houses there are, what amenities they have, and just how many people live in them. Official information on these points is scanty, or relates to only some areas. A Government census was taken in 1931, but that is not much help to us now for a million houses were destroyed or damaged during the war; also the population has increased and standards have changed. There is an urgent need for more up-to-date information about the structure and condition of buildings and the degree of overcrowding, and when we have that information it will surprise some of us.

At present we are obsessed with the housing shortage, with the problem of getting enough physical space under cover. Our preoccupation with housing shortages is natural enough after a war of destruction, a war of making-do with partially damaged and insufficient accommodation; of living with relatives and friends; of being evacuated and taking in people from more dangerous areas. The end of the war brought men and women back from the Forces who wanted to rear families, but found there was not enough houseroom to do so in a reasonable standard of comfort and privacy. For many, the prolonged nagging of these conditions caused more neurosis than the noisier and more dangerous episodes of the war.

But by any reasonable standards there has always been a housing shortage in this country. For centuries a large proportion of the population lived in appalling conditions of overcrowding, insanitation, inconvenience, damp and filth. This was so before ever the industrial revolution brought its smear of congested squalor; behind the facade of elegance described by the articulate

upper classes life in the cottages was often terrible. Creepers hid damp and cracking walls of some, and the mellow exteriors of others, blending with their surroundings, hid from the passer-by the state of the inside. When the rise of industrialism added the horrid works of the get-rich-quick builders who exploited the workers' enormous demand for housing of some kind in the new mining and manufacturing areas, housing conditions reached still lower depths, and these conditions were very widespread. There is no need to describe them here. Others have already painted the lurid picture, but our concern now is that, despite generally higher standards of living and the benefits of Housing and Health Acts, there still exists to reproach our civilization a large part of this legacy of dreadful houses. Perhaps we now build permanent houses with greater knowledge and sense of responsibility than many of our ancestors. Let us hope so, because, as we know only too well, jerry-built houses are apt to last a very long time. Built at the lowest cost to house workers for a new factory, they survive for generations after the original industry and workers have been forgotten. The population grows, and we have not the time, resources, or good taste to replace these houses with better.

This does not apply only to dwelling houses. Once we have built a post office or railway station it is with us for all time, unless it is removed by earthquake or enemy action. We were active in the industrial field before other nations and were building railways, factories and houses in the mass at a time when taste was fairly terrible and what there was was subordinated to profit-making. It is therefore not surprising that our railway stations seem quite atrocious when compared with those at Los Angeles or San Francisco, and that our older post offices compare so badly with those in New Zealand, or with our own newer ones.

There is another point about the permanence of bad houses and, indeed, of all housing, which was too often disregarded in the past, even in the very recent past. That point is the use of land. In times when food growing was secondary to industrial and commercial expansion, factories, houses and towns were built on any land irrespective of its value for farming. Obviously there must be some encroachment on agricultural land, but big areas of first-class land have been needlessly but permanently withdrawn from growing food, where less productive land could have been used. In the past "land ripe for development" often meant the final devastation of good land by concrete.

It is not, however, so much with the public buildings or land, but with domestic accommodation that we are now concerned. A visitor to any of our industrial cities can testify to the slums we have inherited. A traveller in the countryside will have to be more vigilant, for the charm of so many of the houses, and the beauty of their surroundings, can deceive the unwary. A Government Committee reported in 1943:

> "Apart from the actual shortage of cottages, the general standard of accommodation, equipment and services was, and still is, very low. Thousands of cottages (in England and Wales) have no piped water supply, no gas or electric light, no third bedroom and often only one living-room with no separate cooking or scullery accommodation. For the great majority of rural workers a bathroom is a luxury."

Then, according to the British Electrical Development Association, in 1939 about one-third of all dwellings in rural district areas were not electrified. It was estimated that only about 30,000 agricultural holdings out of a total of 365,972 were served with electricity in 1938. Much the same story was told about water supplies and drainage. In June 1939, it was said that out of 11,186 parishes, 3,432 had no piped water supply. Sewerage was even worse. At least 5,186 parishes were entirely without sewerage systems in 1939, and conditions have not changed very much since then.

To some town dwellers taking a summer holiday away from modern conveniences, there may be something romantic about washing under the pump, about going to bed by the light of oil lamp or candle, and about logs tastefully laid for the cooler evenings. The countrywoman has other views, and younger ones who can do so move elsewhere. They know the labour in January of filling, cleaning and trimming a dozen oil lamps, of standing in the rain pumping water into buckets, and of carrying heaps of logs from the shed every day. All this has to be done apart from the ordinary tasks common to any home: cooking,

washing, cleaning, mending, amusing the children, and the rest; and all done with the minimum of assistance from the design of the house and its lack of public services: no electric cooker, no vacuum cleaner, no electric iron. These conditions are common enough in most parts of Britain and they are not so very unusual even within thirty miles of London.

We have certainly inherited some ugly, back-breaking and rheumaticky houses; houses with basements and ill-designed; houses not designed at all but seemingly just constructed as cheaply as possible from a heap of bricks; we tolerate badly converted flats and rooms with fireplaces made between doors and windows. True, the interiors of many old houses have been made comfortable and have beauty rivalling their lovely appearance from outside, and we have a wealth of beautiful new houses and well-constructed flats, but we have a tremendous number of the others.

We are apt, too, to take for granted the lack of convenience and of labour-saving equipment in the home. We are used to things as they are, perhaps we cannot afford the improvements we know to be necessary, or our landlords will not sanction them, and, if it is the place we know and which has our family and belongings, we do not want to move to anything else. This was evident enough during the war when people living in slums in danger areas had sometimes to be persuaded and even coerced to move.

Also, we make trouble for ourselves with our traditional prejudices and fancies. Take, for example, the open fire. We love open fires. Every day for some months in each year we clear away ashes and carry scuttles of coal to perhaps several rooms. Then, according to the quality of the coal and when the fire was last made up, we shiver in a draught or draw our chairs away from such heat that has not gone up the chimney; and we leave a beautiful fire to warm the empty room after we have gone to bed. It is not that our heating engineers and architects are not ingenious. They are, and they have devised all kinds of systems which really heat a house and do it economically, but we still like our open fires.

Another idiosyncrasy which interests and infuriates visitors from civilized countries is the way we test our strength and cunning on the quaintest collection of cisterns and chains. These certainly give individuality to the Englishman's home. It is only when the visitor is leaving after a fairly long stay that he really understands their little ways. But except that we put up with these things, and sometimes are even fond of them, we are not wholly to blame, for we were pioneers of so many once modern ideas, and made our fittings so durable, that we are still using the experimental models which other people have replaced or improved.

Yet, as a whole the nation is well served with gas and electricity. Four out of five households have one of these services; more than half have both. For a country with very little water-power harnessed to generate electricity, and with plenty of other uses for its coal, these proportions are high, although, as we have seen, in the past the companies do not seem to have thought it worth-while spreading their benefits into rural areas. Indeed, even in districts within short distances of towns and cities, electricity companies were sometimes asking country householders to pay as much for connection as their houses originally cost to build. The charges are still high and materials for main services are not plentiful so the manufacturers of lighting sets and of bottled gas and suppliers of fuel oil are doing well. Certainly they are likely to have ample scope for some time to come.

When both gas and electricity are available, most people prefer to cook by gas. Perhaps this

CHART 6

HOUSEHOLDS WITH GAS AND ELECTRICITY SUPPLIES

In total and by social class

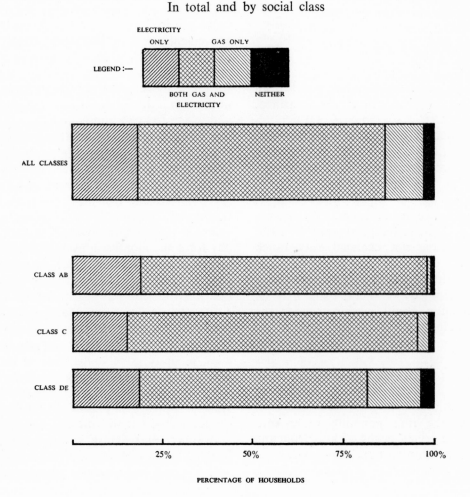

PERCENTAGE OF HOUSEHOLDS

is just another manifestation of the British passion for the naked flame; perhaps it is lack of initiative or of money to change over from something that was installed first. When it comes to ironing clothes the preference is reversed, and for refrigerators neither service is much ahead of the other. In fact, compared with other English-speaking countries, and especially North America, we have scarcely started to use refrigerators. Perhaps we have not the same need for them as our climate is what geographers, with restraint, call temperate. But when it comes to devices for washing clothes and dishes our resistance is not so easily understood. Even although husbands nowadays are sometimes fairly readily enlisted for domestic jobs, their efficiency and patience do not compare with those of the underpaid treasures who toiled for long hours in middle-class households before World War I.

In this apparent lack of enterprise in doing things about home amenities we must not forget our climate. We determine every summer to lag our waterpipes with felt and specially to protect the one on the north-east corner of the house, and when the pipes burst in February we wish we had done so. When cold draughts blow the carpet up we promise to fill up the huge gap under the drawing-room door, but somehow it does not get done. The trouble is that our climate is seldom sufficiently cold or hot or wet or dry long enough for us to prepare for something that may not happen again for months. Our attitude to all this is expressed by the philosophical plumber who was asked by the American woman why our waterpipes were outside the house. He said, "Well, they would make much more mess if they burst inside".

This attitude is common, and few would sacrifice the individuality of their homes in order to live in the roofed machines as some ultra-modern dwellings seem to be. But we are now having to pay more attention to the efficiency of our houses for the simple reason that we have not the labour and energy to go on as we have done in the past. There was a time when the middle and upper classes employed servants to cope with the inconveniences of their houses. There was plenty of this labour and it was reconciled, if not content, to work at very low wages.

Those days are gone. Some of the richer and not-so-rich families do have help of some kind, but not the kind of help that rises at 6 a.m. and works steadily throughout the day and half the night. In 1947 about one in seven well-to-do families had resident domestic assistance, but very few of the middle and lower-middle classes had any help living in the house. Of the lower-middle class wives, only one in five had any help at all in the house even for an hour or two a day. For the wealthy the number of resident maids is still decreasing, and now one-half of well-to-do and middle class families have daily help only and 40 per cent have none. Now that there are so many other jobs open to them, girls and women of other classes do not want to work as domestic servants although the wages offered are sometimes seven or eight times as high as they were a generation or two ago. Who can blame them? Traditionally the social status of the domestic worker is low and, by the very nature of the job and the contact with the employer and her family, the worker is constantly reminded of this. The girls prefer the regular hours of a shop or factory, the company of others of the same age, and meeting people who are not just the friends of the employer. They prefer all this although often they would probably be better off financially, and certainly more comfortable, as a worker in a good house. Also, the wife of the artisan has not the same need now to supplement the earnings of her husband by doing domestic work. Nor do some of them relish working a few hours a day for someone else as well as doing all their own chores, when their old man thinks he is overworked with an 8-hour day, five days a week. These are just some of a whole complex of forces which are making women and girls reluctant to do domestic work for other people.

All these reasons are understandable, but their effect is to make the middle and upper classes, many of whom, the professional people especially, cannot afford the existing scale of wages, revise their ideas of home. Already enormous changes have taken place: from big houses to smaller ones, from houses to flats, and all the time more labour-saving gadgets are being introduced. In spite of this, however, there are too many middle class women, and men too, who are having to spend far too much of their energies in just doing

CHART 7
HOUSEHOLDS WITH ELECTRIC FIRES, VACUUM CLEANERS AND ELECTRIC OR GAS REFRIGERATORS, SPRING 1948

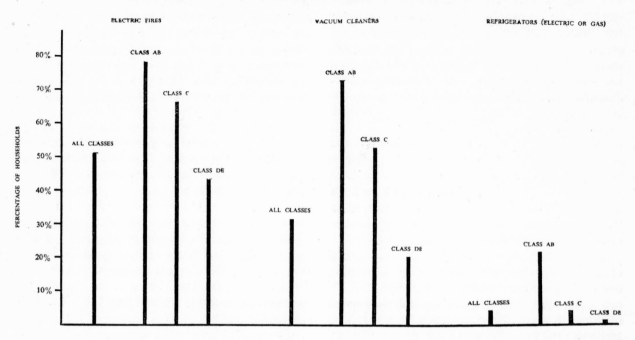

things for and about the house. When the complexities and delays of rationing are added to housework and nursing, life can be a nightmare for these people.

In the circumstances a revolt against parenthood is to be forgiven. The Survey shows how many of the financially better-off people with children have no domestic help. Education has often fitted them more for cultural pursuits than for domestic work. This may be a fault of their education and an error of judgment by their parents, but some might say that to curb cultural development amongst the professional classes could be a loss to the nation. Others would suggest that the talk about middle class cultural pursuits was all their eye; from their observation the lack of domestic help and child-minders merely cut down the length and number of bridge evenings. We are not concerned with arguments like this. Whether they are deprived of bridge or ballet, killing animals or creating masterpieces, there are too many middle class people fastened to the sink. Many have yet to find a way of keeping houses with space and time enough to think.

But they will not find it by grumbling about the working classes. It will come through abandoning some of their prejudices, in more and better equipment in the home, and more neighbourly co-operation.

Then what about those who are paid by the week and do not call themselves middle class? They too would like to see much more labour saving in their houses; for they are financially better-off than they were, the husbands work shorter hours for more money, they know—though some knew only recently—what it is to have leisure and not be too tired to enjoy it. These people insist on higher standards than before and they are willing to pay for them. These higher standards may be better things in their homes: vacuum cleaners, electric irons, washing machines, quick-frozen meals, refrigerators, or just better furniture and fittings. The higher standards which they value may be outside their home: the motor-bike or car, visits to the cinema or football matches, cycling clubs and means of spending a restful or strenuous leisure. Higher wages and shorter hours give means to use the many opportunities for recreation and entertainment outside the home that have appeared in the last thirty years.

The increase in these opportunities has made older heads shake in sorrow at the passing of home life. They need not worry. The British family cherishes its home as much as ever. The woman has plenty of pride in its appearance and organization, the man's flowers and vegetables quietly compete with those next door; the family are glad to ask other people to their homes. True, there is greater freedom to come and go than in Victorian days, but while "going places" is more frequent, the coming home is less reluctant than when the home had the totalitarian atmosphere of rights and obligations and continual duties. Affection for the home is spontaneous, and for that reason it is greater and truer than when home meant prison with hard labour for the woman and irksome rules and regulations for the children.

Tables relating to the foregoing Section will be found on pages 100 to 106

SECTION FIVE

GARDENING INTERLUDE

There are many paradoxes in the Englishman's character, but it is probably in his attitude to the land and to country life that it seems most contradictory. Official statistics tell one story, and the Englishman himself tells another. According to records, Britain has a smaller proportion of its population directly earning its living from the land than any other nation in the world. Only one in twenty of the working population is engaged in agriculture. In the heyday of the industrial and commercial materialism of the nineteenth century, Britain handed over its corn-growing to other countries, and it was as indifferent to the way these countries exploited their soil as it was to spoiling millions of acres of its own best lands. Its people crowded into cities, many of which were built for expediency and without design and some of them wholly ugly and squalid, overhung by a pall of sulphurous smoke. Such a people one would suppose must be blind to all beauty and must have forgotten that they have inherited some of the best land, and the loveliest countryside, in the world. They must have forgotten that flowers grow.

Yet this is not so. Listen to men's conversation in the 8.18 on Monday morning and, later, to the chatter at the office and factory. It will be about gardens. It will be of jobs done despite the difficult week-end weather; of seeds sown; of progress made. There will be discussion of the best methods of growing cucumbers and arguments about the best varieties to grow. There will be boasting, and wonder, and disbelief, but each man will talk confidently of his own plot or garden which differs from all others, and which is the place where he himself is an individual and different from all other men.

For the British are a nation of gardeners. Economics, absentmindedness, choice of vocation, the wife's insistence on electricity and a hundred other reasons may have led them to settle in towns, but whatever they do there for a living most of them still keep a big part of their hearts for their gardens and the countryside. They like making things grow whether it is in a window-box outside the kitchen, or in the dream garden of many acres. Some talk of californian poppies, others call them eschscholtzia. Some take infinite pains with each seedling, and will manure and dust and spray to encourage it and to ward off all of the myriad dangers that threaten each cherished growth; each rose or cabbage will be a miracle of nature's work and man's, but seemingly with nature only a fair second. Others, green-fingered geniuses, will act with instinctive abandon and create a garden envied by all the neighbours.

The garden is where man reigns supreme. In the house he must behave warily and obediently. He is allowed to wash up the dinner things, he can replace the washer on the kitchen tap, he may distemper the hall with the colour chosen by his wife, he can eat what he is given, and sit and read the paper when there are no jobs for him to do. But this is not his kingdom. He can suggest, but he cannot command, and he must be careful where he leaves his shoes or his pipe if harmony is to be preserved. In the garden it is different. Provided he produces vegetables when wanted and flowers for the drawing-room, and leaves space enough to hang out the nappies, he can do as he likes. He can create a formal world with symmetrical beds of tulips, geraniums and asters in their seasons, flanked with privet and peopled by concrete gnomes. Or he can find his pleasure in an ordered wilderness of flowers and shrubs where there is colour all the year.

The garden reflects the temperament of its owner; it also flourishes by his skill, care and industry. Watch how the gardens grow behind a row of new houses. The houses are identical in design, the space behind each is rectangular and they are all the same size. Yet in a season they will tell a great deal about the kind of people who live and work there. The man with faith will plant trees; the far-sighted, who can think of better things to do than pull up weeds, will have paved his paths with stones or concrete; the mountain-minded will have his rockery; the mariner his pool; the unimaginative will have half his plot growing potatoes; the connoisseur will be shifting his cloches from one row of strange plants to another. There is the man who believes everything he sees in his gardening book. His digging has the precision of the diagrams, he measures each application of manure, his peas are exactly two inches apart, and (the prig) his tulips are all the same height. All these gardeners are there. From the railway carriage window you can see something of the spread of ideas through furtive peeping over the fence or just the power of persuasion of the expert. Sometimes three gardens in a row have concrete paths, or the same kind of seed frame, or the same proportion of vegetables. Perhaps this is just an expression of neighbourly co-operation.

You will seldom see a suburban garden neglected. Pride and fear of local talk see to this, but more than anything it is due to the simple and inherent wish to make a garden. It will be made wherever opportunity offers: in a box in a back-yard, in the virgin soil around a prefabricated house, in the devastation of bomb damage, and where there is no space around houses it will be in an allotment. For some people there is no opportunity for gardening; for a few others there is no desire to grow things. They may prefer the great convenience of flat-dwelling and to buy their vegetables and see the charm of gardens without any of the anxiety and hard work. That is their affair or their misfortune, but even of these there are many who, when they can, will get right away to the peace of the countryside. For the British are really country-folk at heart. Although the majority are now crowded in towns, they are not so many generations removed from their rural ancestors, and they are proud of it, and often dream of returning in later life to the cottage set in a garden. In the meantime they make the best of what opportunities come their way.

The gardener is an individualist. He seeks to create something that is different and his own. But he is always experimenting, reading about gardens, listening to and giving advice, comparing notes with other gardeners; for though they are jealous of their results, gardeners are united in making the best use of ideas and in the common battle against slugs, black-fly, wireworms, canker, blight, jays, and cats that must always sit on seed-beds. They are always interested in new fertilizers and new tools and fresh ways of using old ones. They will read and criticize the article about growing beans, and they will really study the advertisements for gadgets and things that might help them to do a better job and with less chance of getting lumbago. Each has his special interest in growing vegetables, in roses, or in the herbaceous border. Some combine gardening with keeping hens because they like hens, or, more likely, because they see in those perverse creatures a useful method of converting worms, beetles, scraps and rubbish into a handy and eatable form. We see these preferences in the crowds at flower shows and other exhibitions where perfection inspires or intimidates the ordinary man.

Whatever may be the individual whims and fancies, the love of gardens is deep-rooted in the British people. They have faith enough to grow trees and make lawns. They find in gardens the satisfaction, variety and recreation they often cannot get from their work. In times of food shortage, too, gardens give a greater sense of security, just as at these times the nation comes to know some of the real value of its agriculture. Whether there is famine or abundance, or whether there are 100 million or 10 million people in Britain, and even if babies drive themselves in atomic prams, the British will find time for gardening and be proud of their countryside.

Tables relating to the foregoing Section will be found on pages 107 to 108

SECTION SIX

EARNING A LIVING

Whether we like it or not, most of us have to spend a very large part of our adult lives working for a living. However much we love our families and homes, or cherish our independence and the things we like doing most, work of some kind rules our lives. What we do for a living, and how we do it, determines how and where we spend the best—or worst—hours of the day, and may even colour the rest of our waking hours. It governs the type of home we have, how much and what kind of food we eat, what we wear and what our children wear, and the type of holidays and luxuries we can afford.

We have some choice in what we do for a living, but very few can avoid doing work of some kind. As individuals we work because we have to work, because we can exchange the value, though usually at someone else's valuation, of our services for the means to live. Our living standards depend on how much we can exchange our services for, and that in turn depends on a great many personal resources as different as skill, energy, luck, honesty and the colour of our hair. In general this applies just as much to the nation as a whole as to an individual citizen. The amount we can produce from our national resources, the skill and energy we use, and the bargains we make in exchanging our products for those of other countries, all these determine the way we live. On production in its many forms depends our diet and all the other physical things that make up our standard of living; on production depends what kind of health service we can afford, what pensions we can look forward to, and the standard of luxury we can offer in our prisons. Production means working for our living.

The British are an industrious race. It is true that young people of each succeeding generation are told by their elders that they have forgotten how to work. Unfortunately, the delirious devo-

tion to duty and toil which is alleged to have existed in days gone by contrasts with the tranquil scene so often painted by authors at the time. The young of every century, and no doubt of every country, have always been the victims of this kind of propaganda, and as we envelop the idle office boy in admonition and cigar smoke we shall likewise exclude from our own success story how and when we gained our prowess at snooker. Now and then, foreigners point scornfully at our own sloth and warn us of our decadence, but events sometimes confound or reassure them. While the Englishman does not love work for its own sake, he usually gets things done when he must, and he does not mistake bustle for business as do many Americans. His trouble is that he needs some fairly big shock, like an enemy staring across the Channel, or the threat of national bankruptcy, really to lure him from his hobbies. He will have plenty of suitable shocks to encourage him for some time yet.

We care about our spare time, but nowadays we cannot afford the luxury of an able-bodied leisured class, people like the French nobles of the eighteenth century who lived by taking a proportion of what others grew, or by levying taxes on them. Civil servants and the armed forces are about the only big class who live wholly on the fruits of taxation, but, whatever else may be said about civil servants, they are certainly not idle. In this country more than nine out of every ten men of all classes and aged 16 and over are working for a living. As this proportion includes all those considered to be past the normal retiring ages of 60 or 65, this means that of those in the prime of life only a tiny percentage are not working, and that percentage will be unable to work because of some disability or another.

For women the figures are very different. At first it looks as though women are apt to leave

CHART 8
PROPORTIONS OF ADULT WOMEN WORKING FULL OR PART-TIME
By marital status and social class

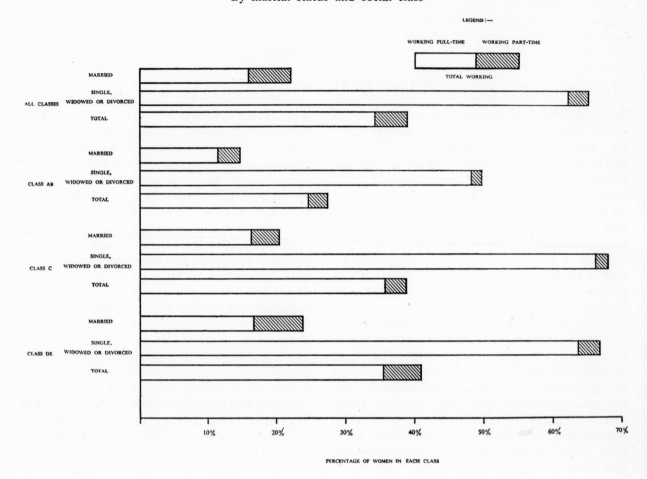

most of the serious work to their menfolk. Only one-third of them are working full-time and apparently only two out of five do any work at all, which goes to prove what many have suspected—that statistics are an iniquitous instrument of man. Certainly, any figures which show only how many women are "working for a living" in the accepted sense of being employed for some financial reward by someone outside the family circle, do not do justice to a hardworking sex. What is surprising is that, with other strong claims on their time for work in the home, there are so many women who go out to earn a living. With women's employment there are, however, some class distinctions. Of the women in the upper and middle classes, less than one in three works outside the home either full-time or part-time, while two in five of the poorer women are working. These proportions refer to all women; the differences between classes are even greater for married women, but if we had figures for earlier years we should probably find that more women of the wealthier families are earning their living now than in the past. There are the jobs to do, and with high taxation and a rising cost of living, fewer middle class people can afford not to do a paid job.

This is a sign of the times and these conditions will continue, but despite the need for women to work in offices, fields and factories, and sometimes their own desire to do so, it is the home, cooking, housework and babies that still govern most women's lives. Young women take jobs almost as readily as young men; nearly three-quarters of girls between 16 and 24 years old are fully employed in paid work, but soon after that most of them have managed, or been persuaded, to abandon that way of life for the usually busier and more responsible one of marriage. Whatever their motives may have been when they first started work, for most girls a job merely spans the period between leaving school and getting married. Moreover, those who do carry on their jobs, whether they are married or unmarried, give them up earlier in life than do men. There are very few women doing paid work from 65 onwards, whereas the majority of men are still plodding on at that age and some will do so until they are removed in an ambulance.

There are fairly obvious reasons for men's longer working life. Few have the dual job of earning their living and being a housekeeper, so they can go on working without other claims on their time, except the claims of leisure and hobbies. More important is that very many of them just cannot afford to retire. Whereas the majority of women working for a living are either keeping just themselves, or are supplementing their husband's earnings, most men have far more financial responsibilities, even after the age of 60. With the changed status of women these differences may possibly decrease even more than they undoubtedly have during the past half-century; but if there is still to be family life, if the race is to continue, and unless women become the equal of men at most jobs outside the home, there are always likely to be fairly big differences in the working lives.

From now onwards there will always be a bigger proportion of women earning a living than there were before the war. Apart from their own inclinations, the country cannot afford to do without their help in industry, commerce, in the professions, and even in the Forces. That was inevitably so during the war, but the need for their work will make them an important feature in the changing pattern of employment in the future, for this pattern will change in the future just as it has in the past. Once, and not much more than a century ago, this country had more

people busy on the land than on all other jobs together. We were even more an agricultural nation than either Australia or New Zealand is now. But the coming of industrialization brought, in a few decades, more changes in the mode and tempo of life here than had occurred in the previous thousand years.

The main events of the nineteenth century are familiar to most people and we need not concern ourselves with history as recent as that when most of us have taken part in a revolution of our own. Before the shock of war came to these islands a new shape of employment was evolving. Agriculture had had plenty of encouragement in World War I, but since then it had steadily lost workers to other industries, until in 1938 less than 5 per cent of our total workers were on the land. Low wages, sometimes non-existent profits and poor housing and other amenities were the main causes of this drift from the land; the increased use of machinery was partly another cause and partly an effect of it. Although Britain had a smaller proportion of its workers engaged in farming than any other country, the movement to the towns was world-wide for much the same reasons as in this country.

Other things were happening here. Workers were going from some other staple industries like coal mining and cotton manufacture to find jobs in general engineering, motor and aircraft manufacture, making wireless sets and other electrical goods. Some of these industries were quite new; others were older ones which were adapting their products to a new demand. Perhaps most striking of all was the way workers were finding their way into those jobs concerned not with making things, but with selling them, and with financing production. If we look at the figures of employment from 1921 onwards we find that the number of people employed in distributive trades, in commerce, banking and insurance gets bigger all through the years, and they seem to draw their workers from several of those big industries which were so important to us in the nineteenth century. Then, in the years between the wars, all kinds of new industries grew up or expanded. Before 1914 we were used to the idea of industrialism in Britain and we had long ago given other countries the job of feeding us for most days of the week, so the changes which took place after

World War I did not seem like the revolution which indeed they were.

World War II showed us something of the strength and weakness of the structure of employment that had grown up. The neglect of agriculture was an obvious weakness. It was neither sensible nor safe, and it has cost a great deal in organization and money to get farming somewhere near to the place which it should have in our national life. The war, and the years after the war, have shown us the folly of letting our coal mining get into a mess, undermanned and badly equipped with machines. After all, coal and the fertility of our land are about the only natural resources we have in any quantity. Coal we must have for heat, light and power in our homes and factories. We cannot now buy our food at bargain prices and, indeed, only part of what we want can be bought at all. In contrast with coal and agriculture, the drift from another staple industry, cotton, could well have been greater than it was. The size and inflexibility of our cotton industry between the wars was in some ways an embarrassment to itself and to the country. Many of its products were no longer able to compete with those of newer textile industries in other countries, yet it stuck to old methods instead of trying to meet changed demands with new ideas.

On the credit side was the development of skill in a great variety of industries. In this country we have plenty of skill and inventiveness and, between the wars, these qualities were put to many good uses. They were applied to dozens of industries and processes in which precision, fine workmanship and well-organized research were wanted. Although we did not equal the Americans in adapting ideas, improving them, and translating them into mass production, we were easily ahead in original invention. The list of things that helped us and our allies in the war is a very long one: radar, television, penicillin, medical and chemical products, fighter-planes and fighter-bombers are just a few items. Our future, too, depends very much on the use of skill and machine craftsmanship. If we can continue to make up for our lack of native raw materials with use of native skill, the things we make will have a high value which will stand us in good stead when we exchange them for food and other products that we must import. Britain is no longer the only workshop of the world, but we can see to it that the world looks first to us for quality goods. So it is healthy and good for Britain that more people are earning their living in specialized engineering industries, chemical manufacture and jobs like that. But there is another change which we are not so certain about.

How much does it matter that a larger proportion of people seem to be taking jobs in distribution, finance, and in Government service? The movement towards distribution, banking and finance was severely checked during the war, but it had been steadily going on for the previous twenty years or so. It was not just due to the attraction of a white collar and the wish to work with a coat on. After all, snob inclinations in themselves cannot create demand for that kind of worker. The fact is, that the 'twenties and 'thirties saw in this country a growing interest in the techniques of selling in all its forms, while banking and insurance, besides expanding with the general growth of economic and social activities in Britain, were doing increasing business for other countries. We could afford to have more people in these occupations. Increased production in industry due to improved methods and machines meant there were more things to handle; the standard of living was rising.

In contrast with distribution and banking the number of people employed by the Government increased enormously during the war, and for many years yet it may remain much bigger than it was at any period between the wars. We must be careful what we say about this. People are apt to take sides when talking about the civil service, and both sides talk a lot of nonsense and use terms like bumbledom, idle bureaucrats, the dead hand of bureaucracy, the heaven of a planned economy, and squandermania, which does little more than put the civil servants on the defensive. Some of this banter does no harm, and could even do good. For although most civil servants are conscientious, hardworking people and are doing an essential job, some of them are just part of the general hangover from wartime organization. When we have settled down to something like the peacetime administration that we need, these people will go elsewhere. Criticism is healthy, too, in keeping in check that minor empire building we suspect goes on sometimes. While the freedom from the anxieties of profit-making may leave the civil servant's brain the clearer for his work, one feels that this organization would be better for some greater spurs to efficiency than exist at present.

But these points divert us from the main issue, which is that as a nation we are insisting on a lot of things being done by the State which once we either did as individuals or did not do at all. Health services, free or cheap meals, unemployment benefits, pensions, educational services, maternity benefits, cash allowances for children—all these have been introduced or expanded in the last generation, and they have come to stay just so long as we can afford them. Nationalized industries also have come to stay. All these activities need workers. Maybe the new workers concerned with nationalized industries will justify themselves by their contribution to production, but just how extensive our social services will be depends in the end on just how much we as a nation can produce. We do not know the answer to this yet; nor have we solved the problems of the right balance and relationship between Government and private industry. We shall do so in the end, and in the meantime we shall need a lot of civil servants. At present one in ten of our working population earns his living in national or local Government work, and this does not include those men and women in the armed forces and auxiliary services.

So we see something of the kind of things we do for a living. Rather more than a third are engaged in engineering or manufacture of one type or another; a little over a million are working on the land, while transport and shipping together employ rather more than that. The number of miners creeps up, but still it is less than just before the war and we have more than twice as many civil servants as miners. Well over a quarter of all the people earning a living are women and some of them do this as well as form part of the silent, hardworking army of housewives who run the homes of Britain. Then there is a group of people in various professions: doctors, lawyers, economists and many others.

What we have described is the general pattern of work, so general that it is an outline drawing with little detail. It tells little of what goes on within the various groups; exactly what things are made or services performed, how many lenses are made for Hollywood cameras, how many hairdressers and candlestick-makers there are. Perhaps some of our occupations would not stand up to limelight, perhaps an X-ray would be too revealing. Nevertheless, we know something of the general trends of employment.

But while doing work is important especially, the motive for doing it is even more important to us as individuals. This is no place to analyse all the reasons why people do the amount or type of work they do, but we can say this about ourselves: that we are not much influenced by slogans which tell us that we must work or want, or that work makes Britain strong. Those general statements and expectations leave us cold. We need something less remote from our immediate comfort and more likely to affect our next meal. We know that if we all worked less or not at all something terrible would happen, but we realize much more that if we personally did not work we should get no pay. As individuals we work not only because we are going to be paid for what we do, but because that pay can be converted into things which we need. There are, of course, other motives for working: good nature, pride, love of the job, prestige, duty, patriotism, and so on—but for most of us the motive is the goods and services we get with our wages and the leisure we are able to afford when the job is done.

Just as there have been broad changes in the types of jobs we have been doing, so there have been changes in the amount we have received for our work. As a whole we are very much better off than we were a century or even fifty years ago. Maybe we are not any happier than we were, but we have certainly more comforts and more material things. For most people the standard of living is higher, much higher, now than it was in 1914. More people are better fed and better clothed, their houses are more comfortable, they have more and better holidays, they are better educated and are a good deal cleaner. Some people are undoubtedly worse off, but it is estimated that the standard of living of the majority in this country has increased by 35 or 40 per cent since just before World War I. Hourly wage rates as a whole are more than three-and-a-half times as high as in 1914—in some jobs like domestic service the rise has been very much more, while retail prices in general have not much more than doubled. Wage earners are getting a bigger share of what is produced and, thanks to inventions, machinery and better methods, there is much more to share and very much greater variety of goods and services.

We have compared present standards with those in 1914. Some of us can actually remember 1914, but more of us know how things were in 1938 and how we ourselves have fared since that year. Many people really admit that they are better off now than before the last war; some are quite sure they are not doing so well, while others, with incomes whittled by taxation in one form or another, but who are buying food at prices which they know are less than they should be, and paying the Government 2s. 3d. a week for the wife's 5s. child allowance from the Government, just do not know how they stand financially, or if they stand at all. Nor is it very easy to help them to find out exactly. The war and the paraphernalia of rationing, controls and shortages make it difficult to compare the things which people buy now with what they bought in 1938. If snoek is an edible substance, with what pre-war foodstuff does it compare? Or is it, like whale steak, one of the goods which the ill wind of war has blown to us?

There are these obvious difficulties in trying to compare present living standards with those of before the war, but we do know enough, or can estimate well enough, to get a general idea of some of the changes that have taken place in the last ten years.

First of all, the total of all private money incomes has just about doubled since 1938. That is an easy way of starting the story but it really tells us nothing of its ending. Comparisons of money incomes are by themselves quite misleading; they show us nothing of how living standards have changed. To find the answer we want we must also know something of where, and to what kind of people, this huge increase in money has gone. We must know what changes there have been in the amount, variety and prices of things which people buy. We must see what new ways a thoughtful Government has devised for relieving us of our hard-earned wages and try to calculate how much we have lost or gained by their ingenuity in using the fruits of taxation.

All these things affect the story, and whether we find the tale stimulating or irritating, tragic or amusing, depends on which character in it we happen to be. For we are all in it somewhere, as the squire at the Hall, his doctor son now treating all too freely, the farm girl on the stile with the foreman, all of us right to the undertaker who studies our longevity with a wistful interest.

Our problem is complicated because scarcely any person is affected in the same way as his neighbour; nor does the price of one thing we need behave like any other. But we can do some grouping and classifying. We saw that the total of private money incomes has just about doubled since 1938. On the other hand, total direct taxation has quadrupled; it increased from £519 million in 1938 to £1,787 million in 1947, but in 1947 very many people were still paying none at all, while others, whose money incomes may not have increased, were paying very many times as much tax as they used to. Generally, that group of people whose wages had risen in the greatest proportion were paying little or no income tax, while others, some of whose incomes were not much bigger than before the war, were paying most of the increased tax. This second group, it is true, had larger incomes to start with, but figures can explain more clearly than words just what has happened.

So far, therefore, we know this: an enormous number of people are getting a bigger share of the enlarged national income than they did of the smaller pre-war one. There are far fewer people with large incomes to spend; taxation has seen to that. There has, in fact, been a lot of levelling up of money incomes, and a good deal of levelling down. Part of the great increase in the total of personal incomes is simply because there are more people earning their living. Then the population is greater, while some people (married women, older men, daughters previously at home, independent people) who started, or returned to, jobs during the war are still carrying on. There is plenty of work and no unemployment, except for short periods when people are changing their jobs. Once our worry was to find enough work for the people who wanted to earn their living; now the difficulty is to get enough workers for all the jobs that need to be done. In 1938 there were more than a quarter-

CHART 9

TOTAL PERSONAL INCOME IN THE UNITED KINGDOM, 1938 AND 1947
Showing distribution between different income-ranges, and the proportions
taken by income tax and surtax

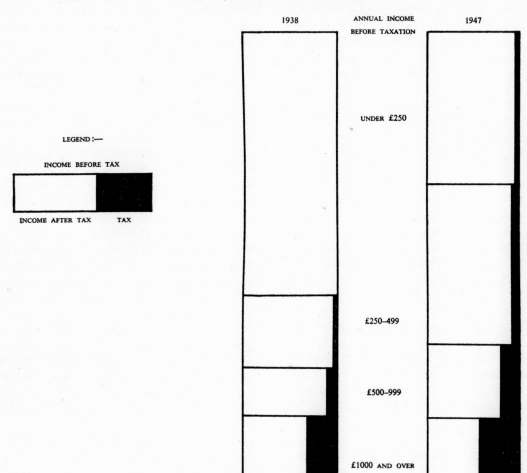

1938   ANNUAL INCOME   1947
BEFORE TAXATION

UNDER £250

LEGEND :—

INCOME BEFORE TAX

INCOME AFTER TAX   TAX

£250–499

£500–999

£1000 AND OVER

of-a-million textile workers out of work, there were as many building workers unemployed and nearly as many miners. Similarly with some other great industries. At present these industries could employ more people than they can get. But to return to the levelling of incomes.

We have seen how very much more money the so-called lower income groups have to spend. More workers account for some of this, but higher wages for much more. As a whole, standard weekly wage rates have increased by about 75 per cent since 1938, while actual earnings, that is payment for overtime worked as well as for the number of hours on which the standard rates are based, have more than doubled. After allowing for taxation, wages accounted for 48 per cent of total personal income in 1948 compared with 39 per cent in 1938.

The wage earner's share has been greater mainly because his work has been urgently wanted. He has produced more, what he has produced has been sold at a higher price, and his trade union has usually been strong enough to see that he had his share of this price. Some workers have gained an altogether different status which reflects the new importance of their industry. Farmers and farm workers, for example, are at last recognized as an essential and highly skilled part of the community. Farm wages have trebled and farmers' net incomes have quadrupled since just before the war and the whole country has gained by the change, gained by the appearance and the prosperity of a countryside with a vigorous and highly productive industry, instead of the quaint, old-fashioned occupation as it was once regarded.

For most salaried workers the change has not been so good. Their incomes have gone up, but not as much as those of the wage earners, yet they pay far higher rates of income tax than before the war. In 1938, salaries after tax were one-quarter of total private incomes; now they are only one-fifth. As a whole people getting their living from profits, interest and rent, have done rather better than salaried workers, but even they have lost a little compared with wage earners.

So, just from the aspect of the amount of money they get now compared with what they had before the war, wage earners have about doubled their income, businessmen have made good profits, but salaried workers have not done so well. Salaries of bank clerks, civil servants, university professors and lecturers, school teachers, solicitor's clerks and the host of other people who have the dignity of being paid monthly, have certainly gone up since the beginning of the war, but they have not risen in the same proportion as wages. Manual workers have been catching up with clerical and professional people, even although the average artisan still gets rather less money than the average middle class worker.

Even if we know how much more or less money people are getting, we still cannot say just whether they are better- or worse-off than before. To get somewhere near the truth we must know also whether people are compelled to spend more than they did in order to get the things they need.

The answer to this depends mainly on how prices have changed. The prices of goods and services as a whole have not increased in as high a proportion as wages, but they have risen faster than salaries. The short answer therefore is that most wage earners are better-off than before the war, but the salaried middle class are worse-off. Wage earners have more to spend than they used to have after paying for essential things like food, clothing and a roof. Most salaried professional people have less to spend after buying necessary things, and some of them have had to cut down a good deal even on these.

That is the short answer. A longer look at the picture shows that the real differences are greater than given in the short answer. Just as wages have risen more than salaries, and some wages more than others, so have the changes in prices been very uneven. Nor, with the mutilation of those economic forces so dear to economists, could it very well be otherwise. Nowadays, there is hardly such a phenomenon as a true price. Purchase tax increases the retail price of some things, subsidies lower the prices of others. Maximum prices prevent some things from costing as much as they would without this control, but other maximum prices probably make things cost more than they would in a free market. It is all very well to say that the 1938 pound sterling is worth only about 12s. now. It is not as easy as that. For food it is worth 16 or 17 shillings; for rent, even more. A pound spent on household goods will buy about as much as 9s. in 1938, but that ounce of tobacco which we used to buy for 11d., and furtively lest we were accused of depriving the baby of its food, now looms up in the horrible, dark shape of 4s. and more, and a tot of whisky or gin will add to the shock rather than relieve it.

There is rough justice in these differences. Essential things like food and certain types of clothing are kept artificially cheap; while goods that are less necessary are made dearer by taxation or duties and optional or luxury goods proportionately much more expensive. Obviously all this affects different people in different ways. Poorer people spend a bigger proportion of their income on food and necessary things than more wealthy people do, and it is right that these things should be reasonably cheap. This arrangement is apt to be rather hard on the middle income groups who pay for their food twice, once in the shops and again to the tax collector, and this despite having to maintain from habit, or because of their jobs, an altogether different standard of essential goods and services than manual workers. The middle class man's office opens at 9 or 9.30 a.m., so he cannot use workman's fares; his working clothes have a lot of accessories like collars and ties, and they must be clean; he wants his children to be as well educated as he was; his work necessitates wide reading, and books cost money; his house is a little bigger than some, but he must have a room to work in, and anyway it would cost more to move. We could give a long list of these special expenses. Some have been reduced, but others cannot be cut out unless he is to give up his job and what is left of his way of life to do something else in which his special training and skill might be of no value. If many people like him did that it would be a loss to the country.

Much has been said about the plight of the salaried middle classes, a good deal of it exaggerated and some of it just sentimental nonsense, but looked at from any economic angle they are certainly worse off than before the war. Their special needs, and some well-established whims, have had little consideration. Like others, they benefit from the health services, but the taxation allowances for children are unrealistically small and the rebate for a wife is not flattering to her present replacement value. About the only group of salaried people that is better off are those younger single men and girls who are in a job but living at home, and married couples where both partners are earning. Taxation allowances greatly favour the childless working partnership, and salaries of junior office workers have risen just as much as, or more than, wages in general, while the cost of their basic needs has often not risen in the same proportion.

The table below shows more clearly what has happened to the various classes of incomes. It shows changes in *real* incomes, i.e. incomes after allowing for taxation and for changes in the purchasing power of the pound.

This redistribution of income is one of the things that has affected the pattern of spending. The dislocation of war, priorities, shortages, diversion of goods for export, rationing, special allowances of milk and all those other new

CLASS OF PRIVATE INCOME	INCREASE OR DECREASE IN PRIVATE INCOME AFTER DIRECT TAXATION SINCE 1938 SHOWN IN TERMS OF THE 1938 PURCHASING POWER OF THE POUND
	£ million
WAGES	+338
SALARIES	—178
PAY AND ALLOWANCES OF ARMED FORCES	+ 51
PROFESSIONAL EARNINGS	— 3
FARMING PROFITS	+ 45
PROFITS OF TRADES AND PARTNERSHIPS	+ 31
TRADING PROFITS OF COMPANIES:	
DISTRIBUTED ..	— 28
RETAINED ..	+134
PROFITS OF PUBLIC ENTERPRISES	+ 21
RENT OF LAND AND BUILDINGS	—160
TOTAL INCREASE	+251

experiences of a meek and law-abiding people have also affected the amount that is spent on goods and services of different kinds. The influences of both of these groups of reasons is seen in the increased purchase of tobacco in spite of its outrageous price. In 1948 people were smoking more tobacco than in 1938. People were buying more things to read and spending much more on entertainment. Partly, these increases were due to the need for some distraction from gloom in the life of a struggling nation; partly they were because other things like clothing and household goods were not available in sufficient quantities; partly because people whose wages once only just covered their essential needs had more money to spend.

Shortages may gradually diminish as time goes on; we shall, we hope, have fewer sorrows to eclipse in tobacco smoke, or to forget in entertainment. Already some goods are more plentiful. Children know what an orange looks like; to have tasted a banana is no longer a sign of senility; there is a prospect of being able to buy a carpet at a price per acre slightly less than a City building site, and already we can get socks for ourselves as well as for our children. Supplies are improving and, with luck and an enormous amount of hard work, we shall one day smile, not just grimly in the face of adversity, but because life is good. One day we shall show our grandchildren the husk of our old clothing ration book and recount to them horrors and privations of our boyhood lives.

In the first three years since the war the amount and the directions of spending have changed a good deal. Just after the war, total expenditure on consumers' goods and services was slightly below what it was in 1938; in 1948 it was about 3 per cent above pre-war, but for most things prices have far outstripped the volume of purchases. People spent far more on tobacco and strong drink, but bought less than in 1946. Nevertheless, the pattern of spending in 1948 showed that essential goods were gaining at the expense of some luxuries. Far more household goods and clothing were bought than in 1946; more food was purchased than in 1938, but the increase was only slight and, allowing for the rise in population, the amount per head was less than pre-war. In contrast to these improvements, private motoring lagged far behind; it was only about one-third of what it was in 1938.

Already we can choose our own brand of cigarettes on a Friday; we are offered the option of Danish, New Zealand and even English butter, and the fishmonger is glad to see us even although we have left our copy of *The Times* at home. Soon we may be able to express our preferences and spend our money without feelings of guilt.

But when those times do come, the pattern of the nation's spending will not be the same as it was before the war. Habits made through necessity, and in times of stress and shortages, will die slowly and some not at all. New joys, new freedoms and new vices found during the war may remain at least for a generation, and all the while manufacturers will be designing fresh things to attract us. Above all, the many people who have known what it is to have a higher standard of living will insist on going on having enough money; if the nation produces enough, and can make good enough bargains with other countries, they will get it. Redistribution of income, levelling of incomes, has come to stay. Wage earners will get a bigger share of produce than they did in days gone by; those who are ill or too old to work will have pensions; no one will be able to retain an income much more than necessary for his reasonable needs. That, certainly, is the principle. Provided levelling of incomes does not involve levelling of people, or does not mean uniformity of abilities and tastes, the principle is right. It must mean, too, great changes in the amount of some things and services some of which will be needed. Fewer luxury yachts, but more pleasure steamers; less caviare, but more butter; fewer diamond tiaras, but more well-designed, reasonably-priced jewellery; in fact, less expensive luxury goods and more of the things needed for the ordinary family.

Tables relating to the foregoing Section will be found on pages 109 to 111

SECTION SEVEN

WELL-EARNED LEISURE

We all know that delicious moment of waking in the grey gloom of dawn when we suddenly realize that we are not going to work to-day after all. Instead of plunging into the tiresome flurry of preparation, the day stretches before us, timeless and our own. Instead of feverishly dismantling our curlers, we settle down in bed once again to end our dream just where we will and not when the 8.18 dictates.

That is the essence of leisure; to have time that is our own. We, in Britain, care for our leisure. It is our consuming interest. We start work in the

morning later than do most other nations; we finish earlier than some. We have not yet succumbed as some other English-speaking countries have to the rigidity of the 40-hour week, but we are moving that way. Trade Unions concern themselves with shortening the working day and week and with getting longer annual holidays, just as they fight for higher wages. This is natural enough. For most people work has become so mechanized, so repetitive, so boring, that the sooner it is over the better. Well-lit factories, good canteens, pleasant company and even the exhilaration of knowing our work is helping Britain to regain solvency cannot much reduce the tedium of seven or so hours doing exactly the same thing: twisting a knob, examining a horde of ball bearings, folding a book-cover; sometimes without knowing what goes on further down the production line.

With much office work it is the same. No wonder each day, as we start work in the morning, we look forward to our elevenses, then to lunch, a break for tea, and to the final goodnight to Miss Scrim, when we can start to live our own lives for a few hours. Each week, Saturday stands brightly ahead to be reached with all speed. Each year, bank holidays gleam like jewels and our summer holiday is like an oasis in the desert of dull routine. So it seems to many, at any rate, though by the sobering logic of simple multiplication their lives thus become concerned only with looking forward to eternal rest.

The principle of leisure is easy to comprehend. To have spare time, doing things we wish to do instead of those we are compelled to do; however we describe it, the idea is much the same. We might have added that leisure was rest from toil, but had we done so we should have disclosed a complete misunderstanding of the Englishman's interpretation of leisure. It would have suggested that leisure was the reverse of toil, and that it was possible to distinguish easily between the effort of work and the effort of leisure.

For some people, that might be possible, but for many the pursuit of leisure unleashes an energy which would not have been suspected by their colleagues in the office or shop or at the work-bench. The clerk who grumbles if he has to stagger with two ledgers to the department upstairs will cheerfully haul his ten-stone girl friend on a rope up a crag in the mountains. The typist reluctantly drooping over her shorthand, in intervals between coffee, lunch and repairing her complexion, is a tireless dynamo of jive after 8 p.m. The business executive, scarcely able at 4.30 to find the effort to think of anyone else to telephone, will be digging his garden with reckless enthusiasm two hours later, and his wife will have to call him often to coax him indoors to eat. Certainly we must keep our minds clear when we are thinking about work, leisure and effort.

Just how we spend our leisure is still mainly our own affair. Perhaps our ideal is to change places with the man watching the hole in the road at night, with his cosy hut, delectable coke fire, the aroma of sizzling sausages and the joy of warm solitude. Maybe our choice is the ecstatic agony of seeing Stanley Matthews hit the crossbar with a terrific drive when Arsenal and Blackpool are one-all two minutes before time. Whether our passion is for mountains or museums, pin-tables or the polka, cricket or croquet, ballet or evening classes in economics, or just the wish to stand and stare, the pursuit of leisure is a huge national occupation, individual sometimes, yet in parts highly organized. Let us look at some of the organization.

As we noted in the last Section, there is now no accredited able-bodied leisured class in Britain. Permanent idleness is no longer a sign of respectability; envy of excessive leisure is now tinged with resentment and words like spiv and drone are revived and applied with bitter emphasis. Leisure has to be earned and there is still some stir in the national conscience if it is not earned honestly, but the job of providing means of occupying people's leisure gives employment to hundreds of thousands of workers part-time and full-time. The list of the various ways in which they do so seems endless. Professional footballers, cricketers, actors, jockeys, theatre workers, clowns; the people who sort out the football pools; hotel staffs and charabanc drivers are just a tiny fraction of the vast army mobilized for our entertainment and pleasure, and this army is not to be confused with its poorer relation which merely defends the country against its enemies. However fascinating her curves and gentle her voice, no top-rank film star could muddle along on a general's salary, no admiral in the Wren's could coax from an ungrateful nation one-tenth of what is gladly paid to a queen of song. Thus is our sense of values. It is one thing to pay the Minister of Fuel and Power £5,000 a year to warm our homes and factories and to give power to industry. We pay very much more for talents that will take our minds off our working life.

In recent years we have relied more and more on other people to fill part of our leisure time, to amuse us, to play our games for us, and even to do our spare time thinking. Every Saturday, for eight months of the year, a million or more people watch scores of teams of paid footballers stage competitions for ninety minutes. Hundreds of thousands of other people watch thousands of amateur teams—soccer, rugby, hockey, netball and the rest. Those watching amateurs have a genuine interest in the fortunes of their teams since they are drawn from their villages, their schools, or their office or works. There is local patriotism and loyalty.

The spectators at the professional matches are different. They are connoisseurs. To them football is art for its own sake. The collection of Scottish, Welsh, Irish and occasional Danish or Italian artists are called "Southampton", "Portsmouth" or "Blackpool" according to the place where their headquarters happen to be. Amongst the spectators there is some high-minded rivalry and preferences such as might exist for the National Gallery or the Tate Gallery. Occasionally these preferences are forcibly expressed, as when the local Scottish centre-forward is put on his nose by the opposing right-back, or when the referee awards a goal to the visiting artists, although forty thousand people could and, indeed, do testify that the ball did not cross the goal-line. When, on a Saturday evening, we are told that it was a good game the chances are that a spectator is telling us that the home side won, or that the result of the match confirmed our informant's pool forecast which happened to coincide with the opinion of the specialist in his daily newspaper.

As with football, so with innumerable other sports: ice hockey, tennis, horse racing and greyhound racing, in which spectators outnumber those taking part by a thousand to one. We seem now to be a nation of spectators. When we do not watch sport we read about it. Daily and weekly newspapers devote acres of space to reports on games and to comments and forecasts of results. There are special sporting papers, while some sports have a whole press to themselves; this is not to mention some other leisure occupations like the theatre, cinema and opera, which together attract millions of people every week.

It is not surprising that a foreign visitor gets the impression that we are preoccupied with sport and amusement. He will shrug his shoulders and take note of another sign of the decline of Britain, but a resident observer could even get worried. He sees that our leisure occupations have taken much of the form of our work. The gregariousness of the factory is transferred to the stadium. The radio relieves us of constructive thought just as the factory machine relieves us of physical effort. We accept standardized amusements produced in the mass just as we clamour for mass-produced clothes and furniture. We are bored with our work, bored to the point of inertia, so that we cannot contrive our own amusements, but must hire someone to distract us. Leisure has become a passive thing, a drug, and not as it should be—a time for recreation when we renew our talents and use the powers which nature gave us. Yet, busy people though we claim to be, we are getting more spare time and more money to spend on it than ever before. The working day gets shorter, the weekend lengthens, soon the 5-day week may be the rule and not the exception, and more and more workers are getting paid annual holidays. The greater output of industry made possible by more and better machines is not bringing benefits, but just more leisure to efface what is left of our individuality and intellect.

Is it really as bad as all that? It could be, and one day it might be. There are great dangers of carrying mass production of anything too far, but the observer, and there are many who talk in this vein, sees and hears only what is most obvious and assumes that what is not obvious does not exist at all. The shouting at the race track drowns the gentler sound of digging in the countless gardens and allotments around. Certainly, we spend more time watching other people do things than we did a generation or so ago. There are more opportunities for doing so; travelling is easier, there is more money, and people are encouraged to go to these events by those who make profits out of them. Another reason is that there are not enough playing fields for all who would like to use them; most schools have too little space to enable enough children to get the idea of doing rather than watching.

Even so, and despite our gloomy observer, we have not been reduced to a nation of uniform morons whose only hobbies, apart from seeing a few people play something, are beer, the radio and gambling. Indeed, we suggest that just as these people are beginning to understand some of the follies of excessive industrialization, so are they getting tired of too much regimentation in their leisure. Let us get a sense of proportion. It is true that professional football and Margaret Lockwood have millions of followers, but football matches usually last only ninety minutes of one day a week, not so many people as all that attend the cinema more than once a week, and a surprising number of people have never seen a single greyhound race. Admittedly, it takes time to get to the match or the cinema and it takes time to recover from the emotional strain of the event, but there is still plenty of spare time left in the week.

Then, while most people go to the cinema now and then, it is only a minority that regularly watches games of any kind. We are apt to be misled by the reports of Saturday attendances and forget to subtract the figures from the total adult population. What do the rest do in their spare time? What do the spectators do in the rest of their spare time? Here are four just men leaving their office; ask them.

This one, Wilson, has a job to do. His son has a birthday next week and he has to finish fitting up the boat he is making for him. Wilson is good at that kind of thing. Some people think he is a craftsman. Anyway, he makes a good deal of his own furniture, and toys for most of his friend's children.

Billson is carrying a violin case. He is playing second in his local orchestra. He would have liked to have been a professional, but he had to earn his living as soon as he left school, so he could not have the training. Perhaps it is better this way. He earns enough for his family and he has time for plenty of music. Now here is Millson, a shy fellow and difficult to know. He reads a lot and spends a lot of time walking in the country looking at country churches. After he

has had tea he is going to a lecture on English architecture.

Finally what about young Dawson, the most junior clerk and not any more conscientious than he need be? You would not think so at 9 a.m., but he is the chap who makes the Youth Club at Croystead such a success. Somehow he manages to get people to take part in all kinds of activities and to like doing so.

Perhaps this is unfair; perhaps these four are not representative. Maybe we *were* a little lucky that we happened to meet just these, but if we looked in at most offices, or shops or factories, and asked the workers we met what they did in their spare time and what they would most like to do if they had the chance, we should get an amazing catalogue of hobbies and aspirations. Machine-minding would not appeal much, but skilled engineering a great deal; the list would consist of everything from breeding whippets to being the mother of six children; from modelling in clay to tub-thumping in Hyde Park. We should discover the zest for the open air, and for doing something which only one person could do that way. We should hear plenty about gardens, just as anyone who discovers England must hear about gardens.

For so many whose spirit of adventure, whose skill and creative urges are frustrated in the routine of their work, leisure is necessarily an escape, and whether we see different lives and new worlds on the screen, dangle on precipices, grow a more luscious rose than our neighbours, or try to create a marrow as big as a blimp, this instinct to escape keeps us sane. Just as Americans try desperately to escape from being nonentities by playing at secret societies, so do we in Britain gamble millions with horses because we should be arrested if we diced with death in our daily work.

IT MAKES A CHANGE

The first crocus marks a cheerful point in the uncertain rhythm of Britain's climate. Nature thus disproves the theory, widely held in March, that our winter is permanent. With faith rekindled, British thoughts turn to holidays.

First comes Easter as a foretaste of leisure. According to the disposition of the moon and the lottery of wind and weather, Easter may be a blaze of flower-spangled glory, or just a chilly stage in the slow climb out of winter. We all know this, but for most of us it is the first reasonable break in our work since Christmas, and we need the break. Also, we remember that there was once an Easter that was fine and warm and if it could happen once, why not again? So with the unreason of natural gamblers, we buy seeds, mend the deckchairs, look to our paint brushes, count our petrol coupons, shake last year's crumbs out of our rucksacks, unfurl our

maps and revel in the luxury of anticipating two or three days in the open air.

Easter is everybody's holiday. It is marked in our diaries when we buy them in December, and by the time Easter Monday is over and we have taken off our fur coats and unpacked our swim suits, our thoughts have gone forward to our summer holiday. This is our own holiday. We may even be able to arrange it when we like, go where we like and for as long as—well, as long as we can afford, or are allowed to be away from work. Most people in Britain have at least a few consecutive days' holiday sometime during the year, and in 1947 more than half the adult population, with a swarm of children, had this holiday away from home. Three out of four upper-middle class and wealthier people went away; and just about half of the manual workers and poorer people also managed to get to the

CHART 10

PROPORTION OF THE "ADULT" POPULATION TAKING HOLIDAYS AWAY FROM HOME IN 1948

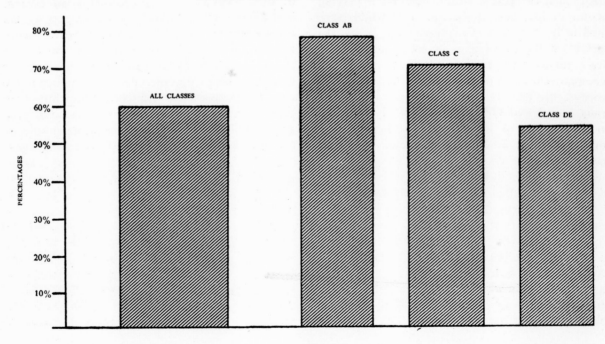

seaside, the country, to London and other places away from the sink, garden and chores.

The kinds of holidays people take are often as surprising as their spare time habits. By the time we have talked over our holidays with friends, colleagues at work and with our neighbours, we have obtained a new sidelight on their character and affluence. If we met them when they are on holiday and have shed their bowler hats and inhibitions, we have some new sidelights on their habits and physique as well. Weekends and evenings are times for new activities; the annual holiday can take us into new worlds, away from the tyranny of the morning train or the washing up; away to new climates, a new life, a time of glorious freedom. At any rate, so it seems on a foggy Monday afternoon in the office.

The holiday spirit and the prospect of going away affects people differently. To some people the whole year is related to the annual holiday. They plan their holiday as though it were a major military operation. Before the autumn leaves have fallen their intelligence services are at work on next year's holiday. Guide books, maps and timetables are laid out. When the objective is determined, the fullest information is obtained and checked by interrogation of visitors who have been there and have survived. Statistics of sunshine are studied and compared with those of other English resorts and it is noted that the Mediterranean can offer no more. This point is confirmed by public relations officers in the various places, and they ought to know as they live in them. After study of information there is a reconnaissance to confirm that there is a Woolworths', to find out whether the natives are friendly and, above all, to find one friendly enough to offer to feed Pa, Ma and two children (quiet, good-mannered, clean, with small appetites) for two weeks in August.

This reconnaissance can be disconcerting to the inexperienced person. He must make allowances for changed appearances due to the early visit which is necessary if he is to get accommodation. The time of the year may account for the absence of bathing machines, near-R.A.F. types in straw hats and tight-belted young women in white, carrying parasols which were in the guide book photographs. If he is optimistic he will assume that the teeming rain will have stopped by the time he actually goes on holiday. Reassured on all points the visitor will return to report to the family, and then to start the real job of getting ready for the trip six months ahead. These preparations will be thorough, right to the final checkings of trains in Bradshaw with those in the ABC and both by the opinion of the enquiries girls at Waterloo.

That is the careful type. We all know him, just as we know the last-minute kind who acts on impulse, piles a few things in a bag the night before going, takes a chance with the train, has faith that there will be room somewhere to stay, and money enough to buy the things he has left behind. This type never seems to return home until he is due, and remains married for quite a long time, so he must get fixed up all right. Between the careful campaigner and the spontaneous, intuitive kind there is every variety of holidaymaker. There is the type who travels light with just a spare shirt and toothbrush and a lot of confidence in his friends; there is the house-moving kind who takes all the clothes he possesses, a medicine chest, tools for every emergency and quite a lot of furniture. It is just as well to be prepared for most things when holidaying in Britain.

Still, we cannot catalogue the strange idiosyncrasies of our fellow men, but we can get some idea of what kind of people go to which places, and when they go. Obviously, money and class have a great deal to do with holiday habits. A bigger proportion of wealthier people go away for holidays than of those who are not so well off. They also have more choice in determining where they go and at what time of the year they take their holidays. Age and sex also have a large influence. We saw that of those who are quite well-off three out of four went for holidays in 1947.

Mainly because of money only one person in fifty of the working class who went away at all went abroad, and most of these probably went to Eire or the Isle of Man. But despite the currency regulations and patriotic exhortations about the balance of payments, one in ten of the wealthier people spend a holiday in another country. Although money is the main thing that governs the length and type of holiday people take, it is not the only factor. Custom, habits, needs of younger children, school holidays of older ones, love of crowds or of preference for different types of scenery, interest in farming: all these have their influence. How much influence they have obviously depends on the sort of lives people normally lead and the kind of work they do. People want a change. The city broker wishes to atone for the past eleven months by harvesting wheat instead of cornering it; the farmer's wife who lives in an atmosphere of paraffin, steaming hen-food and muddy boots may be determined to see the lights of the city from a modern hotel suite; even the barrow boy outside the station may hanker for purer air and push his wares to Brighton.

It is the sea that dominates the holiday programme. Well over half of the adults who took holidays in 1947 went to the seaside. For children the proportion was probably much higher. The seaside holiday was the most popular with adults of all classes and all ages. For a nation still with traces of the spirit of Drake and Grace Darling this is not surprising, and with no place in Britain more than 70 miles from the coast anyone can easily get to a seaside resort of some kind in a day's travel, although many richer or more adventurous persons went much further from their homes than 70 miles. There are other reasons for the lure of the seaside.

Many people really believe that frequent immersion in the water around our coast enables them to withstand the coming winter. When we recall some of these immersions, prefaced by furtive undressings only partly sheltered from the cloudladen gale by a rock or breakwater, the shock of putting our left foot into a receding wave, the breathless plunge and the desperate attempt to restore our circulation and the final glow as we dragged our sand encrusted legs back into our clothes, we know that no one could do this without some fairly powerful beliefs. We can also recall days when the sea murmured gently on the baking sand; when the Gulf Stream really did have some effect on the temperature of the water; when we skipped refreshed to rejoin the children building sand castles; when, in fact, the seaside was all that we had hoped for when we were poring over the guide books.

Do not let us be too modest about our sea-coast. In parts there is a grandeur which the Italian Riviera can scarcely improve upon. There are beaches equal to the Australian Bondi and Manley beaches. There is surf-bathing in the South-west exciting enough for any who like that kind of thing, and without the sinister danger of sharks. The English seaside has plenty to offer to those adaptable enough to lie inert under the broiling sun which may appear during their holiday, or to stride the promenade in the chastening tempest which is just as likely.

Then the seaside resorts are more able to cope with holiday visitors than are most inland towns. It is their job. Some are even designed to do the job, with everything for the visitor whatever the weather may be. Others deliberately retain their native atmosphere of fishing and seaweed. The visitor goes to these places to avoid the crowd and not to swell it, but even some of those resorts which cater for larger numbers of visitors, and advertise their charm and hours of sunshine, have sad deficiencies. Partly this is because, like so many of our railway stations and post offices, they were built when architecture had had a bad relapse and comfort was thought to be ungodly. Not much can be done about the buildings except to blow them up and start again, and that would not conform with the principles of the Economic Survey. But something could be done to provide a means for removing sand and salt from body and clothes after swimming. Some other countries have showerbaths for this, and it is possible to swim there without feeling afterwards as if we had been fried in breadcrumbs. Also, we wonder whether it is always necessary to add to the disciplinary ordeal of our first bathe by providing nothing but hideous boxes to hide our milk-white torso from the gaze of the crowd. We might add some comments on the discomforts of some hotels and boarding-houses, on the lack of drying facilities, on insufficient amenities for children, but the rejoinder would be that these things were no worse in hotels than at home, and the answer would be just.

But these are asides. The fact remains that more holidaymakers go to the seaside than anywhere else. Some like to be awakened by a loudspeaker to a day of increasing jollity in a holiday camp; others prefer to live their own lives and go to sleep on the beach in the afternoon, or listen to the sea lapping the rocks. Probably more people between 35 and 64 than any other

CHART 11
LENGTH OF HOLIDAYS SPENT AWAY FROM HOME, 1947

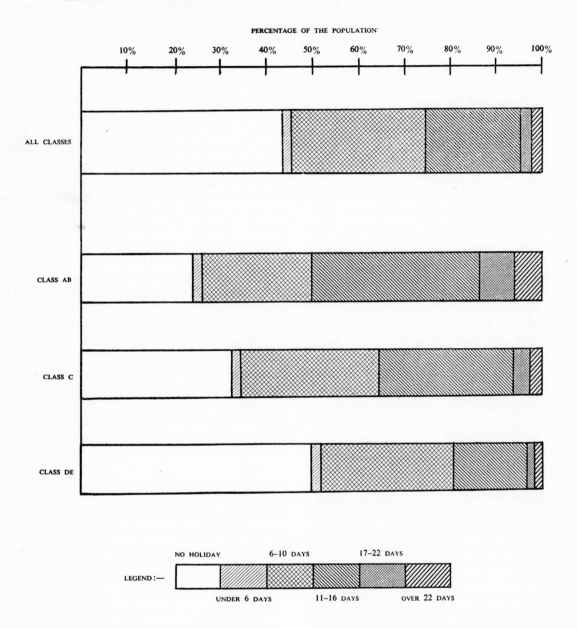

PERCENTAGE OF THE POPULATION

10% 20% 30% 40% 50% 60% 70% 80% 90% 100%

ALL CLASSES

CLASS AB

CLASS C

CLASS DE

LEGEND :—

NO HOLIDAY   6–10 DAYS   17–22 DAYS

UNDER 6 DAYS   11–16 DAYS   OVER 22 DAYS

adults go to the sea, some because they like it, some because they have become used to it, and many because it is the best and easiest way of keeping the children happy.

It is a smaller, but more discerning public that goes into the country for its holidays. The coasts of other countries may equal our own and their seas may be warmer, but the British countryside has no equal. Nature and man have combined to give it a mature and ordered charm that is its own. No other area so small can have such an infinite variety of beauty, changing with each season and with each mile. Beech-clad downs shelter rich lands farmed as well as any in the world. Mountains and lakes give way to fertile plains linking centuries-old villages, each clustered round the church. Villages and farms blend with the landscape of which they are a part, often built of stone quarried within a mile or two of them. Deciduous trees of every kind give a new loveliness to each season, a loveliness that cannot exist in countries which only grow ever-greens. Each county takes pride in its own gifts. For one it is lake and mountain scenery; another is jealous of its lush farming; another of its moorland. Each has its pride and each has good reason for it.

In Britain there is everything for those who love the country. The visitor can climb mountains, fish streams, argue in ancient pubs, help on the farm, stare at a glade through the oaks carpeted with bluebells. He can stay among the soft green hills of Somerset, or choose the wildness and wide horizons of the Essex coast. He can work or play in the country, but he must seek his own excitements. There are no funfairs or amusements organized for his benefit. Countryfolk are busy people and have no time to provide a pageant of Merrie England, but if the visitor knows of country things and can see why the farmer is doing what he is in the field by the copse; if he can distinguish the song of the black-cap, or knows where to find a great spotted woodpecker, or see a heron standing motionless in the stream, every day and hour will be rich for him.

In 1947 about one adult in eight went to the country for a holiday. Some went to help farmers with the harvest, some to stay with relations, others to wander from one youth hostel to another. Not all of them found peace in the country. Some whose rooms adjoined the farmyard and whose sleep was pierced by the chant of geese at dawn may have pined for the peace of Streatham Hill. Not all of them took peace with them, but noisy motors, radio sets and gramophones to compete with morning birdsong and to disturb the stillness of the downland afternoon. Many of them also forgot that broken bottles are dangerous to animals; that gates are not merely to sit on; that by the time their party has dragged fifteen-stone Aunt Gladys through the hedge, the hole they have made is big enough to let Betsy, the farmer's best cow, get into the cabbage field. But most went to the country because they love what they find there, and most of them realize

that there is a serious and important job going on in most of our countryside.

The country appeals to people of all ages and all classes. Many poorer people go because accommodation is probably cheaper than in seaside towns, but some others because they left their old homes and many of their friends and relatives there when they were driven by farming depression, or an urge to find better housing amenities, to take jobs in the towns.

London and other cities also have their attractions for the holidaymaker, but the attraction does not rival that of the country.

July and August are the main holiday months. But older people, freed of the fetters of school holidays, probably take advantage of their wider choice and are, perhaps, even influenced also by the lower charges which are usual in June and September. Those with families are more limited, although it is surprising that youth does not show more enterprise in the time of the year at which it arranges its holidays. Perhaps, when they, too, are disciplined by their children's school regulations they will wish they had seen more of Devon in April and May.

Most of those spending holidays at the seaside and who have a choice at all, naturally go in the months when the sea has lost some of its chill, but there is very little difference in the proportions of those spending holidays at the sea and in the country who go in the various months.

1947 was scarcely a year in which people travelled for the fun of it. Railway carriages needed repair and there were not enough of them. Maintenance was often poor and some-times it was possible to know whether there was sunshine or cloud only by opening the windows. Trains were crowded, stations were worse, and for those who had to travel with young children at weekends the journey could be a nightmare, tiring, cramped and dirty, but this did not deter holidaymakers. Most of them went by train and far too many went on Fridays and Saturdays for their own comfort and the sanity of the railways' workers. Many went on long journeys. One Scotsman or Scotswoman in twenty came to the South-east of England; one-and-a-quarter million people living in the South-east went to Devon, Cornwall and Wales; few

CHART 12

NUMBERS AND PROPORTIONS OF THE "ADULT" POPULATION ACTUALLY ON HOLIDAY AWAY FROM HOME AT ANY PARTICULAR TIME DURING THE HOLIDAY MONTHS

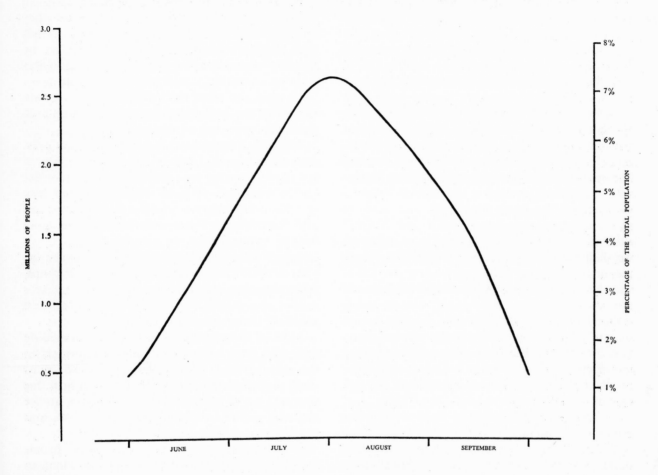

people living in the Midlands seemed to want to stop there at all; only about a quarter of those normally in the North and North-east of England spent their holidays in that region.

This is an enormous reshuffle of population, and our prayers go to the railways who have to cope with most of it at weekends in July and August. If we join the throng ourselves we mingle shame with self-pity and wonder why we did not think of going on a Tuesday in June when we could dream our way in comfort in a corner seat.

Railways took most of the burden, but they did not take all of it. Where money could buy more comfort and convenience it did so. About

half of those in the wealthier classes went by private or hired cars—mostly in their own cars— or by aeroplane, whereas four poorer people out of five went by train or by motor coach. Not that 1947 could be called exactly a gloriously carefree motoring year. It is true that more than half of the upper-middle class and richer households had a car of some kind, but in normal times the allowance of petrol would scarcely have made it worth while putting most of these cars on the road, but 1947 was too soon after the war for people to be rational about domestic economies and the cars were brought into holiday service. A great many of the not-so-rich households also used cars for their holidays—altogether one adult

51

in five, or nearly four-and-a-half million of them plus their children, used their own or hired cars for their holidays. In all classes but the lowest more people went by car than by motor coach, but in all groups but the richest the railway took by far the greatest number of holiday-makers.

Neither bicycles nor motor bicycles come very much into people's plans for annual holidays. Less than 2 per cent went away on them, although no doubt quite a number of people took pedal bicycles by train and used them around their holiday destinations. The trouble is that the push-bike has limits to its capacity for carrying luggage, and its owner's enthusiasm wanes when he alternates the anguish and toil of going up hills with the risk of lumbago in the blast of cold air going down. Push-biking competes with walking as the ideal means of moving about the country-side. Each has advantages over the other and we shall not express our own preferences, but as the main means of locomotion both are better suited to the shorter or weekend holiday than to the more extensive annual break. Moreover, scarcely one adult in three owns a bicycle, and only in the lowest adult age group do more than half own them. The proportion of men owning motor cycles is surprisingly, perhaps fortunately, small—just over 4 per cent; but these 4 per cent cannot be reproached for reticence about their existence. Indeed, there always seem to be many motor cycles about.

We have shown something of the pattern of holidays in 1947. That year can be looked upon only as a rough guide to people's general holiday habits, for in several ways it was not typical of previous years and some later ones may be very different. For one thing, the weather was better during the main holiday months than in almost any we could remember. But we need not stress weather very much as an influence on holiday plans. People who spend their holidays in Britain take the weather in their stride and usually make their plans hoping for fine weather, but determined to go whatever happens.

More important than the weather was the fact that 1947 was only the second complete post-war year. The cost of living was high, but lower than it is now. People had arrears of holidays to make up: wartime civilians had had too little during the previous eight years, and those in the forces had had more time off, but too often had to spend their leaves in the wrong places and away from their families. Numbers of demobilized people had gratuities, or part of them, to spend and no one had really settled down enough after the anxieties and turmoil of war to realize how poor they all were. Then a great many industrial workers were enjoying paid holidays for the first time and others were getting longer paid holidays than they had had before. All these reasons are important, although they naturally affected some people more than others.

Since 1947 there has been one very big change and that is the increase in railway fares and, indeed, in the cost of travel as a whole. This affects our holidays in two ways: directly, it affects the cost of getting to our holiday destination; indirectly, as most of us do a lot of travelling to and from work and in other pursuits throughout the year, higher fares mean less to spend on non-essential things. It is too early to say yet how this is going to cut holiday spending, but the amber light was showing in many resorts in 1948 and 1949, although this was undoubtedly due to the very high cost of accommodation and the higher cost of living generally, as much or more than to the specific rises which had occurred in fares.

The British care for their holidays as much as any race, but for a time at any rate this pattern will be influenced by more cautious spending than in 1947. This may mean shorter holidays; holidays at or nearer home to save fares and petrol; more holidays with friends and relations and, perhaps, for a bigger proportion of middle class and lower middle class people, no holidays at all.

Tables relating to the foregoing Section will be found on pages 112 to 121

GONE UP IN SMOKE

Sir Walter Raleigh certainly started something. Of course, he started several things; so many, in fact, that he was finally beheaded in Old Palace Yard. The ones we remember him for especially, however, are the introduction into this country of an elaborate form of chivalry, of potato growing and of smoking tobacco. The first was sadly modified in times of clothes rationing; the second still goes on, but he would be really proud if he could see just how we are now following his example of smoking. This has become such a success that some of us wish that the events in Old Palace Yard had taken place a little earlier.

The British have been called all kinds of a nation by admiring and envious foreigners: a nation of shopkeepers, gardeners, hypocrites and imperialists, but they have now an outstanding characteristic of spending an enormous amount on smoking. We are all of us accustomed now to huge amounts of this and that in our national income and expenditure, so one more will leave us unmoved, but the picture of what we spend on tobacco is worth a second glance and it might even bring a flush of shame to our cheeks, or at least cause some of us to do some swift domestic calculations. Last year, personal expenditure on tobacco in this country was £772 million. In isolation this is a meaningless statistic, so we shall fit it into the framework of our other expenditure. Our spending on tobacco was nearly a tenth of the total amount we spent on goods and services, necessary things and luxuries of all kinds. Let us look at it more closely. If, just for a moment, we regard tobacco as a fuel, we see that we spent more on this type of fuel than we did for all the coal, electricity, gas, paraffin and other fuels than we used to heat and light our homes and to cook for our families. In fact, we spent twice as much on tobacco as on these fuels.

We spent on tobacco more than one-third of the total expenditure on food; much more than we spent on household goods of all kinds; six times as much as on books, newspapers and magazines, and more even than we paid out in rent and rates.

These comparisons do no more than put into some perspective what most of us know already, that we spend a tremendous amount on tobacco. The comparisons can, however, be misleading unless they are explained a little more. We have been discussing personal expenditure, the total sums spent out of personal income in this country. Thus, as we chain-smoke our way through each day, we may rob our own housekeeping money and deprive our family of its food, but we are not depriving the country as a whole of resources to the extent shown by the statistics. On the contrary, a very large part of the expenditure on tobacco represents customs and excise duties payable to the government. Smokers contributed something like £600 million to the Exchequer in 1948. So if we have any regrets about cutting down milk for our own baby, we can preen ourselves that we helped other people's babies to have subsidized milk, or, if we prefer to look at it that way, we can be proud that as smokers we own and maintain a part of the British Navy. The nation's annual assessment for smoking would, however, have to include other losses of resources such as corn stacks, house and industrial property, commons and other combustible assets consumed by fires caused by smokers.

That is the national aspect. For us as individuals there is much more to smoking than can be shown by national statistics. For one thing, some people smoke more than others, while there are people who do not smoke at all and still seem to enjoy life. When this Survey was carried out, Britain's civilian population aged 16 and over was approaching 37 million. Of these, nearly 21 million smoked pipes or cigarettes and, lest women are wrongly accused of causing all the cigarette shortages, it must be said straightaway that men smokers outnumbered the women by two to one. Four men out of five are smokers; only two women in five smoke. All this means that in 1948 the burden of spending £772 million on this habit, pleasure, vice, solace, drug or, alternatively, of contributing £600 million towards the cost of government, was borne by not

CHART 13

DISTRIBUTION OF TOTAL TOBACCO CONSUMPTION BETWEEN MEN AND WOMEN

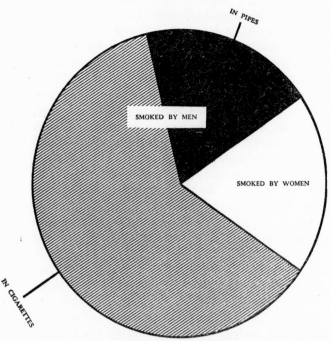

very much more than half of the adult population, and most of these were men.

Despite the enormous amount of money involved, smokers are found in every economic and social class and the proportions of smokers and non-smokers in each class differ very little. Indeed, there is a bigger proportion of men smokers in the working classes than in the others, and the preponderance is especially marked in cigarette smoking. With women, however, we find a larger proportion of smokers in the highest income classes than in the others, although the difference is very small.

So far, we have considered smoking in general, just as a way of ridding ourselves of a great deal of money and of burning away large quantities of vegetable matter, but both for us as a nation and as individuals there is obviously much more to it than this. The terms "smoker" includes the flapper who self-consciously consumes one mild cigarette each day and it includes the addict on the Churchillian scale who is seen without a cigar in his mouth only when he is kissing his wife. It includes the pin-table fiend who leers at each

contrivance with a cigarette stuck to his lower lip, the man who likes to be photographed behind a large pipe, and successful businessmen who breathe affluence and cigar smoke. Then there is the man who makes his own cigarettes. If he is an artist he will coax wisps of fine tobacco into suitable paper, lick the resulting tube and set fire to it in the usual way. The more mechanically-minded, who like a cigarette with tobacco adequately and evenly distributed throughout its length, have a gadget which looks like a miniature mangle with an army blanket in it which seems to do the job very well.

A study of all the types of smokers we know would take a whole book. In this Section we can attempt only a few broad classifications. Age rather than the income classes influences the proportion of smokers, and this influence is more marked for women than for men. A larger proportion of men in the 35–64 age-group are smokers than in any other group; the 16–24 group has, as we should hope though not necessarily expect, the largest proportion of non-smokers. With women it is very different. From ages 16 to 44 nearly every other woman smokes, but the proportion of smokers then falls very rapidly; of those aged 65 and over, only one in six smokes at all. We should have expected this to be so; a great many of the older women were brought up, and lived their earlier years in a period when women were considered to be rather fast if they smoked, so they did not start, and, as among the older women there are many retired spinsters and widows with small incomes, this is a time to give up smoking rather than to begin.

From the results of the Survey it is obvious that to smoke a pipe is a sign of exclusivity or senility. Pipe smokers would prefer to think that they just had mature tastes, but whatever the reasons, two things are striking. Only a small proportion of the men smoke a pipe at all and, of those who do, the overwhelming number are older men of 45 or more. This seems to confirm that pipe smoking is rather more exclusive than cigarette smoking, and this is certainly supported by the illustrations of stories for women where, if it is conceded that the hero has any weaknesses at all, he is usually shown smoking a pipe; that is, when he is on his own. Also, whenever sturdy manhood needs emphasis, the pipe is seldom far away. Then one often hears that doubtful appraisal of masculinity by women: "I like to see a man with a pipe. There is something so solid and secure about him."

In case any pipe smoker is in danger of getting a swollen head, we suggest that he charges his incinerator with home-grown tobacco and takes it along to a London hotel. He has no need to light the thing. Just the appearance of a pipe protruding from his face will bring a polite, gentle, yet very firm request for its removal. To the pipe smoker, this hoodoo on his apparatus is difficult to understand. He might well be aggrieved. His pipe is one of the best; it is hygienic and his tobacco is pure and fragrant. So why the embargo? There it is: he must obey, put his cherished pipe out of sight and sit with no form of retaliation in an atmosphere pungent with smoke from all brands of cigarettes and cigars of doubtful pedigree or no pedigree at all. When he reflects that his preference for pipes is shared by people as distinguished as Sherlock Holmes, Stanley Baldwin and Joe Stalin, he can feel sore. The trouble is, of course, that some pipe smokers are unaware that their apparatus needs cleaning at least every spring and they experiment rather too freely with their tobacco, so that even the flies on the ceiling seek fresh air. Because of this unwholesome minority all pipe smokers must suffer a certain amount of ostracism.

There are some men who smoke both pipes and cigarettes. On average, these people smoke much more tobacco than those who confine themselves to either cigarettes or pipes. The average man who smokes cigarettes only manages to get through fifteen a day, but the cigarette *and* pipe people average nearly twelve cigarettes and a third of an ounce of tobacco, which totals in weight of tobacco much more than the two-fifths of an ounce smoked by the average man who sticks to his pipe. Women as a whole smoke far less each day than men. The average woman smokes just over six cigarettes a day and if she smokes a pipe she says nothing about it. So some of the accusations that women cause all the trouble in our daily hunt for cigarettes is not just, but there is no doubt that there are more women smoking now than there were even a few years ago. More money; more time on their own during the war; access to cigarettes in the services; all these have contributed to the increase.

There is another point which may or may not be related to the increase in women's smoking. It is likely that a bigger proportion of married than unmarried men smoke pipes. Possibly this is due to encouragement by wives who feel better with a tough pipe-smoking chap about, or maybe it is because the husband is less likely to drop ash while cooking the Sunday dinner than if he smoked cigarettes. Most likely, however, the pipe-smoking habit was developed when he found it was the only way he could be sure of having an unmolested supply of tobacco in the house.

We started this Section with some national statistics and a few comparisons. We have seen enough to show that the consumption of tobacco in various ways is one of the principal and most expensive accompaniments of the daily lives of most people. Mainly because of increased duty on tobacco, its retail price has gone up to a height which in 1938 we should have thought would make people give up smoking. Prices have just about quadrupled. Yet consumption of tobacco is higher than it was before the war. It is true that the curve has wavered in the last few years, but in 1948 demand was still well above that of 1938. It meant that about 21 million people were each spending about £37 a year on tobacco; the average man a good deal more and the average woman rather less. There were plenty of people spending over £80 a year on tobacco and some husbands and wives must each have spent as much.

Then smoking involves other expenditure besides just the purchase of tobacco. Matches, lighters and accessories, pipes and cigarette-holders and cases come into this expenditure, and there are other things like the cost of mending holes made by hot embers falling from pipes that affect the smoker's budget. All these expenses must be included.

If a smoker invested a legacy of £5,000 in gilt-edged securities, he would need all the taxed proceeds to pay his smoking bill, but while he evens out his expenditure in small instalments over the year by buying the odd ounce and a packet of twenty, he will go on doing it in much the same cheerful way as he goes on with PAYE, cheerful because he is never quite aware of what is going on.

Tables relating to the foregoing Section will be found on pages 122 to 125

FOR TO-NIGHT WE'LL MERRY BE

Like religion, love and battles, drink has probably inspired plenty of English literature. Yet it is difficult to define our national attitude to drinking. It is lauded in poetry and song and decried in cold and solemn prose; at its best it is a mark of the connoisseur and of good fellowship, but in the eyes of many drink inevitably leads to degradation and penury. This is natural enough. Alcoholic drink has other properties besides the power to quench thirsts; it can raise or lower the spirit, it can loosen the tongue, and it has anaesthetic qualities.

So it is not surprising that people range themselves as individuals or in powerful leagues and societies in defence of their attitudes to the habit of drinking strong liquors. To some it outpoints money as a root of evil; in legislation the concern is largely with the right time and place for drinking; to most of us moderate drinking is an accepted part of life; it is expensive, and otherwise harmless. Traditionally, it has an association with song and this can be embarrassing to those whose natural disposition is to sing, even without the stimulus of alcohol. For example, if you are inspired by the May sunshine and leafy lanes to sing as you drive to the station in the morning, people will think that you are slightly mad, but if, by any chance, you sing when you return at dusk, everyone, and especially the police, will assume that you are drunk and should not be driving at all.

Nor is there always concrete evidence of this alleged association of drink and song. A peep into the saloon bar of a public house will give almost any impression but one of merry-making and song. There will be low conversation punctuated with long pauses for drinking and deep reflection, but song is unlikely. Indeed, if there were any it would probably be frowned on as being disorderly. Even the popping of champagne corks at the exclusive hotel is more likely to be the prelude to over-long set speeches and dazed boredom than to spontaneous bursts of song. Then, to turn from the consumption of liquids in public to that modern way of entertaining friends with the minimum of trouble, the cocktail party. The late-comer will be directed to the vicinity by a great volume of sound, but certainly it will not be music or song. By the time he joins the throng, the earlier chatter will have achieved an amazing crescendo, where each person is competing in voice with his neighbour and many eyes will be liquid from the pall of tobacco smoke —but no singing. Yet we have a fine legacy of our own drinking songs and can draw fully on those of other countries.

Nowadays we are inclined to keep our singing and drinking separate, or rather we stick to our drinking while we leave song to experts. This is a sign of the times, of the period of specialization, but it is not the only feature of our drinking that has changed in the last few generations. There is far less drunkenness now than even thirty years ago. Some would say that this was because alcoholic drinks are weaker or too expensive, or because heads are stronger now. Possibly these may be reasons for greater sobriety, but they are certainly not the main ones. The fact is that our attitude to drinking has changed. There are so many more opportunities in the modern world for expressing our feelings, or of taking our minds off our troubles. Standards of living are higher and in our spare time there is the cinema, the wireless, organized sport and travel available to the descendants of those who might have sought comfort and entertainment by drinking in ribald company. In this respect standards of conduct are higher and there is undoubtedly a greater social stigma in drunkenness than there was in our grandfathers' days. The drunken rowdy is now not a blood but a bore. Drink is expensive, but this is not the main deterrent to excess. We prefer to swoon to the crooner and cloud the issues of modern life in smoke than drown our sorrows in strong drink.

At the risk of incurring the displeasure of the score or so of societies which exist to combat or control the evils of drink, we should say that the present attitude to drinking is healthier than in the past. Women can share the flowing bowl without being written off as hussies. They do not now affect a reluctant sip from their man's glass and, on the pretext of a headache, return to the bottle of gin in their boudoir. They join their husbands at the pub knowing that they are unlikely to be involved in a roughhouse or a brawl. Pubs themselves are designed to be attractive to the moderate and orderly drinker, and sometimes they have furniture other than just a brass rail. There is one licensed house to every 400 people in this country, so there is a fair amount of opportunity for public drinking. That opportunity is well, but not excessively, used.

In 1948 over £750 million was spent on alcoholic drinks. This was about the same as the expendi-ture on tobacco and, although it represented nearly one-tenth of the total personal expenditure on goods and services, the quantity of beer and other drinks consumed was a little less than it was just before the war. So drinkers, like smokers, contribute plenty towards running the country. This expenditure, of course, includes purchases of drinks taken home as well as those "drunk on the premises", but although there are people in every class who drink at home, it is a habit much more common with those who are better off and, taken as a whole, those purchases amount to far less than those made in the pub. This suggests that for most people drinking is less to quench thirst than to share leisure time with old and new

CHART 14

EXTENT TO WHICH PEOPLE DRINK BEER, SPIRITS OR WINES

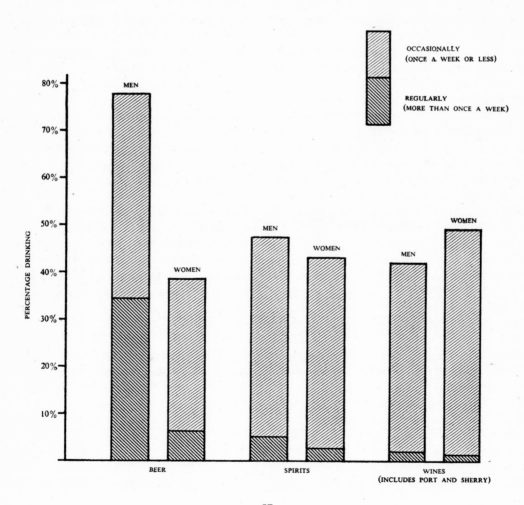

friends. Poorer people have fewer amenities for entertaining at home than upper and middle class people.

Even if they had these amenities, they would probably prefer to meet their cronies at the local for a drink, chat, or a game of darts. It is a tradition of English life and one that is likely to survive the night club and other devices for distracting our thoughts and luring our money.

This tradition of meeting to talk as well as drink at the pub is probably stronger in the country and in small towns than in big cities and industrial areas. It is natural that this should be so. The man working in the field or woods or with the flock on the hill may see few people during the day and may speak to even fewer. By the end of the day he needs company as well as a drink. He knows his company, people like him-

CHART 15

PERCENTAGES OF MEN AND WOMEN WHO DRINK BEER, SPIRITS OR WINES
By social class

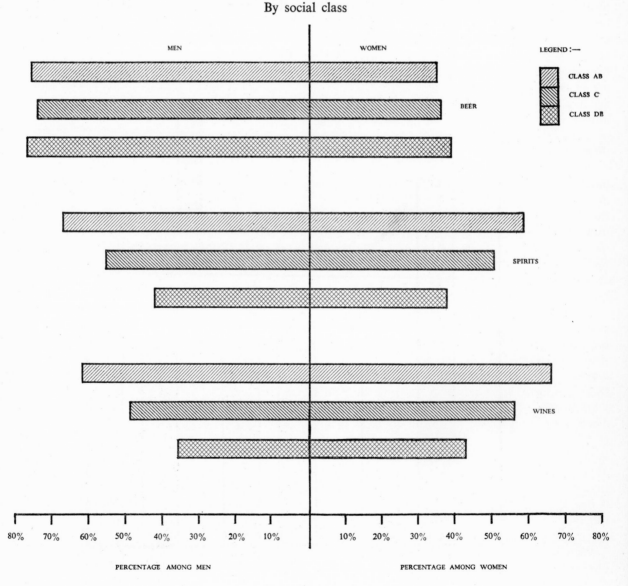

self who live and work in the district, and they have things to talk about; things that matter. The weather is not just an opening gambit for polite conversation as it is in the town and suburb. In the country rain does not merely wet roads and pavements, it makes things grow, and too much of it makes the clay soil by the river unworkable. To the townsman a frost in May can mean only making the choice between overcoat and raincoat; in the country it can cause a loss of thousands of pounds to the apple growers in the parish, and that in turn will affect most people and things around: the farmers, the workers, the shops, and the size of the church collection. People matter, too. Arthur Smith at Robinson's farm can plough better than anyone in the district and he likes talking about ploughing and that kind of thing. He is not like Alfred Smith who disappears every morning from his suburban villa to do some vague job in the City and is a little embarrassed if you ask him about it. In the country people's lives are linked, there are strong local loyalties and plenty of gossip, and the village pub matters a lot to them.

Whether in town or country, beer is drunk much more by men than by women. Less than one woman in ten is a regular beer drinker, while three men in ten, and rather more than that in middle age, drink it regularly, and just about as many again occasionally. Well over one-half of the women in this country do not touch the stuff at all and, a little surprisingly, nor do about a quarter of the men.

There are no comparative figures for years gone by, but it is likely that beer drinking has increased among women and become less with men. Putting this rather more plainly, more women do *some* beer drinking, but probably there are fewer men drinking it at all and those who do drink less on average than their forebears. This is certainly true of consumption in terms of alcohol, though the decrease has not been so great when measured just as a liquid. As anyone at any old-established pub will testify, beer is not the stuff it was. Some have suggested that it is but one more sign of petticoat influence and of the decay of Britain, but we are not going to be involved in any argument on this.

Wine and spirit drinking brings the sexes more closely together statistically as well as socially, but although there is little difference in the proportions of the total number of men and women who never drink wines and spirits at all, there are more men who are regular drinkers. Even so, the differences are not important and only a small proportion of either men or women drink spirits as often as once a week.

Like tobacco, alcoholic drinks are expensive very largely because of excise duties. The increase in price of drink since 1938 has not been as great as that of tobacco. Even so the price has just about trebled. On the other hand the consumption of beer and other alcoholic beverages has fallen slightly despite the increase in population. In alcohol equivalent it has probably gone down more than is shown by the total figures. Just as we pay a penny for our daily newspaper and get only a fraction of the printed matter which we had for the same money in 1938, so we are now getting a rather different brew in our tankards.

Consumption of the different types of alcoholic drinks varies greatly between economic and social classes. Men of all classes drink beer and there is not much difference in the proportions of each class who drink it, but the proportions of the total of women who drink beer increases steadily as incomes diminish.

With wines and spirits it is very different. For both of these classes of drink it is the people who are fairly well off who provide the highest proportion of drinkers. The majority of the wealthier classes drink these things regularly or occasionally, whereas most working class people do not drink them at all. No doubt this was originally due mainly to the differences in incomes, but nowadays these differences in consumption persist just as much because of social and occupational reasons as because of income variations. Manual workers' jobs often still create a thirst; for the wealthier people work, or the thought of it, just stirs up a desire for a drink. The business executive tells his wife that he had to entertain important customers; his wife tells him that Mrs. Poppe-Corkoran dropped in for a sherry and does he realize that they are due to go to the Waddle's cocktail party. These are occasions for the small glass and cigarettes rather than the pint mug and pipe.

In drinking, as with many other social habits, customs are changing and barriers are being removed. Women enter public houses almost as freely as men. Their presence causes no comment; on the contrary, it is likely first to subdue the volume of conversation in the public bar, then perhaps to raise its quality to an even higher level. Those who design the newer licensed houses recognize that they are to be used for meeting and moderate drinking by people of both sexes and all classes, and not just for male orgies. The chucker-out has given place to the uniformed attendant. In the country, and where possible in the towns and suburbs, the newer pubs have car parks. Perhaps all this means a loss of character and individuality, more pin-tables and fewer shove-ha'penny boards, more catering for the passing visitor than for the local population, but that is what people want, and it means more comfort and healthier places altogether. And anyway, there is no fear of our losing our traditions. We all know of a sixteenth-century pub in a village just off the coast road where the beer and the company are the best in England.

Tables relating to the foregoing Section will be found on pages 126 to 132

SECTION ELEVEN

TO PAINT THE LILY

This Section demands a strict objectivity which it is hard to preserve. It is about some of the means used by women to increase, change or maintain their beauty and, while beauty in any form is a delight to contemplate, it can be a thorny subject to discuss. With women's beauty it is even more difficult. There can be no absolute standards; judgment is warped by preferences, by emotion and sometimes determination to make the best of what is around us. Our strong preference for lovely brunettes, vivacious and rumbustious, might make it difficult to be more than lukewarm about the pale delicate beauty so much praised by some others, and just as we have our opinion on Nature's sculpture and use of colour so we must know our mind about if, and how, woman embellishes Nature's rude attempts.

We are, however, concerned not with ends but with means, not with how successful woman is in her efforts to cultivate her physical charms (her own opinion will be final on this), but with how she gets her results. There are some people, both men and women, who consider that even a touch of rouge on a jaded skin creates a painted Jezebel. Of course, their opinion must be respected, but beauty preparations are only a little nearer to the skin than clothes which are an unnatural covering and yet are demanded for decency and can charm the eye.

Whatever opinions may be about this, most women use some kinds of make-up and a large proportion use more than one aid to beauty.

Even so, about a third of all women use no cosmetics at all—nearly five-and-three-quarter million. Perhaps this seems like backwardness in taking advantage of the benefits of science; perhaps it is because of a complacent feeling that nature's work needs no embellishment. Almost certainly British women are not as beauty-conscious as those in some other countries, and especially in other English-speaking countries. They have not the same need to be. At the risk of incurring the charges of insularity and prejudice, it is probably safe to say that the standard of good looks in Britain compares very favourably with those in, say, America, and the lastingly fine natural complexions of our women are as much envied by those in sunbathed countries as the sunshine of those countries is envied by us. Our maligned climate has many advantages and lovely complexions are one of them.

Women in this country may use fewer beauty aids than Americans, but this refers to total use. There are over nine million women of 45 and over and half of these use no cosmetics; the older ones spent their beauty-conscious years in a period when the use of cosmetics was the mark of the fast woman and now their mature charm and dignity needs no artificial assistance.

It is very different with the younger women. Of those between 16 and 24, nine out of ten use face-powder and lipstick and the proportions are only slightly smaller for those aged 25 to 34; after 34 the recourse to these preparations falls

CHART 16
USE OF LIPSTICK
Percentage of women in each social class using lipstick in any one week,
analysed by age

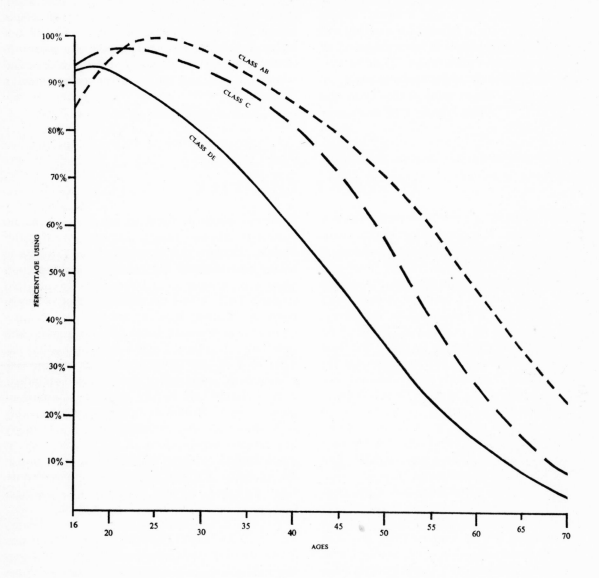

off more sharply. This is for all women, those who are housewives and those who are not. We should expect women's age to determine their attitude to cosmetics as a whole and especially to the use of lipstick and face-powder, although face-powder persists as a comfort even to one in four aged 65 and over. Rouge, too, is used more by the young than the middle aged and elderly, but in any case it is used by fewer in any age-

group than are lipstick or face-powder. Moreover, it is used more by those between 25 and 34 than by younger women or by those in the later age classes. This, too, is understandable and one would dare to suggest that a large part of the increase takes place during the stocktaking period of 29 to about 32 when it is realized, and sometimes admitted, that the twenties are over, and no one has yet mentioned, as he will with conviction, that woman's charm does not really begin until 35. Also it is a time when many women's complexions reflect the greater strains and anxieties of early married life, when earning their living is not just a matter of fixed hours in a 5-day week.

One must be careful about this, for there are some significant differences in the uses of cosmetics by housewives and non-housewives. Generally, those who are not housewives are more beauty conscious than those who have the responsibility of the home. Some might say that this was because the housewife had achieved what she set out to do, to get a partner and the security of a home, and there was now less need to take quite so much trouble, at least not until a seductive distraction necessitated putting on the war paint again. There may be something in this, but more important is whether the woman is going to meet people. Outside the domestic circle the housewife who works for a living outside the home is more beauty conscious than the one who does not. This is so, at least, for working class and lower-middle class women. For women in the higher social strata the differences are small, due partly, perhaps mainly, to the greater social activities of these people. The rivalries of earlier gaieties continue at the cocktail party and the bridge table.

But housewives or not, whether rich or poor, women spend very much more money on their appearance nowadays than in any earlier period. This is especially so for those in the lower income ranges, but it is true for all, except perhaps for a few of those with the highest incomes. The descriptions of Sunday finery and social events amongst poorer people by writers even fifty years ago make odd reading now. The joy of the new ribbon or the gay bonnet, or of the dress decked for an outing which we read about have given place to the appointment for a "perm" (or at least a special "hairdo"), nylons, and all the other accessories considered essential for any event out of the ordinary; and for many these things are considered to be the necessary equipment of everyday life. More money and the greater social opportunities provided by large-scale women's employment in World War I, and during the last generation, have brought this about. Moreover, there has been no lack of enterprise by manufacturers of cosmetics, hairdressers and a host of other people in stimulating women's demand for aids to beauty.

What of the results of all this? Are women more beautiful than they were twenty-five or fifty years ago? For centuries the history of this country has been influenced by beautiful women, and the villages, as well as the courts, have had their share of good looks. But no one could say whether one period had a bigger share than another, nor even whether the Gaiety Girls were more beautiful than Cochran's Young Ladies. It is safe to say, however, that standards as a whole, and especially of poorer people, are higher now than they have ever been. Partly this is due to the generally better health. Healthier parents are having healthier, and fewer, babies; there is more knowledge of diet and of hygiene, and better standards are insisted on at schools and in the home.

All these are sound foundation to good looks. Greater economic and social freedom, greater freedom in dress, more leisure and healthier activities have all helped to build well on that foundation.

Tables relating to the foregoing Section will be found on pages 133 to 138

SOME NEW HABITS

The man in the corner seat avoids further thought and argument on the latest Government proposal by saying that you can't change human nature. He usually gets away with it because you cannot argue with a man like that, and also because he may be right. We have overlaid some of our instincts with a veneer of humanitarianism or propriety and repressed them with by-laws and conventions, but in most of us there is still the urge to love and hate, to be selfish, rich and cruel, to gamble and seek adventure, to be vain or just to be amused. Some folk can still express a few of these urges in their daily work, but for most people adventure and the main zests of life have to be sought in leisure time.

Most work is nowadays moulded by the specialized division of labour, or, as it may seem to most of us, it is mainly dull routine. Yet although our senses are kept in suspense during our work, they are still fundamentally unimpaired. When work is ended we seek excitement, we try to escape to new worlds in which we at any rate do not have to work and, fortunately, most workers have more time and money for recreation than their ancestors had. We have already seen some of the ways this leisure is spent. Sometimes it is in individual hobbies, sometimes in activities shared by crowds of other people, and organized as a profit making business. This large-scale profit-making from sports, pastimes and entertainment is a fairly new feature of our national life. There has always been delight in a spectacle, but the pageants, public executions, fun around the maypole and even the theatre of earlier times were not highly commercialized. Local people usually took the principal part in these affairs, and they occurred infrequently enough to be important events in people's lives.

It is very different now. Quite apart from sports in which one can actually take part if one has the skill and energy, there are an embarrassing number of ways of spending money on entertainment. Theatres, cinemas, so-called funfairs, horse racing, dog racing—indeed, racing of almost every object on legs or wheels—football of different varieties, and a hundred other types of things to watch. But a spectacle is only one thing they provide. Many also satisfy the urge to gamble and in this country it is a very strong urge. It is obviously impossible in this study to look at more than a few of the modern ways of meeting our need for excitement, so we shall examine just three which are as typical as any: the cinema, dog racing and football pools.

As an influence on our lives the cinema is the most important of these. The cinema is described by different people as a good influence and a bad one; as an education, an escape, a drug, a corrupter of morals; as an art, an entertainment; as a place to hold hands; as a pernicious habit and many other things. No doubt it is all of these at some time or another, and for some people at any time it is an extremely popular form of spending a part of one's leisure time. For a great many people, especially young people, it *is* a habit. It is estimated, indeed, that only one person in five does not go to the cinema at all, and most of those who never go are middle aged or elderly. About two out of five adults go to the cinema at least once a week and roughly the same proportion go less often. This means that nearly 30 million people go to the cinema regularly or now and then. Catering for these millions are nearly five thousand cinemas spread over the country. It is exceptional for even a small town not to have at least one cinema, so that most of the population, rural and urban, is able to reach one without much difficulty; and compared with many ways of being entertained, educated, or corrupted, cinema-going is not very costly. A medium-priced seat at a suburban or provincial cinema involves an expenditure equivalent to the cost of playing billiards for an hour, losing two rubbers of bridge at a penny a hundred, ten cigarettes, half a pound of chocolates, a pint and a half of beer, and buying most of a Penguin book. These alternatives have their merits, but the cinema ticket makes us the unchallenged tenant for three hours or more of a comfortable seat from which we can see love made without

CHART 17

HOW OFTEN PEOPLE "USUALLY" GO TO THE CINEMA, SPRING 1949
Analyzed by sex, by social class and by age

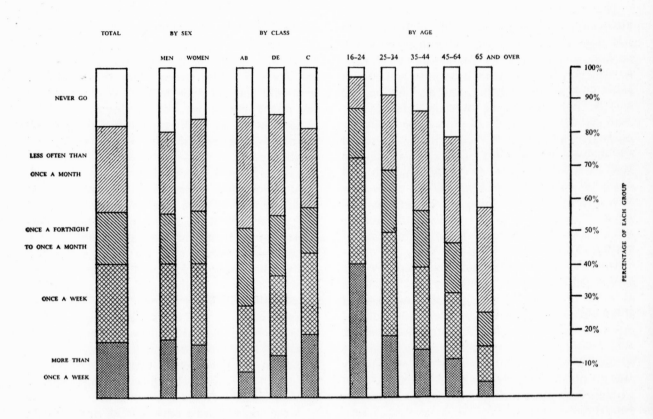

losing ground with our own companion, from which we can thrill with adventure and horror, see the news, laugh with Goofy and be awed by the unearthly versatility of the mighty Wurlitzer organ. All these, and more. With the stimulation of the pictures we can see ourselves as we should like others to see us. As Spencer Tracy triumphing over incredible difficulties as he leads his harassed but glorious band back to safety and admiring womenfolk; as George Arliss, suave and brilliant, the Prime Minister of the century. Our rather high-pitched voice becomes the smooth, seductive huskiness of Lauren Bacall and we forget the sink, the lathe and the shop counter and live for a little while in another world.

Perhaps this is one reason why the cinema especially attracts the very young. For three out of four young men and women aged 16 to 24 go to the cinema at least once a week: more than

one-half of these go twice or more. In the next age-group—25 to 34—far fewer people go as much as twice a week, but just under one-half go at least once a week. Middle-aged and older people go far less than this, which is what we should expect. At 20 we know we can, and probably shall, conquer the world as the hero does in the film; at 45 we realize that the world is putting up a stiff resistance; at 65 we merely tell incredulous youth how we should have done it had we thought it worth while.

There is much more to the comparative attendances than this. Most boys and girls are earning good wages now, many are living at home and have few financial or other responsibilities; they have plenty of leisure and no babies to curtail their activities. They had better go to the cinema while they can. By the time they are 35 and have two young children and a great deal less time and money to spend on leisure pursuits, they will have to plan each cinema outing and, as a consequence, they will probably be more particular about what they see on these occasions.

The feature which stands out in the figures of attendances of people of all ages, but especially with the young, is the regularity of going to the cinema. Nearly 15 million people go at least once a week and probably most of those go to the same cinema every week. It is a habit. They accept whatever programme is provided, good or bad, comedy or tragedy. If they are particular at all it is about the comfort of the seats, the leg room, and accessibility of choc-ices. It is easy to condemn this lack of discrimination as laziness and poor enterprise, but, after all, in this respect it is no worse in principle than other habits like accepting what is provided in a regular daily or weekly paper, or in reading the book of the month chosen by someone else.

Unless accompanied by companions with expensive appetites, going to the cinema is a luxury that can be afforded by most people. Indeed, it is a leisure habit much more popular with people with small incomes than those who are better off. Nearly one-half of those people in the two lowest income groups go at least once a week; the proportions are much less at the other end of the economic scale. Partly this is accounted for by the larger proportion of younger people in the low income section, but it is also because the cinema is accessible to those who cannot afford, or have not developed, more expensive tastes like golf, tennis and bridge clubs and who have no theatres or ballet situated conveniently for them.

Age, income and social class all have a large influence on cinema going, but there is very little difference in the proportions of men and women in these various groups who go. It is no more a habit of the girl then the boy, or of the woman than the man. Probably that is because they go together.

Two other modern habits—football pools and dog racing—are, however, the province of men more than of women. With these habits, however much is said to the contrary, the attraction is mainly the opportunity to gamble. Plenty of people who go to football matches have no financial interest in the result. They go in the

hope of seeing their favourite team win a good game. They may have completed their football pools for the week, but that will not affect their attitude to the game they see on Saturday. The converse is by no means true. Many people who do their pools each week do not go near a match at all and some would not understand it if they did. They may never have known that glorious moment when, after taking a fast pass from the outside-left, you hoodwink the opposing half and net a terrific drive from twenty-five yards range—the goal that puts your side into the next round. They may not appreciate the finesse, or realize the skill that is needed in the game. They merely want an excuse to gamble.

They are not unique. This is a nation of gamblers, although, as with drinking, it has never quite made up its mind about what moral attitude it should take to gambling. Money changes hands on an almost infinite variety of unpredictable events: the result of a horse race, of dog races, outdoor games of all kinds, the inglorious uncertainty of cards, and even the golfer, playing a game which involves physical skill as well as rhetoric, has to have five bob on the round. There is almost every form of gambling except the State Lottery, which was never happy in this country and now is considered respectable enough only for foreigners.

Some of this gambling can undoubtedly be harmful. Like drinking it can become an obsession and in excess it is bad, even if one wins. But although the evil effects of gambling are found in real life, and although the national annual turnover of the main organized forms of gambling is well over £500 million, the average citizen is in little danger of being corrupted by the habit. With so much social and other security he likes his flutter on something a little less certain.

Football pools have special attractions. For a very small outlay a man can exercise his occult powers on a number of future events. If his predictions are wrong, his loss is small, and if he wins he may win enough to give him independence, a cottage in the country and a daily pint of beer for the rest of his life. Win or lose, he has a lot of excitement on Saturday evening and the pleasures of anticipation for some days before that.

It is a poor man's hobby. About half of the

65

CHART 18
FOOTBALL POOLS

PERCENTAGE OF THE POPULATION AGED 21 AND OVER SENDING IN A COUPON IN ANY ONE WEEK, SPRING 1949

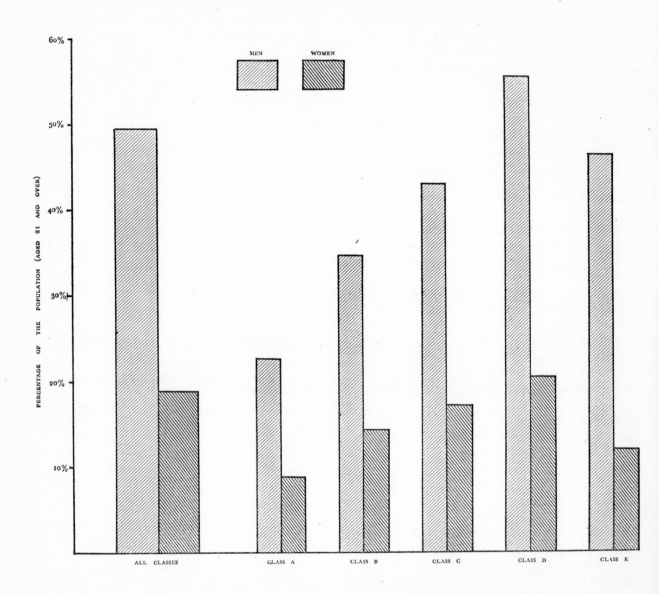

working class men do their pools in season, whereas those wealthier people who gamble do so in other ways. It is also a man's occupation; less than one woman in five goes in for football pools. Perhaps it would be more accurate to say that few women actually send in the pool coupons, though no doubt many more give their menfolk every kind of assistance when they are completing their forecasts. On the other hand, it is probable that a fair proportion of the women who say that they go in for football pools only provide the stake, or part of it, on the coupon filled in by their husband, father or brother.

In all, over eleven million people of 21 and over take part in these pools and it is estimated that they spend between £60 and £70 million on them each year. This total expenditure is very much less than the amount spent on betting either on dogs or horses, but whereas the volume of these other forms of betting has decreased very much in the last two or three years, participation in pools has not. This is probably because it is possible to stake only a little without inconvenience and without incurring the displeasure of a bookmaker, and for that stake we get a more varied and sustained excitement than with some other forms of gambling. For men the average stake is 3s. 10d.; for women it is about one-half of that amount, so men's financial support of the pools is even more than the figures of participation would suggest. Over 80 per cent of the participants spend less than 5s. each week, but the few who stake more than 10s. account for nearly one-fifth of the total amount staked.

CHART 19

FOOTBALL POOLS

AMOUNTS STAKED BY PARTICIPANTS IN ANY ONE WEEK, SPRING 1949

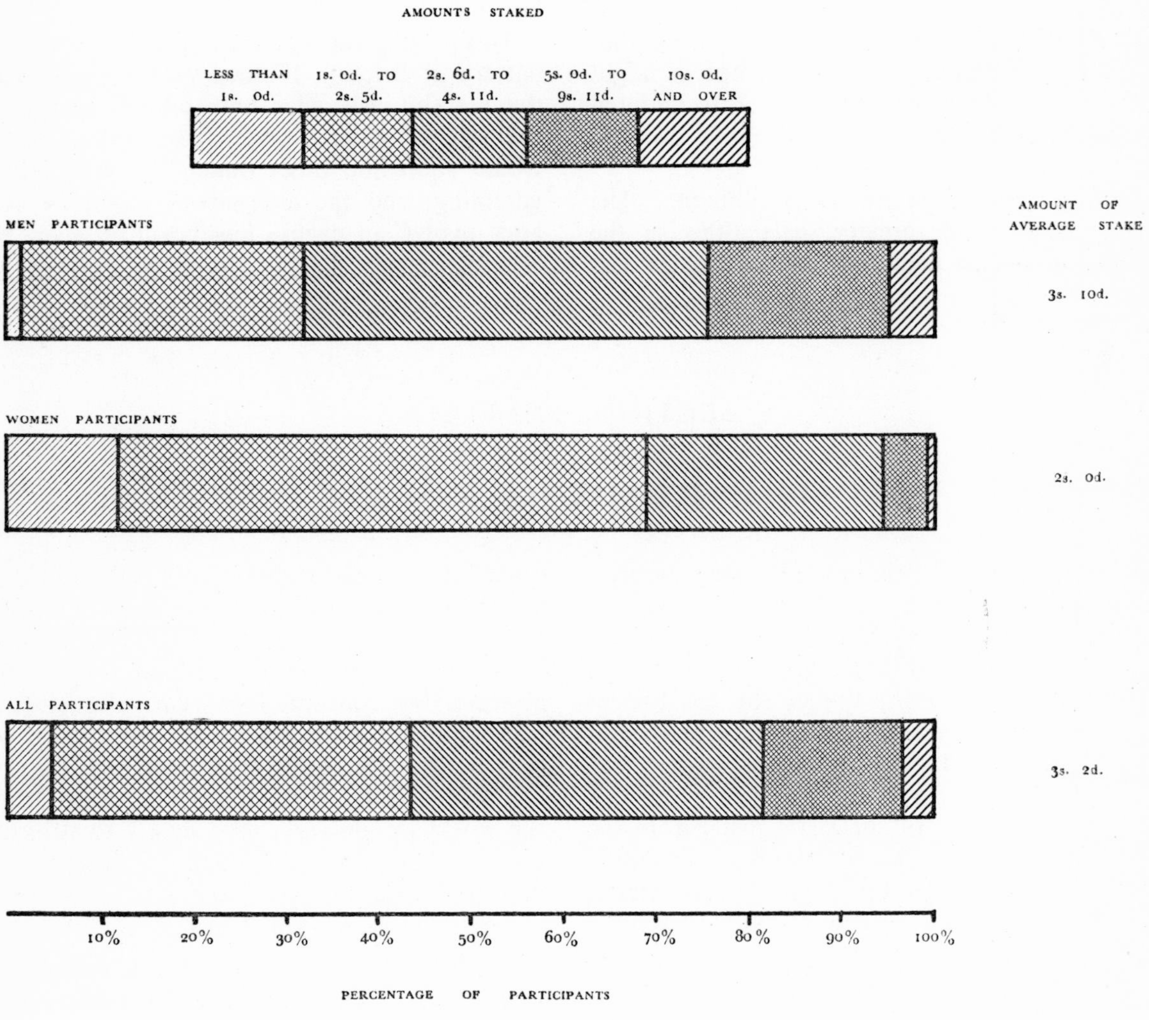

AMOUNTS STAKED

LESS THAN 1s. 0d.	1s. 0d. TO 2s. 5d.	2s. 6d. TO 4s. 11d.	5s. 0d. TO 9s. 11d.	10s. 0d. AND OVER

AMOUNT OF AVERAGE STAKE

MEN PARTICIPANTS — 3s. 10d.

WOMEN PARTICIPANTS — 2s. 0d.

ALL PARTICIPANTS — 3s. 2d.

10% 20% 30% 40% 50% 60% 70% 80% 90% 100%

PERCENTAGE OF PARTICIPANTS

67

These are just some of the facts shown by the Survey. If he is cautious the statistician will leave it to others to analyse, and take sides on, other aspects of pools and of gambling as a whole. For gambling is widely attacked from many sides as a waster of money, time and effort, and as a menace to morals and to the stability of the home. Football pools may be a waste of time, money and effort—and most people taking part in them have thought this when their chosen teams have let them down—but, for the participant, they do not waste much of any of these things, and they are no more a menace to the home and backbone of the nation than most other routine leisure occupations. Indeed, whereas *The Times* cross-word puzzle may put one member of the family in surly isolation from the rest, the filling up of football coupons may unite the group in zealous common endeavour. From the national stand-point the waste of manpower in the pools' staff is a different matter, but the promoters might say that they are redistributing part of the national income. The Board of Inland Revenue does no more.

With greyhound racing it is different. The betting is on a far greater scale although the number of people gambling on dogs is far less than those taking part in football pools. Whereas people go to football matches to see a game, they go to dog races almost entirely to gamble. True the greyhound is a graceful beast and in action it is a delight to watch, but in a whole race meeting the greyhounds are in action only a few minutes. There are big intervals between each race in which sensitive persons can reflect on the aesthetic charm of the spectacle, but these intervals are used mainly for analyses of the health and speed of the dogs in the next race with a view to backing them with money. Despite the immense amount of money spent in gambling on dogs (it is estimated to be well over £200 million a year) it is not a sport that appeals to many. Nineteen out of twenty adults never go to the races at all, and the great majority of people would lose no sleep if the greyhound lost its competitive instincts altogether.

This form of racing has its place in the gambling pattern of Britain. If there were no greyhounds these enthusiasts who now get excitement and the hope of making money from betting on them would soon find other outlets for their zest for gambling, and the alternatives might be worse and involve an excuse less beautiful than greyhounds.

Tables relating to the foregoing Section will be found on pages 139 to 143

SECTION THIRTEEN

THE READING PUBLIC

Not many years ago Britain used more newsprint per head than any other nation, more even than the United States. Her appetite for reading is still great, probably greater than ever, but, as with food and a good many other things, she has had to make do with far less newsprint since the beginning of the war. In 1948 our consumption was nearly 18 pounds per head, less than a third of what it was in any of the years just before the war. So far from being the leading consumer, Britain had fallen far below the United States, Canada and Sweden, and was slightly less than Switzerland.

The standard of education and literacy in these other countries is certainly very high, but it was not these but their command of natural resources or foreign exchange which improved their position in relation to Britain. Indeed, for one of them at least, the consumption seems altogether out of proportion to needs as they are understood by some hard-hit, but still quite literate, European countries. The United States with 6 per cent of the world's population used nearly two-thirds of the world's newsprint in 1948. Anyone who has had to tackle two or three American Sunday newspapers could well believe this and wonder how such a busy people with such small families could ever manage to read more than a tiny fraction of these papers and their numerous supplements for people of all ages.

The British have not, however, lost reading matter in the same proportion as they have lost supplies of paper. The size of their newspapers is still deplorably small and ranks with those of nations whose standard of literacy is far less, but thanks to ingenious make-up born of necessity, and more economical styles of writing, the effects of paper-famine have been lessened. Moreover, the war stimulated the desire and, indeed, the need to read, and for most types of reading matter that demand has been maintained.

In 1948 twice as much was spent on newspapers, books and magazines as in 1938 and, even allowing for the increase in price of some classes of reading matter, the rise in this period was nearly 70 per cent. Partly, of course, this increase was because people get less for their money with each periodical than they used to and so they buy more papers and magazines. Nowadays three people out of four read a national morning newspaper and one in four reads at least two. With general weekly magazines the proportion reading two or more is much higher, nearly one-half of the total adult population.

A larger proportion of men than women read daily papers, but the difference is not great; this applies to Sunday and evening papers as well, but for men and women of all classes Sunday is a big day for reading. Nine out of ten women read a national Sunday paper; more than half of them read two or more. This is so in all classes; indeed, for both men and women, those who are not so well off are apt to buy two or more Sunday newspapers than are those with higher income groups. The reverse is true of the weekday newspapers.

Readership figures of Sunday newspapers are, of course, only a partial guide to the extent of weekend reading. Between the various classes there are wide differences in the reading of general weekly and monthly magazines. A much larger proportion of people of the wealthier classes buy these magazines than do poorer people and, although the days of publication are spread over the week, it is likely that a great part of this reading is done at weekends.

While an overwhelming majority of people of all classes read national daily newspapers, it is not so with local weeklies and twice-weeklies. About one-half of the population reads one only of these papers and about one in ten reads two or more. This is to be expected, although some might be depressed by this evidence of lack of interest in local affairs. The interest does not vary much between the various age and class groups, but readership of these papers, as of national daily newspapers, too, is greater in the South of England and in Wales than in the Midlands and northwards. This does not, however, apply to Sunday newspapers, general weekly and general monthly magazines, nor to women's magazines. The majority of Scots read no national daily, but three in four read Sunday papers and nearly one-half of them—a far bigger proportion than in England and Wales—read three or more. Similarly the Scots are extensive readers of general weekly magazines, and for these again they are more likely than people in other regions to buy more than one of these magazines.

Age and class have a great influence on readership of periodicals in general, but the influence varies according to the type of magazine. A larger proportion of both men and women read general weekly and monthly magazines than in the lower income groups, but the proportions get steadily less as people get older.

The women's magazines need special mention. Of the total of women the majority do not read a women's weekly magazine and only about one in three a monthly one, but class and income greatly affect the proportions. Among working class girls, especially the very young ones, a choice is for weekly rather than monthly magazines. Monthly magazines are relatively far more popular with the better-off women, more than half of whom read at least one, and one in four reads two or more. Again, however, it is the younger women who read them although the fall in proportion as ages increase is not so sharp as for the women's weeklies.

No comment will be made on the readership of individual publications. The tables which follow present the facts eloquently and more economically than could be done in words. It is for this reason that these tables run on directly from this Section, rather than being included in the statistical Section.

I   CLASS ANALYSIS OF READERSHIP
Men and women combined

Women's magazines have been excluded from this table	ALL CLASSES		CLASS AB		CLASS C		CLASS DE	
NUMBER OF INFORMANTS	13,000		2,307		3,536		7,157	
ESTIMATED POPULATION AGED 16 AND OVER	36,800,000		4,200,000		6,450,000		26,150,000	
Readers of:	%	'000	%	'000	%	'000	%	'000
RADIO TIMES	54·2	19,940	69·9	2,940	62·3	4,020	49·7	12,980
NEWS OF THE WORLD	48·3	17,770	24·3	1,020	36·8	2,380	55·0	14,370
PEOPLE	32·8	12,060	18·9	790	29·2	1,890	35·9	9,380
SUNDAY PICTORIAL	31·0	11,430	21·5	900	26·3	1,700	33·8	8,830
DAILY EXPRESS	26·7	9,830	28·0	1,180	29·8	1,930	25·7	6,730
PICTURE POST	26·0	9,560	36·8	1,550	29·8	1,920	23·3	6,090
DAILY MIRROR	25·3	9,320	13·5	570	19·7	1,270	28·6	7,480
SUNDAY EXPRESS	19·8	7,290	35·6	1,500	28·7	1,850	15·1	3,940
ILLUSTRATED	17·4	6,390	21·6	910	19·1	1,230	16·3	4,250
DAILY MAIL	14·6	5,380	23·4	980	18·3	1,180	12·3	3,220
SUNDAY DISPATCH	13·8	5,080	21·1	890	16·4	1,060	12·0	3,130
LONDON EVENING NEWS	12·8	4,710	15·8	660	15·8	1,020	11·6	3,020
JOHN BULL	12·2	4,500	6·8	280	11·4	740	13·3	3,480
LILLIPUT	11·8	4,360	16·3	690	13·2	850	10·8	2,820
EMPIRE NEWS	11·3	4,140	*4·1*	170	7·8	500	13·3	3,470
DAILY HERALD	11·0	4,060	*2·7*	120	7·6	490	13·2	3,460
EVERYBODY'S	10·9	4,010	9·1	390	12·0	780	10·9	2,850
NEWS CHRONICLE	9·3	3,420	9·0	380	11·2	720	8·9	2,320
SUNDAY POST	8·6	3,160	5·5	230	8·6	560	9·1	2,370
WEEKLY NEWS (THOMSONS)	8·3	3,070	*3·0*	130	6·2	400	9·7	2,540
SUNDAY CHRONICLE	7·9	2,890	11·6	490	9·8	630	6·8	1,770
DAILY TELEGRAPH	7·3	2,670	22·9	970	12·7	820	3·4	880
SUNDAY GRAPHIC	7·0	2,590	11·0	460	8·8	570	6·0	1,560
LONDON STAR	6·8	2,510	7·0	290	6·4	420	6·9	1,800
LONDON OPINION	6·8	2,490	9·3	390	8·9	580	5·8	1,520
LONDON EVENING STANDARD	5·0	1,850	12·1	510	7·1	460	3·4	890
PICTUREGOER	4·9	1,800	*3·9*	170	4·4	290	5·2	1,350
PUNCH	4·8	1,780	15·6	660	6·3	410	2·8	720
MEN ONLY	4·8	1,760	6·2	260	5·7	370	4·3	1,140
SUNDAY TIMES	4·6	1,680	20·0	840	7·2	460	*1·4*	370
REYNOLDS NEWS	4·3	1,590	*2·9*	120	3·9	250	4·7	1,220
SUNDAY MAIL	4·1	1,510	*2·4*	100	3·9	250	4·4	1,150
PEOPLE'S FRIEND	3·8	1,410	*1·8*	70	3·6	230	4·2	1,110
DAILY GRAPHIC	3·7	1,360	7·0	300	4·6	290	3·0	770
OBSERVER	3·5	1,290	14·1	600	5·9	380	*1·2*	320
TATLER	3·5	1,270	9·7	410	4·8	310	2·1	560
ILLUSTRATED LONDON NEWS	3·4	1,240	8·9	380	4·4	290	2·2	580
TIT-BITS	3·2	1,180	*1·7*	70	3·7	240	3·3	870
IDEAL HOME	3·2	1,160	6·6	280	4·5	290	2·3	590
STRAND MAGAZINE	3·1	1,120	6·5	270	3·9	250	2·3	600

Percentages in bold type (**26·5**) are subject to a relatively small proportion of error.
Percentages in italic type (*3·7*) are subject to a relatively large proportion of error.

II   CLASS ANALYSIS OF READERSHIP
Men

Women's magazines have been excluded from this table	ALL CLASSES		CLASS AB		CLASS C		CLASS DE	
NUMBER OF INFORMANTS	6,003		1,077		1,630		3,296	
ESTIMATED POPULATION AGED 16 AND OVER	17,000,000		1,950,000		3,000,000		12,050,000	
Readers of:	%	'000	%	'000	%	'000	%	'000
RADIO TIMES	55·0	9,330	70·2	1,380	62·8	1,870	50·5	6,080
NEWS OF THE WORLD	52·2	8,870	27·3	540	39·8	1,180	59·3	7,150
PEOPLE	35·4	6,020	20·5	400	30·2	900	39·1	4,710
SUNDAY PICTORIAL	32·5	5,510	23·3	460	26·5	790	35·4	4,260
DAILY EXPRESS	31·9	5,420	33·3	650	35·1	1,040	30·9	3,720
PICTURE POST	29·1	4,940	39·0	770	32·6	970	26·6	3,200
DAILY MIRROR	24·9	4,230	14·4	280	19·0	570	28·1	3,380
SUNDAY EXPRESS	22·4	3,810	38·5	760	30·6	910	17·8	2,140
ILLUSTRATED	18·9	3,220	22·1	430	20·0	600	18·2	2,190
LILLIPUT	15·6	2,650	20·4	400	16·8	500	14·6	1,750
DAILY MAIL	15·3	2,610	23·7	470	19·4	580	13·0	1,560
SUNDAY DISPATCH	15·2	2,590	22·9	450	18·0	540	13·3	1,600
JOHN BULL	14·3	2,440	8·3	160	11·8	350	15·9	1,920
DAILY HERALD	13·7	2,330	3·5	70	10·1	300	16·3	1,960
LONDON EVENING NEWS	13·7	2,320	17·5	340	17·1	510	12·2	1,470
EMPIRE NEWS	13·2	2,230	5·6	110	9·2	270	15·4	1,850
EVERYBODY'S	13·1	2,220	9·9	200	12·8	380	13·7	1,650
NEWS CHRONICLE	11·2	1,910	10·3	200	12·6	380	11·0	1,330
LONDON OPINION	9·7	1,650	12·6	250	12·0	360	8·7	1,050
SUNDAY POST	8·7	1,480	5·8	110	9·0	270	9·1	1,100
SUNDAY CHRONICLE	8·5	1,450	12·1	240	11·3	340	7·2	870
WEEKLY NEWS (THOMSONS)	8·1	1,380	3·1	60	5·3	160	9·6	1,160
MEN ONLY	8·0	1,370	9·3	180	9·0	270	7·6	920
LONDON STAR	7·5	1,270	7·4	150	6·9	210	7·6	910
SUNDAY GRAPHIC	7·3	1,230	10·0	200	9·2	270	6·3	760
DAILY TELEGRAPH	7·1	1,210	23·6	460	13·1	390	3·0	360
PUNCH	5·6	950	17·1	340	6·9	200	3·4	410
REYNOLDS NEWS	5·6	940	4·2	80	5·2	150	5·9	710
LONDON EVENING STANDARD	5·5	940	12·2	240	8·2	240	3·8	460
SUNDAY MAIL	4·6	790	2·9	60	4·0	120	5·1	610
ILLUSTRATED LONDON NEWS	4·5	760	10·4	200	5·8	170	3·2	380
PICTUREGOER	4·5	760	3·3	70	4·0	120	4·7	570
TIT-BITS	4·4	750	2·4	50	4·3	130	4·8	570
STRAND MAGAZINE	4·2	710	7·7	150	5·2	160	3·3	400
ARGOSY	4·2	700	6·6	130	4·2	130	3·7	450
SUNDAY TIMES	4·0	670	17·1	340	6·7	200	1·2	140
OBSERVER	3·4	580	13·4	260	6·0	180	1·1	140
NEWS REVIEW	3·0	520	5·0	100	4·6	140	2·3	280
TATLER	3·0	520	8·1	160	4·4	130	1·9	230
LISTENER	3·0	510	7·0	140	4·4	130	2·0	240

Percentages in bold type (**26·5**) are subject to a relatively small proportion ot error.
Percentages in italic type (*3·7*) are subject to a relatively large proportion of error.

III   CLASS ANALYSIS OF READERSHIP
All women

	ALL CLASSES		CLASS AB		CLASS C		CLASS DE	
NUMBER OF INFORMANTS	6,997		1,230		1,906		3,861	
ESTIMATED POPULATION AGED 16 AND OVER	19,800,000		2,250,000		3,450,000		14,100,000	
Readers of:	%	'000	%	'000	%	'000	%	'000
RADIO TIMES	**53·5**	10,610	**69·6**	1,560	**61·8**	2,150	**48·9**	6,890
NEWS OF THE WORLD	**44·9**	8,910	**21·6**	490	**34·4**	1,200	**51·3**	7,230
PEOPLE	**30·5**	6,040	**17·4**	390	**28·4**	990	**33·1**	4,660
SUNDAY PICTORIAL	**29·8**	5,910	**19·8**	450	**26·1**	910	**32·3**	4,560
DAILY MIRROR	**25·7**	5,090	**12·8**	290	**20·3**	700	**29·1**	4,100
PICTURE POST	**23·3**	4,620	**34·8**	780	**27·4**	950	**20·5**	2,890
DAILY EXPRESS	**22·2**	4,410	**23·5**	530	**25·3**	880	**21·3**	3,000
SUNDAY EXPRESS	**17·6**	3,480	**33·0**	740	**27·1**	940	**12·8**	1,800
WOMAN	**16·3**	3,230	**14·8**	330	**19·6**	680	**15·7**	2,220
ILLUSTRATED	**16·0**	3,170	**21·2**	480	**18·3**	640	**14·6**	2,060
DAILY MAIL	**14·0**	2,780	**23·1**	520	**17·3**	600	**11·7**	1,650
WOMAN'S OWN	**13·9**	2,750	**10·6**	240	**14·5**	500	**14·2**	2,000
SUNDAY DISPATCH	**12·6**	2,490	**19·5**	440	**15·1**	520	**10·8**	1,530
LONDON EVENING NEWS	**12·0**	2,390	**14·3**	320	**14·6**	510	**11·0**	1,560
WOMAN'S WEEKLY	**10·9**	2,160	*7·1*	160	**11·3**	390	**11·4**	1,610
JOHN BULL	**10·4**	2,060	*5·4*	120	**11·0**	380	**11·1**	1,560
EMPIRE NEWS	**9·6**	1,910	*2·8*	60	**6·6**	230	**11·5**	1,620
EVERYBODY'S	**9·0**	1,790	**8·5**	190	**11·3**	390	**8·5**	1,200
DAILY HERALD	**8·8**	1,740	*2·0*	50	**5·5**	190	**10·6**	1,500
LILLIPUT	**8·6**	1,700	**12·7**	280	**10·1**	350	**7·6**	1,070
WEEKLY NEWS (THOMSONS)	**8·5**	1,690	*2·9*	70	**7·0**	240	**9·8**	1,380
SUNDAY POST	**8·5**	1,680	*5·3*	120	**8·3**	290	**9·0**	1,270
WOMAN AND HOME	**8·0**	1,580	**9·4**	210	**9·7**	340	**7·3**	1,030
GOOD HOUSEKEEPING	**7·7**	1,530	**17·2**	390	**10·9**	380	**5·4**	760
NEWS CHRONICLE	**7·6**	1,520	**7·8**	180	**10·0**	350	**7·0**	990
DAILY TELEGRAPH	**7·4**	1,460	**22·4**	500	**12·4**	430	**3·7**	530
SUNDAY CHRONICLE	**7·3**	1,440	**11·2**	250	**8·5**	300	**6·3**	890
SUNDAY GRAPHIC	**6·8**	1,350	**11·8**	260	**8·3**	290	**5·6**	800
LONDON STAR	**6·3**	1,240	*6·6*	150	**6·0**	210	**6·3**	880
WOMAN'S ILLUSTRATED	**5·7**	1,130	*4·5*	100	**5·8**	200	**5·9**	830
VOGUE	**5·4**	1,070	**13·3**	300	**8·4**	290	**3·4**	480
PEOPLE'S FRIEND	**5·4**	1,060	*2·4*	50	**5·5**	190	**5·8**	820
STITCHCRAFT	**5·3**	1,060	*6·3*	140	**6·8**	240	**4·8**	680
PICTUREGOER	**5·3**	1,050	*4·5*	100	*4·8*	170	**5·5**	780
RED LETTER	**5·3**	1,040	*	*	*2·6*	90	**6·7**	950
HOUSEWIFE	**5·1**	1,020	**8·9**	200	**7·1**	250	**4·1**	570
SUNDAY TIMES	**5·1**	1,010	**22·6**	510	**7·6**	260	*1·7*	230
WOMAN'S JOURNAL	**4·8**	960	**13·4**	300	**6·3**	220	**3·1**	440
LONDON EVENING STANDARD	**4·6**	910	**12·0**	270	**6·1**	210	**3·1**	430
HOME NOTES	**4·5**	880	*4·0*	90	*4·1*	140	**4·6**	650

Percentages in bold type (**26·5**) are subject to a relatively small proportion of error.
Percentages in italic type (*3·7*) are subject to a relatively large proportion of error.
*=Either less that 1·0% or less than 10,000 readers.

IV CLASS ANALYSIS OF READERSHIP
Housewives

	ALL CLASSES		CLASS AB		CLASS C		CLASS DE	
NUMBER OF INFORMANTS	5,235		946		1,440		2,849	
ESTIMATED POPULATION AGED 16 AND OVER	14,750,000		1,700,000		2,650,000		10,400,000	
Readers of:	%	'000	%	'000	%	'000	%	'000
RADIO TIMES	**52·8**	7,790	**68·9**	1,190	**62·2**	1,630	**47·8**	4,970
NEWS OF THE WORLD	**45·3**	6,690	**20·0**	350	**33·0**	870	**52·7**	5,480
PEOPLE	**30·2**	4,460	**16·3**	280	**27·6**	720	**33·2**	3,450
SUNDAY PICTORIAL	**28·8**	4,250	**19·1**	330	**24·2**	640	**31·5**	3,280
DAILY MIRROR ..	**24·4**	3,610	**12·2**	210	**19·6**	510	**27·7**	2,880
DAILY EXPRESS	**22·7**	3,350	**23·3**	400	**25·6**	670	**21·9**	2,270
PICTURE POST	**21·1**	3,110	**31·6**	550	**25·1**	660	**18·3**	1,900
SUNDAY EXPRESS	**17·4**	2,570	**33·2**	570	**27·2**	710	**12·3**	1,280
WOMAN	**14·3**	2,110	**13·1**	230	**17·6**	460	**13·6**	1,420
ILLUSTRATED	**14·2**	2,100	**17·9**	310	**16·5**	430	**13·1**	1,360
DAILY MAIL	**13·9**	2,050	**22·5**	390	**17·8**	470	**11·5**	1,190
SUNDAY DISPATCH	**12·7**	1,880	**20·0**	350	**15·1**	400	**10·9**	1,140
LONDON EVENING NEWS ..	**12·3**	1,820	**14·0**	240	**14·7**	390	**11·4**	1,190
WOMAN'S OWN	**10·9**	1,610	*8·8*	150	**11·7**	310	**11·0**	1,150
EMPIRE NEWS	**10·0**	1,480	*2·7*	50	**7·4**	190	**11·9**	1,230
JOHN BULL	**10·0**	1,470	*5·4*	90	**10·3**	270	**10·6**	1,110
WOMAN'S WEEKLY .:	**9·3**	1,370	*6·7*	120	**9·0**	240	**9·8**	1,020
DAILY HERALD	**9·2**	1,360	*1·9*	30	**5·6**	150	**11·4**	1,180
SUNDAY POST	**9·0**	1,330	*6·1*	110	**8·3**	220	**9·7**	1,010
WEEKLY NEWS (THOMSONS) ..	**8·7**	1,280	*3·0*	50	**6·7**	180	**10·1**	1,050
NEWS CHRONICLE	**8·2**	1,220	*8·4*	140	**10·1**	260	**7·8**	810
EVERYBODY'S	**8·0**	1,190	*7·7*	130	**10·9**	290	**7·4**	770
WOMAN AND HOME	**7·9**	1,160	**9·8**	170	**9·9**	260	**7·1**	730
DAILY TELEGRAPH	**7·7**	1,130	**23·0**	400	**13·7**	360	*3·6*	370
LILLIPUT	**7·6**	1,130	**11·3**	200	**8·7**	230	**6·7**	700
GOOD HOUSEKEEPING	**7·6**	1,120	**17·4**	300	**10·1**	260	**5·3**	550
SUNDAY CHRONICLE	**7·1**	1,060	**11·4**	200	**8·9**	230	**6·0**	620
SUNDAY GRAPHIC	**6·4**	950	**11·8**	200	**7·8**	200	**5·2**	540
LONDON STAR	**5·9**	880	*6·2*	110	**5·6**	150	**6·0**	620
PEOPLE'S FRIEND	**5·4**	800	*2·7*	50	**5·0**	130	**5·9**	620
SUNDAY TIMES	**5·4**	790	**24·1**	420	**8·5**	220	*1·5*	150
HOUSEWIFE	**5·3**	790	*9·2*	160	**7·6**	200	**4·1**	430
LONDON EVENING STANDARD ..	**5·0**	730	**12·5**	220	**6·9**	180	*3·2*	340
WOMAN'S ILLUSTRATED	**4·6**	680	*4·0*	70	*5·1*	130	**4·6**	480
WOMAN'S JOURNAL	**4·4**	660	**13·3**	230	*5·9*	160	*2·6*	270
RED LETTER	**4·4**	640	*	*	*1·9*	50	**5·7**	590
DAILY GRAPHIC	**4·3**	640	*8·8*	150	*5·1*	140	*3·4*	350
STITCHCRAFT	**4·3**	640	*6·6*	110	*5·4*	140	*3·7*	380
VOGUE	**4·1**	600	**11·1**	190	**6·9**	180	*2·2*	230
SUNDAY MAIL	**3·9**	580	*2·4*	40	**4·2**	110	**4·1**	430

Percentages in bold type (**26·5**) are subject to a relatively small proportion of error.
Percentages in italic type (*3·7*) are subject to a relatively large proportion of error.
*=Either less than 1·0% or less than 10,000 readers.

V REGIONAL ANALYSIS OF READERSHIP
Men and women combined

Women's magazines have been excluded from this table	TOTAL ALL REGIONS	SOUTH-EAST	SOUTH-WEST & WALES	MIDLANDS	NORTH-WEST	NORTH-EAST & NORTH	SCOTLAND
			REGIONS (for definitions see page 88)				
NUMBER OF INFORMANTS	13,000	4,572	1,455	2,029	1,682	1,872	1,390
ESTIMATED POPULATION AGED 16 AND OVER	36,800,000	12,600,000	4,150,000	5,850,000	4,850,000	5,450,000	3,900,000
Readers of:	%	%	%	%	%	%	%
RADIO TIMES	54·2	57·0	61·1	58·0	50·0	53·0	39·1
NEWS OF THE WORLD	48·3	50·7	56·1	51·7	38·5	48·6	39·1
PEOPLE	32·8	31·6	36·6	35·6	32·1	38·5	21·0
SUNDAY PICTORIAL	31·0	37·5	40·3	36·7	15·5	27·6	16·0
DAILY EXPRESS	26·7	25·1	26·8	25·2	27·8	21·1	40·4
PICTURE POST	26·0	27·6	30·7	23·5	23·3	26·4	22·3
DAILY MIRROR	25·3	35·8	28·0	29·9	13·3	18·4	6·4
SUNDAY EXPRESS	19·8	22·0	23·4	16·9	16·6	16·5	22·0
ILLUSTRATED	17·4	17·0	17·6	18·4	16·4	17·5	17·7
DAILY MAIL	14·6	13·7	15·8	17·6	15·0	17·0	8·2
SUNDAY DISPATCH	13·8	15·7	17·9	13·2	12·8	12·4	7·6
LONDON EVENING NEWS	12·8	36·2	3·6	*	*	*	*
JOHN BULL	12·2	11·0	12·4	12·3	13·1	16·0	9·7
LILLIPUT	11·8	14·6	11·3	8·6	10·6	13·1	8·1
EMPIRE NEWS	11·3	1·4	6·2	13·2	33·0	19·0	7·4
DAILY HERALD	11·0	10·8	14·8	13·4	10·0	12·6	3·2
EVERYBODY'S	10·9	10·8	12·5	11·4	9·8	11·2	9·6
NEWS CHRONICLE	9·3	13·0	11·7	7·8	8·7	7·2	*
SUNDAY POST	8·6	*	*	*	*	1·4	77·3
WEEKLY NEWS (THOMSONS)	8·3	*	3·0	4·8	8·3	12·9	37·2
SUNDAY CHRONICLE	7·9	2·1	5·1	7·1	23·0	12·6	5·1
DAILY TELEGRAPH	7·3	14·1	8·2	4·2	2·6	2·9	*
SUNDAY GRAPHIC	7·0	8·4	9·3	6·9	5·6	6·1	3·3
LONDON STAR	6·8	19·6	*	*	*	*	*
LONDON OPINION	6·8	8·6	6·2	5·3	5·1	7·3	5·0
LONDON EVENING STANDARD	5·0	14·3	1·0	*	*	*	*
PICTUREGOER	4·9	5·1	6·7	4·0	3·6	6·3	3·2
PUNCH	4·8	6·7	6·1	3·0	3·3	4·2	3·1
MEN ONLY	4·8	5·7	4·3	4·1	3·9	5·0	4·4
SUNDAY TIMES	4·6	6·9	5·8	2·5	3·4	2·7	2·8
REYNOLDS NEWS	4·3	3·8	6·7	4·6	3·1	5·3	3·3
SUNDAY MAIL	4·1	*	*	*	*	*	37·7
PEOPLE'S FRIEND	3·8	*	*	1·1	1·4	3·6	25·9
DAILY GRAPHIC	3·7	5·5	4·2	4·0	3·4	1·5	*
OBSERVER	3·5	4·9	4·2	2·5	2·7	2·3	2·5
TATLER	3·5	4·0	4·8	3·0	2·5	3·5	2·3
ILLUSTRATED LONDON NEWS	3·4	4·2	3·6	2·9	3·1	2·9	2·2
TIT-BITS	3·2	2·9	3·2	2·9	3·6	5·1	1·5
IDEAL HOME	3·2	3·4	3·0	3·5	2·7	3·3	2·4
STRAND MAGAZINE	3·1	3·5	3·3	1·7	2·8	3·1	3·4

Percentages in bold type (26·5) are subject to a relatively small proportion of error.
Percentages in italic type (3·7) are subject to a relatively large proportion of error.
*=Either less than 1·0% or less than 10,000 readers.

VI ANALYSIS OF READERSHIP BY AGE
Men and women combined—all classes

Women's magazines have been excluded from this table	TOTAL ALL AGE-GROUPS		AGE-GROUPS							
			16–24		25–44		45–64		65 AND OVER	
NUMBER OF INFORMANTS	13,000		1,850		5,101		4,222		1,827	
ESTIMATED POPULATION AGED 16 AND OVER	36,800,000		5,450,000		14,800,000		11,500,000		5,050,000	
Readers of:	%	'000	%	'000	%	'000	%	'000	%	'000
RADIO TIMES	54·2	19,940	52·8	2,870	56·7	8,390	53·8	6,190	49·2	2,500
NEWS OF THE WORLD	48·3	17,770	54·1	2,940	52·2	7,720	46·1	5,300	35·6	1,810
PEOPLE	32·8	12,060	33·7	1,830	33·7	4,990	33·9	3,900	26·4	1,340
SUNDAY PICTORIAL	31·0	11,430	39·8	2,170	36·6	5,420	26·7	3,070	15·2	770
DAILY EXPRESS	26·7	9,830	22·8	1,240	28·6	4,230	27·9	3,210	22·7	1,150
PICTURE POST	26·0	9,560	32·6	1,770	28·0	4,150	24·3	2,790	16·8	850
DAILY MIRROR	25·3	9,320	37·4	2,030	29·9	4,420	20·1	2,310	10·8	550
SUNDAY EXPRESS	19·8	7,290	15·7	850	20·2	2,990	21·4	2,460	19·5	990
ILLUSTRATED	17·4	6,390	24·7	1,340	18·5	2,740	15·8	1,810	9·8	500
DAILY MAIL	14·6	5,380	12·9	700	13·2	1,950	15·6	1,790	18·6	950
SUNDAY DISPATCH	13·8	5,080	12·7	690	13·9	2,050	14·6	1,670	13·1	660
LONDON EVENING NEWS	12·8	4,710	11·8	640	12·5	1,840	14·2	1,630	11·6	590
JOHN BULL	12·2	4,500	13·6	740	13·1	1,940	11·5	1,330	9·7	490
LILLIPUT	11·8	4,360	17·0	920	14·7	2,170	9·5	1,090	3·4	170
EMPIRE NEWS	11·3	4,140	11·6	630	11·8	1,740	11·5	1,320	8·9	450
DAILY HERALD	11·0	4,060	9·1	490	11·1	1,650	12·8	1,470	8·8	450
EVERYBODY'S	10·9	4,010	14·2	770	11·2	1,660	10·1	1,160	8·3	420
NEWS CHRONICLE	9·3	3,420	5·9	320	8·2	1,210	11·1	1,280	12·2	620
SUNDAY POST	8·6	3,160	9·3	510	8·9	1,310	8·5	970	7·2	370
WEEKLY NEWS (THOMSONS)	8·3	3,070	10·2	560	9·6	1,410	7·3	840	5·1	260
SUNDAY CHRONICLE	7·9	2,890	5·7	310	6·8	1,000	9·6	1,100	9·4	480
DAILY TELEGRAPH	7·3	2,670	4·0	220	6·2	910	8·3	950	11·7	590
SUNDAY GRAPHIC	7·0	2,590	6·5	350	7·0	1,040	7·5	860	6·5	330
LONDON STAR	6·8	2,510	7·6	410	6·9	1,020	7·5	860	4·3	220
LONDON OPINION	6·8	2,490	11·1	610	8·2	1,210	4·7	540	2·5	130
LONDON EVENING STANDARD	5·0	1,850	4·1	220	4·8	710	5·6	640	5·5	280
PICTUREGOER	4·9	1,800	11·7	640	5·0	730	3·5	400	*	*
PUNCH	4·8	1,780	5·7	310	4·3	640	4·9	560	5·4	280
MEN ONLY	4·8	1,760	6·9	380	7·1	1,050	2·5	280	1·1	60
SUNDAY TIMES	4·6	1,680	2·6	140	3·5	510	5·5	630	7·8	400
REYNOLDS NEWS	4·3	1,590	4·1	220	4·3	640	4·9	560	3·3	170
SUNDAY MAIL	4·1	1,510	4·7	260	4·6	680	4·1	470	2·1	100
PEOPLE'S FRIEND	3·8	1,410	5·1	280	3·4	500	4·1	470	3·5	180
DAILY GRAPHIC	3·7	1,360	2·7	150	3·1	460	4·3	490	5·2	260
OBSERVER	3·5	1,290	1·8	100	3·5	510	4·0	460	4·4	220
TATLER	3·5	1,270	3·4	180	3·6	540	3·6	410	2·8	140
ILLUSTRATED LONDON NEWS	3·4	1,240	3·6	200	3·2	470	3·7	420	2·9	150
TIT-BITS	3·2	1,180	4·6	250	3·5	510	2·7	320	1·9	100
IDEAL HOME	3·2	1,160	3·6	200	3·9	580	2·8	320	1·4	70
STRAND MAGAZINE	3·1	1,120	3·9	210	3·1	460	3·1	350	2·0	100

Percentages in bold type (**26·5**) are subject to a relatively small proportion of error.
Percentages in italic type (*3·7*) are subject to a relatively large proportion of error.
*=Either less than 1·0% or less than 10,000 readers.

VII   ANALYSIS OF READERSHIP BY AGE

Men—all social classes

Women's magazines have been excluded from this table	TOTAL ALL AGE-GROUPS		AGE-GROUPS							
			16–24		25–44		45–64		65 AND OVER	
NUMBER OF INFORMANTS	6,003		818		2,465		1,950		770	
ESTIMATED POPULATION AGED 16 AND OVER	17,000,000		2,350,000		7,200,000		5,300,000		2,150,000	
Readers of:	%	'000	%	'000	%	'000	%	'000	%	'000
RADIO TIMES	55·0	9,330	55·9	1,320	58·2	4,190	53·5	2,820	46·8	1,010
NEWS OF THE WORLD	52·2	8,870	56·1	1,330	54·9	3,950	50·4	2,660	43·5	940
PEOPLE	35·4	6,020	36·7	870	37·0	2,660	35·1	1,850	29·6	640
SUNDAY PICTORIAL	32·5	5,510	40·2	950	38·7	2,780	28·5	1,500	12·8	280
DAILY EXPRESS	31·9	5,420	30·0	710	33·0	2,370	33·5	1,760	26·6	570
PICTURE POST	29·1	4,940	37·1	880	32·2	2,310	26·0	1,370	17·5	380
DAILY MIRROR	24·9	4,230	37·7	890	29·5	2,120	19·1	1,010	9·8	210
SUNDAY EXPRESS	22·4	3,810	19·1	450	22·5	1,620	24·2	1,270	21·4	460
ILLUSTRATED	18·9	3,220	28·7	680	20·3	1,460	16·7	880	9·1	200
LILLIPUT	15·6	2,650	23·2	550	19·8	1,420	11·8	620	3·0	60
DAILY MAIL	15·3	2,610	15·7	370	13·7	990	15·7	830	19·3	420
SUNDAY DISPATCH	15·2	2,590	15·7	370	15·4	1,100	15·4	810	13·9	300
JOHN BULL	14·3	2,440	15·2	360	15·9	1,140	13·1	690	11·4	240
DAILY HERALD	13·7	2,330	10·7	250	13·9	1,000	15·3	810	12·6	270
LONDON EVENING NEWS	13·7	2,320	13·0	310	12·9	930	15·3	810	12·7	270
EMPIRE NEWS	13·2	2,230	14·0	330	13·4	960	13·4	710	11·1	240
EVERYBODY'S	13·1	2,220	16·7	400	13·8	1,000	11·6	610	10·3	220
NEWS CHRONICLE	11·2	1,910	7·9	190	10·0	720	12·8	680	15·0	320
LONDON OPINION	9·7	1,650	15·4	370	11·7	840	6·9	370	4·0	90
SUNDAY POST	8·7	1,480	9·0	210	9·1	650	8·8	470	6·9	150
SUNDAY CHRONICLE	8·5	1,450	6·8	160	7·6	540	10·4	550	9·2	200
WEEKLY NEWS (THOMSONS)	8·1	1,380	9·6	230	9·5	680	6·8	360	5·0	110
MEN ONLY	8·0	1,370	12·0	280	11·7	840	4·0	210	1·5	30
LONDON STAR	7·5	1,270	6·9	160	7·3	520	8·6	450	5·9	130
SUNDAY GRAPHIC	7·3	1,230	6·9	160	7·2	520	7·8	410	6·5	140
DAILY TELEGRAPH	7·1	1,210	4·4	100	6·3	450	7·9	420	10·9	240
PUNCH	5·6	950	6·8	160	4·9	350	5·6	300	6·6	140
REYNOLDS NEWS	5·6	940	5·9	140	5·5	400	5·8	310	4·8	100
LONDON EVENING STANDARD	5·5	940	5·8	140	5·0	360	5·9	310	6·3	140
SUNDAY MAIL	4·6	790	5·6	130	4·8	340	4·8	250	2·6	60
ILLUSTRATED LONDON NEWS	4·5	760	5·5	130	3·9	280	4·9	260	4·3	90
PICTUREGOER	4·5	760	10·3	240	4·7	330	3·1	160	*	*
TIT-BITS	4·4	750	6·4	150	4·3	310	4·2	220	3·3	70
STRAND MAGAZINE	4·2	710	5·6	130	3·9	280	4·5	240	3·0	60
ARGOSY	4·2	700	5·7	140	5·6	400	2·7	140	1·0	20
SUNDAY TIMES	4·0	670	2·9	70	2·6	190	4·9	260	7·6	160
OBSERVER	3·4	580	2·5	60	3·1	220	3·7	200	4·5	100
NEWS REVIEW	3·0	520	3·1	70	3·9	280	2·4	130	1·6	30
TATLER	3·0	520	2·8	70	3·2	230	2·8	150	3·2	70
LISTENER	3·0	510	2·8	70	3·5	250	2·7	140	2·6	60

Percentages in bold type (**26·5**) are subject to a relatively small proportion of error.
Percentages in italic type (*3·7*) are subject to a relatively large proportion of error.
*=Either less than 1·0% or less than 10,000 readers.

VIII ANALYSIS OF READERSHIP BY AGE

Women—all social classes

	TOTAL ALL AGE-GROUPS		AGE-GROUPS							
			16–24		25–44		45–64		65 AND OVER	
NUMBER OF INFORMANTS	6,997		1,032		2,636		2,272		1,057	
ESTIMATED POPULATION AGED 16 AND OVER	19,800,000		3,100,000		7,600,000		6,200,000		2,900,000	
Readers of:	%	'000	%	'000	%	'000	%	'000	%	'000
RADIO TIMES	53·5	10,610	50·3	1,550	55·2	4,200	54·2	3,370	51·1	1,490
NEWS OF THE WORLD ..	44·9	8,910	52·5	1,610	49·6	3,780	42·5	2,650	29·9	870
PEOPLE	30·5	6,040	31·4	970	30·6	2,330	32·9	2,040	24·1	700
SUNDAY PICTORIAL	29·8	5,910	39·6	1,220	34·7	2,640	25·1	1,560	17·0	500
DAILY MIRROR	25·7	5,090	37·2	1,140	30·3	2,300	21·0	1,310	11·6	340
PICTURE POST	23·3	4,620	29·2	900	24·1	1,830	22·8	1,420	16·3	470
DAILY EXPRESS	22·2	4,410	17·2	530	24·4	1,860	23·3	1,450	19·8	580
SUNDAY EXPRESS	17·6	3,480	13·1	400	18·1	1,370	19·0	1,180	18·0	530
WOMAN	16·3	3,230	23·1	710	19·6	1,490	12·9	800	7·7	230
ILLUSTRATED	16·0	3,170	21·6	660	16·8	1,280	15·0	930	10·4	300
DAILY MAIL	14·0	2,780	10·6	330	12·6	960	15·4	960	18·1	530
WOMAN'S OWN	13·9	2,750	27·3	840	14·5	1,100	10·1	630	5·8	170
SUNDAY DISPATCH ..	12·6	2,490	10·3	320	12·4	950	13·8	860	12·5	370
LONDON EVENING NEWS ..	12·0	2,390	10·9	340	12·0	910	13·2	820	10·8	320
WOMAN'S WEEKLY ..	10·9	2,160	17·1	520	9·9	750	11·1	690	6·6	190
JOHN BULL	10·4	2,060	12·3	380	10·5	800	10·3	640	8·5	250
EMPIRE NEWS	9·6	1,910	9·9	300	10·2	780	9·9	620	7·3	210
EVERYBODY'S	9·0	1,790	12·2	380	8·7	660	8·8	550	6·8	200
DAILY HERALD	8·8	1,740	7·9	240	8·6	650	10·7	660	6·1	180
LILLIPUT	8·6	1,700	12·2	380	9·9	750	7·5	470	3·8	110
WEEKLY NEWS (THOMSONS) ..	8·5	1,690	10·6	330	9·6	730	7·7	480	5·3	150
SUNDAY POST	8·5	1,680	9·5	290	8·7	660	8·2	510	7·5	220
WOMAN AND HOME ..	8·0	1,580	7·5	230	8·6	650	8·9	550	4·9	140
GOOD HOUSEKEEPING ..	7·7	1,530	6·2	190	8·9	680	8·5	530	4·4	130
NEWS CHRONICLE ..	7·6	1,520	4·3	130	6·4	490	9·7	600	10·1	290
DAILY TELEGRAPH ..	7·4	1,460	3·6	110	6·0	460	8·6	530	12·3	360
SUNDAY CHRONICLE ..	7·3	1,440	4·8	150	6·0	460	8·9	550	9·6	280
SUNDAY GRAPHIC ..	6·8	1,350	6·2	190	6·8	510	7·3	450	6·6	190
LONDON STAR	6·3	1,240	8·1	250	6·5	500	6·5	410	3·1	90
WOMAN'S ILLUSTRATED ..	5·7	1,130	10·0	310	5·8	440	4·8	300	2·6	80
VOGUE	5·4	1,070	7·8	240	6·3	480	4·8	300	1·9	60
PEOPLE'S FRIEND ..	5·4	1,060	7·4	230	4·8	370	5·4	340	4·4	130
STITCHCRAFT	5·3	1,060	8·4	260	6·1	470	4·1	260	2·6	70
PICTUREGOER	5·3	1,050	12·8	390	5·3	400	3·8	240	*	*
RED LETTER	5·3	1,040	12·1	370	5·1	390	3·3	210	2·0	60
HOUSEWIFE	5·1	1,020	4·6	140	6·5	490	4·4	270	3·8	110
SUNDAY TIMES	5·1	1,010	2·4	70	4·3	330	6·0	370	7·9	230
WOMAN'S JOURNAL	4·8	960	4·2	130	5·1	390	5·5	340	3·5	100
LONDON EVENING STANDARD	4·6	910	2·9	90	4·6	350	5·3	330	4·9	140
HOME NOTES	4·5	880	7·4	230	4·9	370	3·3	210	2·8	80

Percentages in bold type (**26·5**) are subject to a relatively small proportion of error.
Percentages in italic type (*3·7*) are subject to a relatively large proportion of error.
*=Either less than 1·0% or less than 10,000 readers.

IX   ANALYSIS OF READERSHIP BY PARENTHOOD

Male householders—by social class

Women's magazines have been excluded from this table	HAVING CHILDREN UNDER 16 AT HOME							
	ALL CLASSES		CLASS AB		CLASS C		CLASS DE	
NUMBER OF INFORMANTS	1,896		326		515		1,055	
ESTIMATED POPULATION AGED 16 AND OVER	5,400,000		600,000		950,000		3,850,000	
Readers of:	%	'000	%	'000	%	'000	%	'000
RADIO TIMES	**57·2**	3,080	**74·2**	440	**67·8**	640	**52·0**	2,000
NEWS OF THE WORLD	**55·5**	2,990	**32·2**	190	**41·9**	390	**62·5**	2,410
PEOPLE	**36·7**	1,980	*18·1*	110	**31·5**	300	**40·9**	1,570
SUNDAY PICTORIAL	**36·5**	1,960	**24·2**	140	**30·1**	280	**39·9**	1,540
DAILY EXPRESS	**32·4**	1,750	**37·4**	220	**36·9**	350	**30·5**	1,180
PICTURE POST	**28·5**	1,540	**38·0**	230	**28·9**	270	**26·9**	1,040
DAILY MIRROR	**28·5**	1,540	*13·8*	80	**21·4**	200	**32·5**	1,250
SUNDAY EXPRESS	**21·4**	1,150	**45·7**	270	**29·3**	280	**16·2**	620
ILLUSTRATED	**16·9**	910	*21·8*	130	**18·1**	170	**15·8**	610
LILLIPUT	**16·4**	880	*20·9*	120	**17·1**	160	**15·5**	600
JOHN BULL	**15·3**	830	*8·3*	50	*11·5*	110	**17·3**	670
SUNDAY DISPATCH	**14·8**	800	**24·5**	150	*16·7*	160	**13·4**	520
DAILY HERALD	**14·2**	760	*5·5*	30	*11·5*	110	**13·2**	510
DAILY MAIL	**13·2**	710	*21·8*	130	*16·5*	160	**11·1**	430
EMPIRE NEWS	**12·6**	680	*5·5*	30	*8·0*	80	**14·8**	570
LONDON EVENING NEWS ..	**12·5**	680	*16·3*	100	*16·5*	160	**11·0**	420
EVERYBODY'S	**12·0**	650	*9·2*	60	*11·3*	110	**12·6**	490
LONDON OPINION	**9·9**	530	*11·0*	70	*10·7*	100	**9·6**	370
NEWS CHRONICLE	**9·7**	520	*9·2*	60	*11·1*	100	**9·4**	360
SUNDAY POST	**9·3**	500	*7·4*	40	*9·9*	90	**9·5**	370
WEEKLY NEWS (THOMSONS) ..	**9·0**	480	*3·1*	20	*5·6*	50	**10·7**	410
MEN ONLY	**8·3**	450	*9·5*	60	*8·2*	80	*8·2*	310
SUNDAY CHRONICLE	**7·8**	420	*11·7*	70	*10·5*	100	**6·5**	250
LONDON STAR	**6·6**	350	*7·7*	50	*6·4*	60	*6·4*	250
SUNDAY GRAPHIC	**6·3**	340	*9·5*	60	*8·5*	80	**5·2**	200
DAILY TELEGRAPH	**6·0**	320	*23·0*	140	*12·8*	120	*1·7*	70
PUNCH	*4·8*	260	*16·3*	100	*4·9*	50	*3·0*	120
LONDON EVENING STANDARD ..	*4·8*	260	*11·0*	70	*7·0*	70	*3·3*	130
SUNDAY MAIL	*4·7*	250	*2·8*	20	*4·9*	50	*4·9*	190
REYNOLDS NEWS	*4·5*	240	*4·6*	30	*3·7*	40	*4·6*	180
ARGOSY	*4·4*	240	*6·1*	40	*4·3*	40	*4·2*	160
PICTUREGOER	*4·3*	230	*1·8*	10	*3·9*	40	*4·8*	190
STRAND MAGAZINE	*3·9*	210	*8·9*	50	*4·5*	40	*3·0*	120
TIT-BITS	*3·9*	210	*2·1*	10	*3·7*	40	*4·3*	160
FARMERS WEEKLY	*3·4*	180	*5·5*	30	*2·1*	20	*3·3*	130
ILLUSTRATED LONDON NEWS ..	*3·2*	170	*7·7*	50	*5·0*	50	*2·1*	80
NEWS REVIEW	*3·2*	170	*5·2*	30	*4·1*	40	*2·7*	100
WIDE WORLD MAGAZINE ..	*3·1*	170	*3·4*	20	*2·7*	30	*3·1*	120
TATLER	*2·9*	160	*8·3*	50	*4·1*	40	*2·0*	80
DAILY GRAPHIC	*2·9*	160	*5·2*	30	*3·5*	30	*2·4*	90

Percentages in bold type (**26·5**) are subject to a relatively small proportion of error.
Percentages in italic type (*3·7*) are subject to a relatively large proportion of error.

X ANALYSIS OF READERSHIP BY PARENTHOOD
Housewives—by social class

| | HAVING CHILDREN UNDER 16 AT HOME | | | | | | | |
	TOTAL ALL CLASSES		CLASS AB		CLASS C		CLASS DE	
NUMBER OF INFORMANTS	2,132		310		514		1,308	
ESTIMATED POPULATION AGED 16 AND OVER	6,300,000		550,000		950,000		4,800,000	
Readers of:	%	'000	%	'000	%	'000	%	'000
NEWS OF THE WORLD	**54·9**	3,450	*25·8*	150	**42·0**	390	**60·9**	2,910
RADIO TIMES	**49·9**	3,140	**72·9**	410	**63·8**	600	**44·5**	2,130
SUNDAY PICTORIAL	**36·6**	2,300	*22·6*	130	**31·1**	290	**39·3**	1,880
PEOPLE	**31·9**	2,000	*18·4*	100	**29·2**	270	**34·0**	1,620
DAILY MIRROR	**31·7**	1,990	*17·4*	100	**26·5**	250	**34·5**	1,650
DAILY EXPRESS	**24·0**	1,510	**28·1**	160	**30·3**	280	**22·3**	1,070
PICTURE POST	**19·7**	1,240	**32·3**	180	**25·9**	240	**17·0**	810
WOMAN	**15·6**	980	*15·5*	90	**21·2**	200	**14·5**	690
SUNDAY EXPRESS	**15·2**	950	**38·4**	220	**27·8**	260	*9·9*	470
ILLUSTRATED	**14·2**	890	*19·4*	110	**19·5**	180	**12·5**	600
EMPIRE NEWS	**12·2**	770	*	*	*9·9*	90	**13·7**	650
WOMAN'S OWN	**12·2**	760	*11·9*	70	*13·8*	130	**11·9**	570
LONDON EVENING NEWS ..	**11·5**	720	*14·2*	80	*14·6*	140	**10·6**	510
SUNDAY DISPATCH ..	**11·3**	710	*16·1*	90	*11·7*	110	**10·6**	510
DAILY HERALD	**10·5**	660	*	*	*7·2*	70	**12·2**	580
JOHN BULL	**10·4**	660	*5·6*	30	*12·6*	120	**10·6**	500
SUNDAY POST	**10·1**	640	*6·8*	40	*9·1*	90	**10·7**	510
WEEKLY NEWS (THOMSONS) ..	**9·9**	620	*	*	*7·6*	70	**10·9**	520
WOMAN'S WEEKLY	**9·0**	560	*6·1*	30	*10·1*	90	**9·1**	430
EVERYBODY'S	**8·3**	520	*5·8*	30	*13·2*	120	**7·6**	370
LILLIPUT	**7·8**	490	*13·9*	80	*9·5*	90	*6·8*	320
WOMAN AND HOME ..	**7·4**	460	*10·3*	60	*11·1*	100	*6·3*	300
LONDON STAR	**7·0**	440	*8·4*	50	*6·2*	60	*7·0*	330
RED LETTER	**6·8**	430	*	*	*	*	*8·3*	390
NEWS CHRONICLE	**6·5**	410	*8·4*	50	*8·9*	80	*5·7*	270
GOOD HOUSEKEEPING ..	**6·4**	400	*19·7*	110	*8·9*	80	*4·4*	210
SUNDAY CHRONICLE ..	**5·8**	370	*10·6*	60	*7·4*	70	*5·0*	240
PEOPLE'S FRIEND	**5·7**	360	*	*	*4·7*	40	*6·3*	300
HOUSEWIFE	**5·5**	350	*12·6*	70	*8·8*	80	*4·1*	190
SUNDAY GRAPHIC	**5·5**	350	*10·6*	60	*6·4*	60	*4·7*	230
WOMAN'S ILLUSTRATED ..	**5·1**	320	*11·9*	70	*6·0*	60	*5·0*	240
SUNDAY MAIL	*5·0*	310	*	*	*4·3*	40	*5·4*	260
PICTUREGOER	*4·7*	300	*3·9*	20	*2·9*	30	*5·2*	250
SILVER STAR	*4·7*	290	*	*	*	*	*5·8*	280
DAILY TELEGRAPH	*4·4*	270	*19·7*	110	*10·7*	100	*1·3*	60
WOMAN'S COMPANION ..	*4·2*	260	*	*	*4·1*	40	*4·6*	220
LONDON EVENING STANDARD ..	*4·0*	250	*11·3*	60	*7·0*	60	*2·6*	120
WIFE AND HOME	*4·0*	250	*6·1*	30	*4·7*	40	*3·6*	170
STITCHCRAFT	*3·7*	230	*7·7*	40	*6·0*	60	*2·6*	120
TRUE ROMANCES	*3·7*	230	*	*	*	*	*4·2*	200

Percentages in bold type (**26·5**) are subject to a relatively small proportion of error.
Percentages in italic type (*3·7*) are subject to a relatively large proportion of error.
*=Either less than 1·0% or less than 10,000 readers.

XI EXTENT TO WHICH DIFFERENT TYPES OF PERIODICALS ARE READ

Men and women combined—by regions

	TOTAL ALL REGIONS	REGIONS (FOR DEFINITIONS SEE PAGE 88)					
		SOUTH-EAST	SOUTH-WEST AND WALES	MIDLANDS	NORTH-WEST	NORTH-EAST AND NORTH	SCOTLAND
NUMBER OF INFORMANTS	13,000	4,572	1,455	2,029	1,682	1,872	1,390
ESTIMATED POPULATION AGED 16 AND OVER	36,800,000	12,600,000	4,150,000	5,850,000	4,850,000	5,450,000	3,900,000
Percentage of Population	%	%	%	%	%	%	%
Morning Newspapers:							
READING NO NATIONAL	22·4	8·7	16·8	20·2	33·2	33·4	46·5
READING NONE AT ALL	13·7	8·3	11·4	15·7	17·6	19·4	17·3
READING ONE ONLY	61·7	65·0	62·3	61·4	59·7	59·6	57·0
READING TWO	19·9	22·4	19·8	18·3	18·2	16·9	20·3
READING THREE OR MORE	4·7	4·3	6·5	4·6	4·5	4·1	5·4
TOTAL READING ANY NATIONAL	77·6	91·3	83·2	79·8	66·8	66·6	53·5
Sunday Newspapers:							
READING NO NATIONAL	10·0	7·3	8·8	8·4	6·9	9·2	27·0
READING NONE AT ALL	7·6	7·3	8·8	8·3	6·9	7·9	7·4
READING ONE ONLY	28·2	32·2	21·8	28·3	34·1	26·0	17·8
READING TWO	36·0	38·5	37·2	36·7	34·5	34·3	29·5
READING THREE OR MORE	28·2	22·0	32·2	26·7	24·5	31·8	45·3
TOTAL READING ANY NATIONAL	90·0	92·7	91·2	91·6	93·1	90·8	73·0
Evening Newspapers:							
READING NONE AT ALL	32·0	32·7	46·4	32·7	24·9	21·0	37·9
READING ONE ONLY	60·8	55·3	51·1	62·5	68·6	75·3	55·5
READING TWO OR MORE	7·2	12·0	2·5	4·8	6·5	3·7	6·6
TOTAL READING ANY	68·0	67·3	53·6	67·3	75·1	79·0	62·1
Local Weeklies or Bi-weeklies:							
READING NONE AT ALL	42·7	31·0	27·3	51·7	47·1	57·6	56·7
READING ONE ONLY	48·0	58·4	58·5	43·3	40·1	35·0	39·0
READING TWO OR MORE	9·3	10·6	14·2	5·0	12·8	7·4	4·3
TOTAL READING ANY	57·3	69·0	72·7	48·3	52·9	42·4	43·3

General Weekly Magazines:						
READING NONE AT ALL	23·9	23·8	19·3	24·2	28·7	24·3	22·2
READING ONE ONLY	30·1	31·1	30·4	34·2	29·4	26·5	25·7
READING TWO	19·4	18·9	20·4	18·4	19·5	19·9	20·6
READING THREE OR MORE	26·6	26·2	29·9	23·2	22·4	29·3	31·5
TOTAL READING ANY	76·1	76·2	80·7	75·8	71·3	75·7	77·8
General Monthly Magazines:						
READING NONE AT ALL	75·7	72·1	76·2	81·2	78·7	73·2	78·7
READING ONE ONLY	15·0	16·9	15·1	11·7	13·3	16·3	13·7
READING TWO	6·1	7·2	5·7	4·6	5·4	6·8	5·2
READING THREE OR MORE	3·2	3·8	3·0	2·5	2·6	3·7	2·4
TOTAL READING ANY	24·3	27·9	23·8	18·8	21·3	26·8	21·3
NUMBER OF FEMALE INFORMANTS	6,997	2,488	780	1,092	907	981	749
ESTIMATED FEMALE POPULATION AGED 16 AND OVER	19,800,000	6,900,000	2,200,000	3,150,000	2,600,000	2,850,000	2,100,000
Percentage of Women	%	%	%	%	%	%	%
Women's Weekly Magazines:						
READING NONE AT ALL	53·8	54·4	50·3	52·2	59·4	49·5	56·5
READING ONE ONLY	25·7	26·4	27·0	26·8	25·7	23·7	23·5
READING TWO	12·7	11·9	14·5	13·1	9·1	16·8	11·8
READING THREE OR MORE	7·8	7·3	8·2	7·9	5·8	10·0	8·2
TOTAL READING ANY	46·2	45·6	49·7	47·8	40·6	50·5	43·5
Women's Monthly Magazines:						
READING NONE AT ALL	65·4	64·1	59·8	71·4	71·4	61·6	63·6
READING ONE ONLY	19·1	20·1	22·1	15·4	15·6	20·4	20·9
READING TWO	9·1	9·1	10·3	7·6	7·7	11·2	9·1
READING THREE OR MORE	6·4	6·7	7·8	5·6	5·3	6·8	6·4
TOTAL READING ANY	34·6	35·9	40·2	28·6	28·6	38·4	36·4

XII EXTENT TO WHICH DIFFERENT TYPES OF PERIODICALS ARE READ

By social class and by age-group—Men

	ALL CLASSES AND AGES	BY SOCIAL CLASS			BY AGE-GROUP				
		AB	C	DE	16-24	25-34	35-44	45-64	65 AND OVER
NUMBER OF INFORMANTS	6,003	1,077	1,630	3,296	818	1,148	1,317	1,950	770
ESTIMATED POPULATION AGED 16 AND OVER	17,000,000	1,950,000	3,000,000	12,050,000	2,350,000	3,500,000	3,700,000	5,300,000	2,150,000
Percentage of Population	%	%	%	%	%	%	%	%	%
Morning Newspapers:									
READING NO NATIONAL ..	18·0	15·3	14·9	19·2	20·3	15·6	18·6	16·8	21·5
READING NONE AT ALL ..	9·1	4·7	6·4	10·5	12·7	8·1	9·7	7·3	10·1
READING ONE ONLY ..	61·8	50·9	60·9	63·8	58·8	63·6	61·5	62·8	60·2
READING TWO	22·5	32·7	25·8	20·1	21·1	22·1	22·9	22·9	23·4
READING THREE OR MORE ..	6·6	11·7	6·9	5·6	7·4	6·2	5·9	7·0	6·3
TOTAL READING ANY NATIONAL	82·0	84·7	85·1	80·8	79·7	84·4	81·4	83·2	78·5
Sunday Newspapers:									
READING NO NATIONAL ..	7·3	9·2	9·2	6·6	7·4	6·1	6·1	7·1	11·8
READING NONE AT ALL ..	5·3	8·1	6·7	4·4	5·1	4·0	4·3	5·0	9·7
READING ONE ONLY ..	25·4	28·5	28·5	24·2	22·1	23·7	24·1	26·2	32·3
READING TWO	36·6	32·3	34·8	37·7	35·7	36·9	37·3	35·3	38·8
READING THREE OR MORE ..	32·7	31·1	30·0	33·7	37·1	35·4	34·3	33·5	19·2
TOTAL READING ANY NATIONAL	92·7	90·8	90·8	93·4	92·6	93·9	93·9	92·9	88·2
Evening Newspapers:									
READING NONE AT ALL ..	26·3	23·0	22·4	27·8	26·2	26·4	25·9	24·8	30·7
READING ONE ONLY ..	64·7	60·7	65·7	65·1	65·1	66·2	64·1	65·3	61·7
READING TWO OR MORE ..	9·0	16·3	11·9	7·1	8·7	7·4	10·0	9·9	7·6
TOTAL READING ANY	73·7	77·0	77·6	72·2	73·8	73·6	74·1	75·2	69·3

Local Weeklies or Bi-weeklies:

READING NONE AT ALL ..	41·8	40·0	40·6	42·4	44·6	42·6	41·2	39·6	43·9
READING ONE ONLY ..	48·5	47·9	49·9	48·2	47·2	47·9	50·0	49·8	44·7
READING TWO OR MORE ..	9·7	12·1	9·5	9·4	8·2	9·5	8·8	10·6	11·4
TOTAL READING ANY ..	58·2	60·0	59·4	57·6	55·4	57·4	58·8	60·4	56·1

General Weekly or Bi-weekly Magazines:

READING NONE AT ALL ..	21·7	10·9	18·1	24·4	15·7	16·8	21·0	22·4	36·0
READING ONE ONLY ..	28·1	23·9	28·5	28·7	21·8	28·4	28·5	30·3	28·5
READING TWO ..	20·2	23·0	21·0	19·6	23·8	19·1	20·8	21·1	14·8
READING THREE OR MORE ..	30·0	42·2	32·4	27·3	38·7	35·7	29·7	26·2	20·7
TOTAL READING ANY ..	78·3	89·1	81·9	75·6	84·3	83·2	79·0	77·6	64·0

General Monthly Magazines:

READING NONE AT ALL ..	69·1	58·7	65·9	71·5	57·4	57·0	68·7	74·8	88·0
READING ONE ONLY ..	18·4	22·9	19·5	17·4	24·1	23·2	18·5	16·7	8·1
READING TWO ..	8·0	10·7	8·9	7·4	11·3	12·4	8·4	5·9	2·3
READING THREE OR MORE ..	4·5	7·7	5·7	3·7	7·2	7·4	4·4	2·6	1·6
TOTAL READING ANY ..	30·9	41·3	34·1	28·5	42·6	43·0	31·3	25·2	12·0

XIII EXTENT TO WHICH DIFFERENT TYPES OF PERIODICALS ARE READ

By social class and by age-group—All Women

	ALL CLASSES AND AGES	BY SOCIAL CLASS			BY AGE-GROUP				
		AB	C	DE	16-24	25-34	35-44	45-64	65 AND OVER
NUMBER OF INFORMANTS	6,997	1,230	1,906	3,861	1,032	1,247	1,389	2,772	1,057
ESTIMATED POPULATION AGED 16 AND OVER	19,500,000	2,250,000	3,450,000	14,100,000	3,100,000	3,700,000	3,900,000	6,200,000	2,900,000
Percentage of Population	%	%	%	%	%	%	%	%	%
Morning Newspapers:									
READING NO NATIONAL	26·1	19·6	22·7	28·0	29·5	24·2	23·7	25·4	29·6
READING NONE AT ALL	17·6	9·6	12·3	20·2	22·9	17·8	15·3	16·0	18·3
READING ONE ONLY	61·7	53·3	63·7	62·5	62·8	64·3	63·7	59·3	59·6
READING TWO	17·6	29·1	19·9	15·2	12·2	15·8	17·7	20·7	18·8
READING THREE OR MORE	3·1	8·0	4·1	2·1	2·1	2·1	3·3	4·0	3·3
TOTAL READING ANY NATIONAL	73·9	80·4	77·3	72·0	70·5	75·8	76·3	74·6	70·4
Sunday Newspapers:									
READING NO NATIONAL	12·2	11·2	13·0	12·2	10·0	9·7	10·7	12·5	19·1
READING NONE AT ALL	9·7	9·8	10·9	9·4	7·2	7·3	8·1	10·2	16·4
READING ONE ONLY	30·6	30·6	31·0	30·6	30·0	27·0	30·7	29·3	38·6
READING TWO	35·5	37·5	32·7	35·7	36·6	38·1	35·5	35·9	29·6
READING THREE OR MORE	24·2	22·1	25·4	24·3	26·2	27·6	25·7	24·6	15·4
TOTAL READING ANY NATIONAL	87·8	88·8	87·0	87·8	90·0	90·3	89·3	87·5	80·9
Evening Newspapers:									
READING NONE AT ALL	36·9	32·0	32·8	38·7	39·2	33·8	34·8	36·4	42·5
READING ONE ONLY	57·3	56·5	60·2	56·7	55·7	61·7	59·2	56·4	52·6
READING TWO OR MORE	5·8	11·5	7·0	4·6	5·1	4·5	6·0	7·2	4·9
TOTAL READING ANY	63·1	68·0	67·2	61·3	60·8	66·2	65·2	63·6	57·5
Local Weeklies or Bi-weeklies:									
READING NONE AT ALL	43·5	42·5	41·7	44·1	46·3	43·0	43·2	42·3	43·9
READING ONE ONLY	47·7	49·5	50·4	46·7	44·9	49·0	47·0	48·9	47·4
READING TWO OR MORE	8·8	8·0	7·9	9·2	8·8	8·0	9·8	8·8	8·7
TOTAL READING ANY	56·5	57·5	58·3	55·9	53·7	57·0	56·8	57·7	56·1

General Weeklies or Bi-weeklies:

READING NONE AT ALL ..	25·7	13·3	18·5	29·5	22·6	23·8	24·2	26·1	32·8
READING ONE ONLY ..	31·8	26·3	31·6	32·6	26·2	33·2	33·3	31·2	34·8
READING TWO	18·7	23·3	21·9	17·2	20·1	17·6	18·7	19·5	16·7
READING THREE OR MORE ..	23·8	37·1	28·0	20·7	31·1	25·4	23·8	23·2	15·7
TOTAL READING ANY ..	74·3	86·7	81·5	70·5	77·4	76·2	75·8	73·9	67·2

General Monthly Magazines:

READING NONE AT ALL ..	81·5	66·5	76·0	85·2	76·4	75·7	81·5	83·3	90·2
READING ONE ONLY ..	12·1	18·8	14·4	10·5	14·5	15·4	11·9	11·5	6·8
READING TWO	4·4	9·8	6·7	3·0	6·2	6·0	4·5	3·7	2·2
READING THREE OR MORE ..	2·0	4·9	2·9	1·3	2·9	2·9	2·1	1·5	1·0
TOTAL READING ANY ..	18·5	33·5	24·0	14·8	23·6	24·3	18·5	16·7	9·8

Women's Weekly Magazines:

READING NONE AT ALL ..	53·8	64·7	54·8	51·8	32·4	46·3	52·6	60·9	72·1
READING ONE ONLY ..	25·7	22·4	26·4	26·1	27·0	31·1	28·7	23·3	18·7
READING TWO	12·7	9·3	12·0	13·4	21·4	14·9	11·8	10·4	7·0
READING THREE OR MORE ..	7·8	3·6	6·8	8·7	19·2	7·7	6·9	5·4	2·2
TOTAL READING ANY ..	46·2	35·3	45·2	48·2	67·6	53·7	47·4	39·1	27·9

Women's Monthly Magazines:

READING NONE AT ALL ..	65·3	48·0	56·9	70·2	56·0	60·2	62·7	67·9	79·7
READING ONE ONLY ..	19·2	25·7	23·4	17·0	23·7	20·5	19·6	18·4	13·5
READING TWO	9·1	14·1	11·6	7·7	11·3	10·9	11·5	7·6	4·5
READING THREE OR MORE ..	6·4	12·2	8·1	5·1	9·0	8·4	6·2	6·1	2·3
TOTAL READING ANY ..	34·7	52·0	43·1	29·8	44·0	39·8	37·3	32·1	20·3

PREFACE TO THE TABLES

The majority of the tables which follow are based upon the results of *The Hulton Readership Survey 1949*, in which 13,000 informants (6,997 women and 6,003 men) were interviewed in England, Wales and Scotland. The remaining tables are either from the 1948 Survey—the relevant questions having been dropped in 1949—or from official sources. In such cases, the origins are quoted at the foot of the tables. With the exception that in 1948 there was a slightly smaller sample (5,848 men, 6,766 women) the description of the 1949 Survey, which follows, applies to both.

The Hulton Readership Survey is designed, primarily, to give advertisers and advertising agencies a reliable guide to the readership of the most important newspapers and periodicals published in this country, analysed by class and age, and many other factors which make up the pattern of social circumstances and behaviour.

In the course of such a survey, vast quantities of data of sociological importance are collected. Some of these statistics have already been published in the Readership Surveys of 1947, 1948 and 1949, but only in skeleton form; this is the first occasion on which they have all been made available, analysed in as much detail as the size of the sub-samples warrant.

The sample

The population which the sample was designed to represent was that of civilian men and women, aged 16 and over, in Great Britain, in the first quarter of 1949.

The technique used in selecting the sample was that known as "Quota-Sampling" i.e., certain factors, which are correlated with the population variables to be estimated, were used as stratifying characteristics. Stratification for this Survey was by sex, by age, by social class, by size and type of locality, by region and by marital status, in combination with each other. Investigators were given a "quota" specifying the number of informants to be interviewed from each sub-group formed by the combination of these characteristics, the size of each sub-group in the sample being quantitatively related to its size in the population.

For instance, the proportion of the total number of informants who were interviewed in Scotland was the same as the proportion of the total "adult" civilian population which lived in Scotland. The proportions of informants in the upper, middle and lower-middle classes, however, were twice as great as in the whole population, since these groups would otherwise have been too small to permit detailed analysis, but the results were weighted-back so that the correct proportions would be restored. In effect, therefore, a sample was selected which was a miniature of the entire civilian population of Great Britain aged 16 and over.

Much of the information needed to stratify a population in the way described above is not available from official records, but the extensive original data collected by Research Services Ltd.—who were responsible for planning, carrying out and supervising the field-work, and for the machine tabulation of the results—permitted the selection of a sample as representative as is possible.

The composition of the sample, by sex, social class and age is given in the table on page 88, and needs no further explanation.

Field-work control

All field-work was carried out under rigid supervision by full-time professional investigators, and supervisory recalls were made amongst some 10 per cent of informants. Completed questionnaires were subjected to close scrutiny, and only those which constituted a full return of a valid interview, and were internally consistent, were passed for tabulation.

"Rounding-off"

It will be noticed that the "grossed up" figures, besides the percentages, are "rounded-off" to the nearest 10,000. It follows, therefore, that certain of the totals are not the exact sum of the constituent parts, as is shown in the following imaginary example:

Class	Actual Figures	"Rounded-off" Figures
AB	113,333	110,000
C	173,333	170,000
DE	713,334	710,000
Total	1,000,000	990,000

The first total is correctly given as 1,000,000 but the sum of rounded-off parts is 10,000 less.

Definitions

In reading the tables, the following definitions should be borne in mind:

HEAD OF HOUSEHOLD: Man normally responsible for rent or general upkeep of household.

HOUSEWIFE: Woman responsible for "keeping house" in the household in which she lives. She may be married or unmarried; at home all day or in a job; living alone or in a multi-person family.

HOUSEHOLD (OR ACTUAL FAMILY): One or more persons, of which one is responsible for rent or general upkeep, with a right to sole or shared use of cooking facilities. The term excludes persons living in hotels, boarding houses, hostels, etc., friends living together and other communal systems where there is no allocable responsibility (of the order of 1 per cent of families) and biological families which live as subordinate members of some other family (e.g. newly-married couples living with their parents).

"ADULT": A person aged 16 years or more.

"CHILD": A child aged 5 or more but less than 16.

"INFANT": A child under the age of 5 years.

SOCIAL CLASS is defined in the following table:

THE SOCIAL CLASSES

CLASS	DESCRIPTION	BRIEF DEFINITION	PERCENTAGE OF FAMILIES IN EACH CLASS	USUAL INCOME LEVEL OF HEAD OF HOUSEHOLD
A	THE WELL-TO-DO	Head of household a successful business or professional man, or a senior civil servant, or having considerable private means.	3½ per cent	Over £1,000 a year
B	THE MIDDLE-CLASS	Heads of households in younger age-groups will probably graduate later to Class A; those in older groups occupy the less senior positions in business and the professions, or the middle grades of the Civil Service.	7½ per cent	£650 to £1,000 a year
C	THE LOWER MIDDLE-CLASS	The families of the more highly-skilled workers, small tradespeople, and black-coated workers in the more important clerical grades.	17 per cent	£400 to £649 a year
D	THE WORKING CLASS	The families of the great bulk of manual workers and of clerical workers in the less responsible positions.	63 per cent	£225 to £399 a year
E	THE POOR	Pensioners, widows with families, and those who through periods of sickness or unemployment, or lack of opportunity, are unable to reach the higher grades.	9 per cent	Under £225 a year

As defined for the purposes of the Survey (investigators are very precisely briefed in this matter), "class" is a blending of social background and income; the income ranges quoted are typical of the incomes of persons in the corresponding classes (or of the heads of households in the families to which they belong) but do not necessarily apply in every case—for example, a Church of England clergyman, in receipt of less than £400 per annum, is not classed in D Grade.

THE SAMPLE, BY SEX, CLASS AND AGE-GROUP

	MEN AGED						WOMEN AGED					
	16–24	25–34	35–44	45–64	65 AND OVER	ALL AGES	16–24	25–34	35–44	45–64	65 AND OVER	ALL AGES
CLASS:												
A	46	20	71	164	59	360	44	46	86	141	83	400
B	91	86	169	304	67	717	103	105	171	309	142	830
C	203	283	364	546	234	1,630	234	307	391	685	289	1,906
D	412	663	638	850	342	2,905	563	704	673	1,027	423	3,390
E	66	96	75	86	68	391	88	85	68	110	120	471
ALL CLASSES	818	1,148	1,317	1,950	770	6,003	1,032	1,247	1,389	2,272	1,057	6,997

DEFINITION OF THE REGIONS

REGIONS USED IN THIS SURVEY	REGISTRAR GENERAL'S REGIONS	COMPOSITION BY COUNTIES
SOUTH-EAST	LONDON & SOUTH-EASTERN EASTERN SOUTHERN	Greater London, Kent, Surrey, Sussex. Bedfordshire, Cambridgeshire, Ely, remainder of Essex and Hertfordshire, Huntingdonshire, Norfolk, Suffolk. Berkshire, Buckinghamshire, Dorset, Hampshire, Isle of Wight, Oxfordshire.
SOUTH-WEST AND WALES	SOUTH-WESTERN WALES	Cornwall, Devonshire, Gloucestershire, Somerset, Wiltshire. All Welsh counties (including Monmouthshire).
MIDLANDS	NORTH-MIDLAND MIDLAND	Derbyshire (less High Peak district), Leicestershire, Northamptonshire, Nottinghamshire, Lincolnshire, Peterborough, Rutlandshire. Herefordshire, Shropshire, Staffordshire, Warwickshire, Worcestershire.
NORTH-WEST	NORTH-WESTERN	Cheshire, Lancashire, High Peak district of Derbyshire.
NORTH-EAST AND NORTH	EAST AND WEST RIDINGS NORTHERN	East and West Ridings of Yorkshire. Cumberland, Durham, Northumberland, Westmorland, North Riding of Yorkshire.
SCOTLAND	SCOTLAND	All Scottish counties.

1 POPULATION OF GREAT BRITAIN
1921–1948

YEAR	POPULATION MID-YEAR (THOUSANDS)			PERCENTAGE INCREASE OVER PREVIOUS YEAR		
	MALE	FEMALE	TOTAL	MALE	FEMALE	TOTAL
1921	20,423	22,346	42,769	—	—	—
1931	21,459	23,336	44,795	0·51	0·44	0·47
1935	21,885	23,713	45,598	0·50	0·40	0·45
1938	22,197	24,011	46,208	0·48	0·42	0·45
1939	22,332	24,135	46,467	0·61	0·52	0·56
1940	22,632	24,257	46,889	*	0·51	*
1941	22,600	24,275	46,875	-0·14	0·07	-0·03
1942	22,656	24,383	47,039	0·25	0·44	0·35
1943	22,770	24,530	47,300	0·50	0·60	0·55
1944	22,975	24,652	47,627	0·90	0·50	0·69
1945	23,025	24,766	47,791	0·22	0·46	0·34
1946	23,149	24,836	47,985	0·54	0·28	0·41
1947	23,304	24,884	48,188	0·67	0·19	0·42
1948	23,593	25,078	48,671	1·24	0·78	1·00

*See Note (ii) below

Source: Registrars General

(1) Figures for 1921 and 1931 are at census dates. Figures from there on are mid-year estimates.

(ii) Figures from 1940 onwards include all members of the Armed Forces and Merchant Navy. They are therefore not fully comparable (for males) with the previous years.

(iii) Percentage increases between 1921/31, 1931/35 and 1935/38 are average yearly increases.

2 POPULATION OF THE STANDARD REGIONS

	ACTUAL POPULATION (THOUSANDS)			PERCENTAGE OF TOTAL POPULATION %		
	1921	1931	1948*	1921	1931	1948*
GREATER LONDON (Met. police district)	7,480	8,204	8,332	18·3	18·3	17·5
LONDON AND THE SOUTH-EAST	9,487	10,329	10,761	22·2	23·1	22·7
EASTERN	2,223	2,433	2,910	5·2	5·4	6·1
SOUTHERN	1,954	2,135	2,454	4·6	4·8	5·2
SOUTH-WESTERN	2,546	2,615	2,854	5·9	5·8	6·0
WALES	2,657	2,594	2,513	6·2	5·8	5·3
MIDLAND	3,501	3,742	4,294	8·2	8·4	9·0
NORTH MIDLAND	2,763	2,958	3,258	6·5	6·6	6·9
NORTH-WESTERN	6,010	6,185	6,278	14·0	13·8	13·2
EAST AND WEST RIDINGS	3,726	3,920	4,007	8·7	8·7	8·5
NORTHERN	3,020	3,041	3,031	7·1	6·8	6·4
SCOTLAND	4,882	4,843	5,060	11·4	10·8	10·7
TOTAL ..	42,769	44,795	47,420	100·0	100·0	100·0

Source: Registrars General

*Civilians only (excluding members of the Armed Forces and Merchant Navy) at 31st March, 1948

3 AGE DISTRIBUTION OF POPULATION OF GREAT BRITAIN
1901–1948

AGE	1901					
	MALES		FEMALES		TOTAL	
	'000	%	'000	%	'000	%
0–4	2,123	11·9	2,126	11·1	4,249	11·5
5–14	3,897	21·7	3,893	20·4	7,790	21·0
15–24	3,521	19·7	3,736	19·6	7,257	19·6
25–34	2,818	15·7	3,132	16·4	5,950	16·1
35–44	2,183	12·2	2,336	12·2	4,519	12·2
45–64	2,609	14·6	2,889	15·1	5,498	14·9
65 & over	748	4·2	986	5·2	1,734	4·7
TOTAL	17,899	100·0	19,098	100·0	36,997	100·0

AGE	1931					
	MALES		FEMALES		TOTAL	
	'000	%	'000	%	'000	%
0–4	1,724	8·0	1,690	7·2	3,414	7·6
5–14	3,742	17·4	3,669	15·7	7,411	16·5
15–24	3,834	17·9	3,956	17·0	7,790	17·4
25–34	3,410	15·9	3,739	16·0	7,149	16·0
35–44	2,790	13·0	3,284	14·1	6,074	13·6
45–64	4,533	21·1	5,105	21·9	9,638	21·5
65 & over	1,426	6·7	1,893	8·1	3,319	7·4
TOTAL	21,459	100·0	23,336	100·0	44,795	100·0

AGE	1948*					
	MALES		FEMALES		TOTAL	
	'000	%	'000	%	'000	%
0–4	2,135	9·0	2,031	8·1	4,166	8·5
5–14	3,319	14·0	3,203	12·7	6,522	13·3
15–24	3,415	14·4	3,336	13·3	6,751	13·8
25–34	3,642	15·4	3,621	14·4	7,263	14·9
35–44	3,743	15·8	3,812	15·2	7,555	15·5
45–64	5,249	22·2	6,128	24·3	11,377	23·3
65 & over	2,190	9·2	3,024	12·0	5,214	10·7
TOTAL	23,693	100·0	25,155	100·0	48,848	100·0

Source: Registrars General

*Estimate at 31st December, which includes Armed Forces and Merchant Seamen

4 ACTUAL AND NATURAL INCREASES
IN THE POPULATION OF GREAT BRITAIN 1921–1948

AVERAGE OF YEARS	AVERAGE ANNUAL PERCENTAGE INCREASE FROM		
	EXCESS OF BIRTHS OVER DEATHS (NATURAL INCREASE)	MIGRATION	TOTAL (ACTUAL INCREASE)
	%	%	%
1921–1931	0·61	−0·14	0·47
1931–1939	0·32	0·14	0·46
1939–1946	0·29	0·12	0·41
1946–1948	0·83	*	*

Source: Registrars General

(i) Populations in 1921 and 1931 are at census dates: in 1946, mid-year.

(ii) Figures for 1939–1946 are affected by deaths of Service personnel occurring outside Great Britain—approximately 250,000.

*Not yet available.

5 BIRTH AND DEATH RATES IN GREAT BRITAIN

YEAR	BIRTHS PER 1,000 POPULATION	DEATHS PER 1,000 POPULATION		
		MALE	FEMALE	TOTAL
1920–22	23·0	13·5	11·8	12·6
1931	16·1	12·8	14·4	13·6
1935	15·1	12·6	11·2	11·9
1938	15·4	12·6	11·0	11·8
1939	15·1	12·9	11·4	12·1
1940	14·4	14·7	12·9	13·8
1941	14·3	13·6	11·9	12·7
1942	15·8	12·2	10·7	11·4
1943	16·5	12·5	11·2	11·8
1944	17·8	12·2	10·8	11·5
1945	16·1	12·0	10·8	11·4
1946	19·3	12·2	10·9	11·5
1947	20·6	13·0	11·3	12·1
1948	18·0	11·6	10·2	10·9

Source: Registrars General

6 INFANT MORTALITY IN GREAT BRITAIN

Death of infants under 1 year of age per 1,000 live births

YEAR	1920–1922	1930–1932	1935	1938	1939	1940	1941	1942	1943	1944	1945	1946	1947	1948
DEATHS PER 1,000	82	67	60	55	53	60	63	62	51	47	47	43	41	36

Source: Registrars General

7   EXPECTATION OF LIFE

| AGE | AVERAGE FUTURE LIFETIME IN YEARS | | | |
| | 1931 | | 1921 | |
	MALES	FEMALES	MALES	FEMALES
5 YEARS	60·11	63·24	55·81	61·67
10 ,,	55·79	58·87	54·64	57·53
20 ,,	46·81	49·88	45·78	48·73
30 ,,	38·21	41·22	37·40	40·26
40 ,,	29·62	32·55	29·19	27·73
50 ,,	21·60	24·18	21·36	23·69
60 ,,	14·43	16·50	14·36	16·22
70 ,,	8·62	10·02	8·75	9·95

Source: Registrar General

Columns headed 1931 are from English Life Table No. 10, based on 1931 Census and deaths of 1930–1932 and columns headed 1921 are based on English Life Table No. 9, based on 1921 Census and deaths of 1920–1922.

TABLE TO SECTION THREE

8   ANNUAL MARRIAGE RATE IN GREAT BRITAIN

YEAR	1930–1932	1938	1939	1940	1941	1942	1943	1944	1945	1946	1947	1948
MARRIAGES PER 1,000 POPULATION	7·6	8·6	10·3	11·0	9·3	9·3	7·1	7·2	9·3	9·0	9·1	9·0

Source: Registrars General

9 MARITAL STATUS OF THE "ADULT" CIVILIAN POPULATION OF GREAT BRITAIN—1ST QUARTER, 1949

(a) by social class

CLASS	MEN						WOMEN					
	MARRIED		SINGLE, WIDOWED OR DIVORCED				MARRIED		SINGLE, WIDOWED OR DIVORCED			
			EXPECTING TO MARRY		OTHER				EXPECTING TO MARRY		OTHER	
	%	'000	%	'000	%	'000	%	'000	%	'000	%	'000
AB ..	70·9	1,390	1·9	40	27·2	530	63·3	1,420	1·5	30	35·2	790
C ..	68·7	2,040	1·7	50	29·6	880	61·9	2,150	1·5	50	36·6	1,270
DE ..	66·5	8,000	2·1	250	31·4	3,780	59·6	8,410	1·6	220	38·8	5,470
ALL CLASSES	67·4	11,440	2·0	340	30·6	5,200	60·4	11,980	1·6	310	38·0	7,530

(b) by age

AGE	MEN						WOMEN					
	MARRIED		SINGLE, WIDOWED OR DIVORCED				MARRIED		SINGLE, WIDOWED OR DIVORCED			
			EXPECTING TO MARRY		OTHER				EXPECTING TO MARRY		OTHER	
	%	'000	%	'000	%	'000	%	'000	%	'000	%	'000
16–24 ..	12·5	290	5·9	140	81·6	1,930	25·4	780	5·3	160	69·3	2,130
25–34 ..	69·7	2,430	3·5	120	26·8	930	74·0	2,750	2·7	100	23·3	870
35–44 ..	82·7	3,070	1·5	50	15·8	590	78·3	3,050	*	*	20·9	810
45–64 ..	81·2	4,280	*	*	18·4	970	70·5	4,390	*	*	29·4	1,830
65 & OVER	63·8	1,370	*	*	36·1	780	35·1	1,020	*	*	64·9	1,890
ALL AGES ..	67·4	11,440	2·0	340	30·6	5,200	60·4	11,980	1·6	310	38·0	7,530

1. "Expecting to marry" means expecting to marry in the next six months

*=Either less than 0·5% or less than 10,000

10 FAMILY COMPOSITION—1ST QUARTER, 1949
By social class

CLASS		MULTI-PERSON FAMILIES CONSISTING OF				SINGLE-PERSON FAMILIES CONSISTING OF			TOTAL ALL FAMILIES
		HEADS OF HOUSE-HOLDS IN FAMILIES WITH HOUSE-WIVES	HEADS OF HOUSE-HOLDS IN OTHER FAMILIES WITHOUT HOUSE-WIVES	HOUSE-WIVES IN OTHER FAMILIES WITHOUT HEADS OF HOUSE-HOLDS	TOTAL	HEADS OF HOUSE-HOLDS LIVING ALONE	HOUSE-WIVES LIVING ALONE	TOTAL	
		'000	'000	'000	'000	'000	'000	'000	'000
AB	WITH CHILDREN ONLY	300	*	10	320	—	—	—	320
	WITH INFANTS ONLY ..	120	*	*	130	—	—	—	130
	WITH BOTH CHILDREN AND INFANTS ..	120	*	*	120	—	—	—	120
	WITH ANY CHILDREN ..	420	*	20	440	—	—	—	440
	WITH ANY INFANTS ..	240	*	10	250	—	—	—	250
	Total with children or infants	540	*	20	570	—	—	—	570
	NO CHILDREN OR INFANTS	940	10	140	1,080	40	90	120	1,200
	TOTAL	1,480	10	160	1,650	40	90	120	1,770
C	WITH CHILDREN ONLY	490	*	20	520	—	—	—	520
	WITH INFANTS ONLY ..	210	*	*	210	—	—	—	210
	WITH BOTH CHILDREN AND INFANTS ..	210	*	10	210	—	—	—	210
	WITH ANY CHILDREN ..	700	*	30	730	—	—	—	730
	WITH ANY INFANTS ..	420	*	10	420	—	—	—	420
	Total with children or infants	910	*	30	940	—	—	—	940
	NO CHILDREN OR INFANTS	1,210	10	300	1,520	90	180	270	1,790
	TOTAL	2,120	20	330	2,470	90	180	270	2,730
DE	WITH CHILDREN ONLY	2,190	10	130	2,340	—	—	—	2,340
	WITH INFANTS ONLY ..	1,350	*	30	1,380	—	—	—	1,380
	WITH BOTH CHILDREN AND INFANTS ..	1,040	*	30	1,070	—	—	—	1,070
	WITH ANY CHILDREN ..	3,240	10	160	3,410	—	—	—	3,410
	WITH ANY INFANTS ..	2,390	*	60	2,450	—	—	—	2,450
	Total with children or infants	4,590	20	190	4,790	—	—	—	4,790
	NO CHILDREN OR INFANTS	3,220	60	1,530	4,810	370	880	1,250	6,050
	TOTAL	7,800	80	1,270	9,600	370	880	1,250	10,850
ALL CLASS-ES	WITH CHILDREN ONLY	2,990	20	170	3,180	—	—	—	3,180
	WITH INFANTS ONLY ..	1,680	10	30	1,720	—	—	—	1,720
	WITH BOTH CHILDREN AND INFANTS ..	1,370	*	40	1,400	—	—	—	1,400
	WITH ANY CHILDREN ..	4,360	20	210	4,580	—	—	—	4,580
	WITH ANY INFANTS ..	3,050	10	70	3,130	—	—	—	3,130
	Total with children or infants	6,040	30	240	6,310	—	—	—	6,310
	NO CHILDREN OR INFANTS	5,370	80	1,969	7,410	490	1,150	1,640	9,050
	TOTAL	11,400	110	2,210	13,720	490	1,150	1,640	15,360

*=Less than 10,000

11(a) DISTRIBUTION OF MEN BETWEEN TYPES OF FAMILY—1ST QUARTER, 1949

By social class, domestic status and age

		HEADS OF HOUSEHOLDS					
		LIVING ALONE		LIVING IN FAMILIES		TOTAL	
		%	'000	%	'000	%	'000
CLASS AB	..	1·9	40	76·0	1,490	77·9	1,530
C ..	..	2·9	90	71·7	2,130	74·6	2,220
DE	..	3·0	370	65·5	7,880	68·5	8,250
AGE 16–24	..	*	10	8·3	200	8·6	200
25–34	..	0·8	30	58·2	2,020	59·0	2,050
35–44	..	2·3	80	81·9	3,030	84·2	3,120
45–64	..	3·8	200	87·7	4,620	91·5	4,820
65 & OVER		7·9	170	75·9	1,640	83·8	1,810
TOTAL		2·9	490	67·8	11,510	70·7	12,000

		NON-HEADS OF HOUSEHOLDS					
		LIVING IN HOTEL/HOSTEL, ETC.		LIVING IN FAMILIES		TOTAL	
		%	'000	%	'000	%	'000
CLASS AB	..	2·0	40	20·1	400	22·1	440
C ..	..	2·1	60	23·3	690	25·4	750
DE	..	2·0	240	29·5	3,550	31·5	3,790
AGE 16–24	..	2·4	60	89·0	2,110	91·4	2,160
25–34	..	2·0	70	39·0	1,360	41·0	1,430
35–44	..	2·2	80	13·6	510	15·8	590
45–64	..	1·6	80	6·9	370	8·5	450
65 & OVER		2·4	50	13·8	300	16·2	350
TOTAL		2·0	350	27·3	4,630	29·3	4,980

		ALL MEN					
		LIVING ALONE OR IN HOTEL/HOSTEL, ETC.		LIVING IN MULTI-PERSON FAMILIES		TOTAL	
		%	'000	%	'000	%	'000
CLASS AB	..	3·9	80	96·1	1,890	100·0	1,970
C ..	..	5·0	150	95·0	2,820	100·0	2,980
DE	..	5·0	610	95·0	11,430	100·0	12,040
AGE 16–24	..	2·7	70	97·3	2,300	100·0	2,370
25–34	..	2·8	100	97·2	3,380	100·0	3,480
35–44	..	4·5	170	95·5	3,540	100·0	3,710
45–64	..	5·4	280	94·6	4,990	100·0	5,270
65 & OVER		10·3	220	89·7	1,930	100·0	2,150
TOTAL		4·9	830	95·1	16,140	100·0	16,980

*=Either less than 0·5% or less than 10,000

11(b) DISTRIBUTION OF WOMEN BETWEEN TYPES OF FAMILY—1ST QUARTER, 1949

By social class, domestic status and age

	HOUSEWIVES					
	LIVING ALONE		LIVING IN FAMILIES		TOTAL	
	%	'000	%	'000	%	'000
CLASS AB	3·8	90	73·1	1,640	76·9	1,730
C	5·1	180	70·4	2,450	75·5	2,630
DE	6·3	880	67·5	9,520	73·8	10,400
AGE 16–24	*	*	20·0	610	20·0	610
25–34	1·7	60	70·2	2,610	71·9	2,670
35–44	3·1	120	83·1	3,230	86·2	3,350
45–64	7·0	430	84·6	5,270	91·6	5,700
65 & OVER	18·1	530	64·7	1,890	82·8	2,420
TOTAL	5·8	1,150	68·7	13,610	74·5	14,760

	NON-HOUSEWIVES					
	LIVING IN HOTEL/HOSTEL, ETC.		LIVING IN FAMILIES		TOTAL	
	%	'000	%	'000	%	'000
CLASS AB	1·9	40	21·2	480	23·1	520
C	1·4	50	23·1	800	24·5	850
DE	0·8	120	25·4	3,570	26·2	3,700
AGE 16–24	1·8	60	78·2	2,400	80·0	2,460
25–34	1·3	50	26·8	1,000	28·1	1,040
35–44	1·4	50	12·4	490	13·8	540
45–64	0·6	40	7·8	490	8·4	520
65 & OVER	0·6	20	16·6	490	17·2	500
TOTAL	1·0	210	24·5	4,850	25·5	5,060

	ALL WOMEN					
	LIVING ALONE OR IN HOTEL/HOSTEL, ETC.		LIVING IN MULTI-PERSON FAMILIES		TOTAL	
	%	'000	%	'000	%	'000
CLASS AB	5·7	130	94·3	2,120	100·0	2,250
C	6·5	230	93·5	3,250	100·0	3,480
DE	7·1	1,000	92·9	13,090	100·0	14,100
AGE 16–24	1·8	60	98·2	3,020	100·0	3,070
25–34	3·0	110	97·0	3,610	100·0	3,720
35–44	4·5	170	95·5	3,720	100·0	3,890
45–64	7·6	470	92·4	5,750	100·0	6,220
65 & OVER	18·7	550	81·3	2,380	100·0	2,920
TOTAL	6·8	1,360	93·2	18,470	100·0	19,820

*=Either less than 0·5% or less than 10,000

12   FAMILY SIZE—ALL FAMILIES—1ST QUARTER, 1949
By social class and age of housewife
or of head of household in families in which there is no housewife

| | | FAMILY CONSISTING OF | | | | | | | | | |
| | | 1 PERSON | | 2 PERSONS | | 3 PERSONS | | 4 PERSONS | | 5 OR MORE PERSONS | | TOTAL | |
		%	'000	%	'000	%	'000	%	'000	%	'000	%	'000
CLASS:													
AB ..	..	6·9	120	33·3	590	30·3	540	18·7	330	10·8	190	100·0	1,770
C ..	..	9·8	270	33·4	910	26·7	730	18·8	510	11·3	3,090	100·0	2,730
DE ..	..	11·5	1,250	27·1	2,940	24·3	2,640	18·4	2,000	18·7	2,020	100·0	10,850
AGE:													
16–24	..	1·2	10	33·6	210	38·3	240	13·7	90	13·2	80	100·0	620
25–34	..	3·4	90	18·7	510	32·5	880	27·3	740	18·1	490	100·0	2,720
35–44	..	5·9	200	18·3	630	24·8	860	25·3	870	25·7	890	100·0	3,460
45–64	..	10·7	630	32·8	1,950	24·7	1,470	16·6	990	15·2	910	100·0	5,940
65 AND OVER		26·8	700	43·9	1,140	17·5	460	5·8	150	6·0	160	100·0	2,610
ALL CLASSES AND AGES ..		10·7	1,640	29·0	4,440	25·4	3,910	18·5	2,840	16·4	2,520	100·0	15,360

13   FAMILY STRUCTURE—1ST QUARTER, 1949
The most frequently occurring combinations of persons
By social class

| | ALL CLASSES | | CLASS AB | | CLASS C | | CLASS DE | |
	%	'000	%	'000	%	'000	%	'000
FAMILIES								
With no children or infants, and								
1 MAN	3·2	490	2·0	40	3·2	90	3·4	370
1 WOMAN	7·5	1,150	4·8	90	6·6	180	8·1	880
1 MAN AND 1 WOMAN	23·7	3,630	27·8	490	27·3	750	22·1	2,390
1 MAN AND 2 WOMEN	6·3	970	12·2	220	6·9	190	5·2	560
2 MEN AND 1 WOMAN	5·1	790	6·2	110	5·8	160	4·8	520
OTHER COMBINATIONS	13·1	2,020	14·8	260	15·7	430	12·3	1,330
TOTAL FAMILIES WITH NO CHILDREN OR INFANTS	58·9	9,050	67·8	1,200	65·5	1,790	55·9	6,050
With children and/or infants, and								
1 MAN	*	*	*	*	*	*	*	*
1 WOMAN	1·0	140	1·0	10	1·0	30	1·0	110
1 MAN AND 1 WOMAN	25·1	3,850	19·8	350	23·4	640	26·4	2,860
1 MAN AND 2 WOMEN	4·0	610	5·0	90	2·9	80	4·1	440
2 MEN AND 1 WOMAN	3·6	550	2·4	40	2·4	60	4·0	440
OTHER COMBINATIONS	7·4	1,140	4·0	70	4·8	130	8·6	940
TOTAL FAMILIES WITH CHILDREN AND/OR INFANTS	41·1	6,310	32·2	570	34·5	940	44·1	4,790
TOTAL ALL FAMILIES	100·0	15,360	100·0	1,770	100·0	2,730	100·0	10,850

*=Either less than 0·5% or less than 10,000

14 AVERAGE FAMILY SIZE—1ST QUARTER, 1949
Families of more than one person
By social class

	ALL CLASSES	CLASS AB	CLASS C	CLASS DE
MEN	1·17	1·14	1·14	1·19
WOMEN	1·35	1·28	1·32	1·36
TOTAL ADULTS	2·52	2·42	2·46	2·55
MALE CHILDREN	0·25	0·18	0·20	0·28
MALE INFANTS	0·14	0·08	0·09	0·16
TOTAL MALE CHILDREN AND INFANTS	0·39	0·26	0·29	0·44
FEMALE CHILDREN	0·25	0·20	0·20	0·28
FEMALE INFANTS	0·15	0·10	0·11	0·16
TOTAL FEMALE CHILDREN AND INFANTS	0·40	0·30	0·31	0·44
TOTAL CHILDREN AND INFANTS	0·79	0·56	0·60	0·88
TOTAL IN FAMILY	3·31	2·98	3·06	3·44

15(a) OWNERSHIP OF DOGS AND NUMBER OF DOGS OWNED—1ST QUARTER, 1949
By social class of owning family

	ALL CLASSES		CLASS AB		CLASS C		CLASS DE	
	%	'000	%	'000	%	'000	%	'000
Families owning:								
1 DOG	91·5	3,080	86·0	430	86·9	510	93·9	2,150
2 DOGS	6·7	230	10·3	50	10·6	60	5·0	110
3 DOGS OR MORE	1·8	60	3·7	20	2·5	10	1·1	30
TOTAL DOG-OWNING FAMILIES	100·0	3,370	100·0	500	100·0	580	100·0	2,290
TOTAL DOG POPULATION	3,790,000		620,000		690,000		2,490,000	
AVERAGE NUMBER PER DOG-OWNING FAMILY	1·12		1·24		1·18		1·08	

15(b) OWNERSHIP OF CATS AND NUMBER OF CATS OWNED—1ST QUARTER, 1949
By social class of owning family

	ALL CLASSES		CLASS AB		CLASS C		CLASS DE	
	%	'000	%	'000	%	'000	%	'000
Families owning:								
1 CAT	84·7	3,670	82·3	370	84·0	580	85·2	2,710
2 CATS	11·3	490	10·9	50	10·8	70	11·5	370
3 CATS OR MORE	4·0	170	6·8	30	5·2	40	3·3	110
TOTAL CAT-OWNING FAMILIES	100·0	4,330	100·0	450	100·0	690	100·0	3,190
TOTAL CAT POPULATION	5,260,000		590,000		870,000		3,800,000	
AVERAGE NUMBER PER CAT-OWNING FAMILY	1·27		1·31		1·25		1·19	

15(c) OWNERSHIP OF CAGE-BIRDS AND NUMBER OF CAGE-BIRDS OWNED —1ST QUARTER, 1949
By social class of owning family

	ALL CLASSES		CLASS AB		CLASS C		CLASS DE	
	%	'000	%	'000	%	'000	%	'000
Families owning:								
1 CAGE-BIRD	82·8	470	84·9	50	79·6	90	83·4	330
MORE THAN ONE	17·2	100	15·1	10	20·4	20	16·6	70
TOTAL CAGE-BIRD OWNING FAMILIES	100·0	570	100·0	60	100·0	110	100·0	400
TOTAL CAGE-BIRD POPULATION	910,000		80,000		180,000		650,000	
AVERAGE NUMBER PER CAGE-BIRD OWNING FAMILY	1·61		1·36		1·66		1·64	

NOTE: Multi-person families with heads of households but no housewives are excluded

16 PROPORTIONS AND NUMBERS OF FAMILIES WITH PETS —1ST QUARTER, 1949

By social class

Families with:	ALL CLASSES		CLASS AB		CLASS C		CLASS DE	
	%	'000	%	'000	%	'000	%	'000
DOGS AND NO CATS	14·6	2,220	18·7	330	14·2	390	13·9	1,490
CATS AND NO DOGS	20·8	3,180	16·4	290	18·3	500	22·2	2,390
BOTH DOGS AND CATS	7·6	1,150	9·3	160	7·3	200	7·4	790
DOGS AT ALL	22·2	3,370	28·0	490	21·5	590	21·3	2,290
CATS AT ALL	28·4	4,330	25·7	450	25·6	700	29·6	3,180
CAGE-BIRDS AT ALL	3·7	570	3·4	60	4·0	110	3·7	400
NEITHER CATS, DOGS NOR CAGE-BIRDS ..	57·0	8,700	55·6	980	60·2	1,630	56·5	6,100
ALL FAMILIES	100·0	15,250	100·0	1,760	100·0	2,720	100·0	10,770

NOTE: Multi-person families with heads of households but no housewives are excluded

TABLE TO SECTION FOUR

17 ACTUAL AND POTENTIAL HOME OWNERS—1ST QUARTER, 1949

By social class

Families:	ALL CLASSES	CLASS AB	CLASS C	CLASS DE
	'000	'000	'000	'000
OWNING THEIR OWN HOUSES	4,990	1,240	1,420	2,330
LIVING IN SELF-CONTAINED HOUSES OR FLATS, RENTED UNFURNISHED ..	9,230	490	1,160	7,580
TOTAL ACTUAL HOME OWNERS	14,220	1,730	2,580	9,910
LIVING IN RENTED ACCOMMODATION FURNISHED OR SHARED	1,140	40	150	940
LIVING TEMPORARILY WITH ANOTHER FAMILY, BUT HOPING TO MOVE ..	580	10	40	530
COUPLES PLANNING TO MARRY WITHIN NEXT 6 MONTHS	310	40	50	220
TOTAL POTENTIAL HOME OWNERS	2,020	90	240	1,690
TOTAL EXISTING FAMILIES	15,360	1,770	2,730	10,850

NOTES: (i) Total existing families is the sum of "Actual home owners" and families living in rented accommodation, furnished or shared.

(ii) "Shared accommodation" means that the kitchen and certain other facilities are shared.

18   FAMILY ACCOMMODATION—1ST QUARTER, 1949
By social class

CLASS			FAMILY LIVING IN							
			COMPLETE HOUSE		SHARED HOUSE		SELF-CONTAINED FLAT		TOTAL	
			%	'000	%	'000	%	'000	%	'000
AB	OWNING		67·3	1,200	0·8	10	1·9	30	70·0	1,240
	RENTING FURNISHED ..		0·6	10	0·6	10	0·6	10	1·8	30
	RENTING UNFURNISHED		17·1	300	0·5	10	10·6	190	28·2	500
	TOTAL		85·0	1,510	1·9	30	13·1	230	100·0	1,770
C	OWNING		49·3	1,350	1·0	30	1·6	40	51·9	1,420
	RENTING FURNISHED ..		0·8	20	1·3	40	1·5	40	3·6	100
	RENTING UNFURNISHED		27·8	760	2·1	50	14·6	400	44·5	1,210
	TOTAL		77·9	2,130	4·4	120	17·7	480	100·0	2,730
DE	OWNING		20·6	2,230	0·5	50	*	*	21·5	2,330
	RENTING FURNISHED ..		0·9	100	1·8	200	0·8	90	3·5	390
	RENTING UNFURNISHED		52·6	5,710	5·1	550	17·3	1,870	75·0	8,130
	TOTAL		74·1	8,040	7·4	800	18·5	2,010	100·0	10,850
ALL CLASSES	OWNING		31·1	4,770	0·6	100	0·8	120	32·5	4,990
	RENTING FURNISHED ..		0·9	130	1·6	250	0·9	140	3·4	520
	RENTING UNFURNISHED		44·0	6,770	4·0	620	16·1	2,460	64·1	9,850
	TOTAL		76·0	11,670	6·2	970	17·8	2,720	100·0	15,360

*=Either less than 0·5% or less than 10,000

NOTE: "Shared houses" are those in which the kitchen and certain other facilities are shared

19 PROPORTIONS AND NUMBERS OF FAMILIES WITH DOMESTIC ASSISTANCE—1ST QUARTER, 1948†

All families: By social class

	ALL CLASSES		CLASS AB		CLASS C		CLASS DE	
Employing:	%	'000	%	'000	%	'000	%	'000
RESIDENTS ONLY	1·2	180	8·4	140	1·3	30	*	*
RESIDENTS AND NON-RESIDENTS	0·5	70	4·2	60	*	*	*	*
NON-RESIDENTS ONLY	10·4	1,530	47·4	760	17·3	430	3·2	340
TOTAL WITH ANY DOMESTIC ASSISTANCE	12·1	1,780	60·0	960	18·7	470	3·3	350
TOTAL WITH RESIDENT STAFF	1·7	250	12·6	200	1·4	40	*	*
TOTAL WITH NON-RESIDENT STAFF	10·8	1,600	51·6	820	17·4	440	3·2	340
ANY FULL-TIME	1·5	220	10·8	170	1·2	30	*	*
PART-TIME ONLY	9·3	1,380	40·8	650	16·2	410	3·0	320

*=Either less than 0·5% or less than 10,000

†This Table, and *Tables* 20 and 21 are based on data from *The Hulton Readership Survey* 1948. Questions relating to domestic assistance were not asked in the 1949 Survey.

20 PROPORTIONS OF FAMILIES WITH ANY DOMESTIC ASSISTANCE —1ST QUARTER, 1948†

All families: By social class and family type

	ALL CLASSES	CLASS AB	CLASS C	CLASS DE
	%	%	%	%
ALL FAMILIES	12·1	60·0	18·7	3·3
FAMILY SIZE:				
1–4 PERSONS	12·8	58·5	19·7	3·8
5 OR MORE PERSONS	8·8	69·4	11·4	1·4
FAMILIES WITH:				
CHILDREN UNDER 16 YEARS	9·1	61·6	13·1	1·0
NO CHILDREN UNDER 16 YEARS ..	13·9	59·1	22·3	4·8

† See note to *Table* 19

21 PROPORTIONS OF FAMILIES WITH RESIDENT DOMESTIC ASSISTANCE —1ST QUARTER, 1948†

All families: By social class and family type

	ALL CLASSES	CLASS AB	CLASS C	CLASS DE
	%	%	%	%
ALL FAMILIES	1·7	12·6	1·4	*
FAMILY SIZE:				
1–4 PERSONS	1·4	9·2	1·3	*
5 OR MORE PERSONS	3·1	31·3	*	*
FAMILIES WITH:				
CHILDREN UNDER 16 YEARS	1·8	16·3	0·6	*
NO CHILDREN UNDER 16 YEARS ..	1·6	10·5	1·9	*

*=Either less than 0·5% or less than 10,000
†See note to *Table* 19

22 PROPORTIONS AND NUMBERS OF HOUSEHOLDS WITH GAS AND/OR ELECTRICITY SUPPLY—1ST QUARTER, 1949

By social class

	ALL CLASSES		CLASS AB		CLASS C		CLASS DE	
Households with:	%	'000	%	'000	%	'000	%	'000
GAS SUPPLY ONLY	10·9	1,680	0·9	160	3·6	100	14·4	1,570
ELECTRICITY SUPPLY ONLY	18·2	2,800	19·4	350	15·6	430	18·7	2,030
WITH BOTH GAS AND ELECTRICITY SUPPLY	67·9	10,420	78·9	1,400	79·6	2,180	63·1	6,850
TOTAL WITH GAS SUPPLY	78·8	12,100	79·8	1,420	83·2	2,280	77·5	8,410
TOTAL WITH ELECTRICITY SUPPLY ..	86·1	13,220	98·3	1,750	95·2	2,600	81·5	8,870
TOTAL WITH NEITHER GAS NOR ELECTRICITY SUPPLY	3·0	460	0·8	10	1·2	30	3·8	410
TOTAL	100·0	15,360	100·0	1,770	100·0	2,730	100·0	10,850

23 DOMESTIC ELECTRICAL EQUIPMENT USED IN FAMILIES WITH ELECTRICITY SUPPLY—1ST QUARTER, 1948†

By social class

Using:	ALL CLASSES		CLASS AB		CLASS C		CLASS DE	
	%	'000	%	'000	%	'000	%	'000
ELECTRIC IRON	86·2	10,500	96·1	1,480	92·5	2,160	82·6	6,870
,, FIRE(S)	63·5	7,740	89·3	1,370	77·0	1,800	55·0	4,570
,, VACUUM-CLEANER	39·8	4,810	82·8	1,270	60·5	1,410	25·6	2,130
,, COOKER	18·7	2,280	21·3	330	22·7	530	17·1	1,420
,, WATER-HEATER	16·2	1,970	37·9	580	21·3	500	10·8	890
,, WASHING-MACHINE	3·6	430	9·3	140	4·6	110	2·2	180
NONE OF ABOVE	9·5	1,150	2·0	30	4·1	100	12·3	1,030
TOTAL FAMILIES WITH ELECTRICITY SUPPLY	100·0	12,190	100·0	1,540	100·0	2,340	100·0	8,310

†This Table is based upon *The Hulton Readership Survey* 1948; the questions were not asked in the 1949 Survey

24 COOKING FUEL WITH RESPECT TO FUEL SUPPLY —1ST QUARTER, 1948†

By social class

	Cooking with:	ALL CLASSES		CLASS AB		CLASS C		CLASS DE	
		%	*'000*	*%*	*'000*	*%*	*'000*	*%*	*'000*
ALL FAMILIES	GAS ONLY	62·9	9,320	68·8	1,100	68·0	1,720	60·8	6,500
	ELECTRICITY ONLY	13·8	2,050	17·1	270	18·4	470	12·2	1,310
	GAS AT ALL	67·5	10,000	72·6	1,160	70·8	1,790	65·9	7,050
	ELECTRICITY AT ALL	15·3	2,260	20·1	320	20·7	520	13·3	1,420
	COAL ONLY	14·0	2,080	5·8	90	6·1	160	17·1	1,830
	OTHER FUELS OR COMBINATIONS OF FUELS*	3·6	530	2·9	50	2·7	70	3·9	420
	ALL FAMILIES	100·0	14,820	100·0	1,600	100·0	2,530	100·0	10,690
ALL FAMILIES WITH A GAS SUPPLY	COOKING WITH GAS AT ALL ..	86·2	10,000	89·4	1,160	88·5	1,790	85·1	7,050
	NOT COOKING WITH GAS ..	13·8	1,600	10·6	140	11·5	230	14·9	1,230
	ALL FAMILIES WITH A GAS SUPPLY	100·0	11,600	100·0	1,300	100·0	2,020	100·0	8,280
ALL FAMILIES WITH AN ELECTRICITY SUPPLY	COOKING WITH ELECTRICITY AT ALL	18·6	2,260	20·9	320	22·3	520	17·1	1,420
	NOT COOKING WITH ELECTRICITY AT ALL	81·4	9,920	79·1	1,220	77·7	1,820	82·9	6,890
	ALL FAMILIES WITH AN ELECTRICITY SUPPLY	100·0	12,180	100·0	1,540	100·0	2,340	100·0	8,310
FAMILIES WITH BOTH GAS AND ELECTRICITY SUPPLY	COOKING WITH GAS BUT NOT ELECTRICITY	87·1	8,380	87·9	1,120	88·0	1,650	86·8	5,600
	COOKING WITH ELECTRICITY BUT NOT GAS	6·8	650	8·0	100	9·2	170	5·8	380
	COOKING WITH BOTH	0·6	60	1·7	20	0·5	10	0·5	30
	COOKING WITH NEITHER ..	5·5	520	2·4	30	2·3	40	6·9	450
	ALL FAMILIES WITH BOTH GAS AND ELECTRICITY SUPPLY	100·0	9,610	100·0	1,270	100·0	1,880	100·0	6,460

*"Other combinations" includes coal and calor gas, coal and paraffin, etc.

†Based upon *The Hulton Readership Survey* 1948. Questions about cooking fuel were not asked in the 1949 Survey

25   COOKING FUEL USED BY FAMILIES HAVING NEITHER GAS NOR ELECTRICITY SUPPLY—1ST QUARTER, 1948†

| | COOKING WITH | | | | | |
	COAL ONLY	OIL ONLY	COAL AND OIL	CALOR GAS ONLY	COAL AND CALOR GAS	OTHER COMBINATIONS
	% '000	% '000	% '000	% '000	% '000	% '000
ALL CLASSES	60·3 390	23·5 150	9·9 60	4·8 30	* *	0·9 10

*=Either less than 0·5% or less than 10,000
†See note to *Table* 24

26   USE OF REFRIGERATOR—1ST QUARTER, 1948†

By social class and type of power supply

	ALL CLASSES		CLASS AB		CLASS C		CLASS DE	
All householders:	%	'000	%	'000	%	'000	%	'000
USING ELECTRIC REFRIGERATOR ..	1·9	370	16·7	270	2·7	70	*	*
USING GAS REFRIGERATOR	1·6	240	7·1	110	2·0	50	0·9	130
TOTAL USING ANY REFRIGERATOR	3·5	660	23·8	380	4·7	120	1·1	160
ALL HOUSEHOLDS WITH GAS SUPPLY USING GAS REFRIGERATOR	2·5	290	8·7	110	2·5	50	1·6	130
ALL HOUSEHOLDS WITH ELECTRICITY SUPPLY USING ELECTRIC REFRIGERATOR ..	3·0	370	17·3	270	2·9	70	*	*
ALL HOUSEHOLDS WITH BOTH GAS AND ELECTRICITY SUPPLY USING GAS REFRIGERATOR	3·7	290	8·6	110	2·7	·50	2·0	130
USING ELECTRIC REFRIGERATOR ..	3·9	300	16·5	210	3·1	60	0·5	30

*=Either less than 0·5% or less than 10,000
†Based upon *The Hulton Readership Survey* 1948. Questions on refrigerator ownership were not asked in the 1949 Survey

27   THE MALE GARDENER—1ST QUARTER, 1949

By domestic status, social class and age

| | | GARDENING REGULARLY | | | | | | TOTAL GARDENING REGULARLY | | GARDENING OCCASION-ALLY | | TOTAL GARDENING AT ALL | |
| | | IN GARDENS | | ON ALLOTMENTS | | IN BOTH | | | | | | | |
		%	'000	%	'000	%	'000	%	'000	%	'000	%	'000
HEADS OF HOUSE-HOLD	CLASS:												
	AB ..	14·3	660	*	*	7·8	60	12·8	720	14·3	250	13·1	970
	C	20·3	930	7·8	20	12·4	90	18·5	1,050	20·1	350	18·9	1,400
	DE ..	65·4	2,990	91·0	280	79·8	610	68·7	3,890	65·6	1,150	68·0	5,030
	AGE:												
	16–24 ..	1·8	80	*	*	1·0	10	1·6	90	4·1	70	2·2	160
	25–34 ..	16·5	760	22·2	70	18·8	140	17·1	970	26·8	470	19·4	1,440
	35–44 ..	28·6	1,310	26·3	80	26·1	200	28·1	1,590	23·7	410	27·1	2,000
	45–64 ..	41·1	1,880	32·9	100	46·1	350	41·3	2,340	35·0	610	39·8	2,950
	65 & OVER	12·1	560	17·4	50	8·0	60	11·9	670	10·4	180	11·5	850
	ALL CLASSES AND AGES ..	100·0	4,580	100·0	300	100·0	770	100·0	5,650	100·0	1,750	100·0	7,400
NON-HEADS OF HOUSE-HOLD	CLASS:												
	AB ..	10·1	110	*	*	7·2	10	9·3	130	11·3	130	10·2	260
	C	18·3	200	8·9	10	15·3	30	17·3	240	17·6	200	17·4	440
	DE ..	71·6	800	88·9	70	77·5	160	73·4	1,030	71·1	790	72·4	1,820
	AGE:												
	16–24 ..	26·8	300	13·3	10	29·7	60	26·4	370	52·1	580	37·8	950
	25–34 ..	19·3	220	8·9	10	17·1	30	18·4	260	21·1	230	19·5	490
	35–44 ..	11·3	130	8·9	10	17·1	30	12·0	170	7·9	90	10·2	260
	45–64 ..	25·0	280	48·9	40	27·1	50	26·7	370	10·5	120	19·6	490
	65 & OVER	17·6	200	20·0	20	9·0	20	16·5	230	8·4	90	12·9	320
	ALL CLASSES AND AGES ..	100·0	1,120	100·0	80	100·0	200	100·0	1,400	100·0	1,110	100·0	2,510
ALL MEN	CLASS:												
	AB ..	13·5	770	1·4	10	7·7	70	12·1	850	13·2	380	12·4	1,230
	C	19·9	1,130	8·0	30	13·0	130	18·3	1,290	19·2	550	18·5	1,840
	DE ..	66·6	3,790	90·6	350	79·3	770	69·6	4,910	67·6	1,940	69·1	6,850
	AGE:												
	16–24 ..	6·7	380	3·8	10	7·0	70	6·5	460	22·7	650	11·2	1,110
	25–34 ..	17·0	970	19·3	70	18·4	180	17·4	1,230	24·6	700	19·4	1,930
	35–44 ..	25·2	1,440	22·7	90	24·2	240	24·9	1,760	17·6	500	22·8	2,260
	45–64 ..	37·9	2,160	36·3	140	42·1	410	38·4	2,710	25·5	730	34·7	3,440
	65 & OVER	13·2	750	17·9	70	8·3	80	12·8	900	9·6	280	11·9	1,180
	ALL CLASSES AND AGES ..	100·0	5,700	100·0	390	100·0	970	100·0	7,060	100·0	2,860	100·0	9,920

*=Either less than 0·5% or less than 10,000

Informants gardening "regularly" do so as a matter of habit or routine; "occasional" gardeners take no continuous interest in gardening

28 THE FEMALE GARDENER—1ST QUARTER, 1949

By domestic status, social class and age

| | | GARDENING REGULARLY | | | | | | TOTAL GARDENING REGULARLY | | GARDENING OCCASION-ALLY | | TOTAL GARDENING AT ALL | |
		IN GARDENS		ON ALLOTMENTS		IN BOTH							
		%	'000	%	'000	%	'000	%	'000	%	'000	%	'000
HOUSE-WIFE	CLASS:												
	AB ..	19·7	510	*	*	15·7	30	19·2	550	13·0	320	16·4	860
	C	25·0	650	11·1	10	17·6	30	24·3	690	19·5	470	22·1	1,160
	DE ..	55·3	1,440	81·5	40	66·7	120	56·5	1,610	67·5	1,640	61·5	3,240
	AGE:												
	16–24 ..	3·9	100	22·2	10	*	*	3·9	110	6·7	160	5·2	270
	25–34 ..	21·1	550	22·2	10	14·7	30	20·7	590	24·3	590	22·4	1,180
	35–44 ..	27·0	700	14·8	10	42·2	80	27·8	790	28·1	680	27·9	1,470
	45–64 ..	40·7	1,060	33·3	20	37·3	70	40·4	1,150	34·5	840	37·7	1,980
	65 & OVER	7·3	190	*	*	5·8	10	7·2	200	6·4	160	6·8	360
	ALL CLASSES AND AGES ..	100·0	2,610	100·0	50	100·0	190	100·0	2,840	100·0	2,420	100·0	5,270
NON-HOUSE-WIFE	CLASS:												
	AB ..	12·7	180	*	*	*	*	12·7	190	11·3	200	11·9	390
	C	18·6	270	30·0	10	22·2	10	18·8	280	18·7	330	18·7	610
	DE ..	68·7	990	60·0	10	66·7	20	68·5	1,020	70·0	1,220	69·4	2,240
	AGE:												
	16–24 ..	10·8	160	*	*	38·9	10	11·5	170	38·0	660	25·9	840
	25–34 ..	11·2	160	*	*	27·8	10	11·4	170	14·2	250	12·9	420
	35–44 ..	15·1	220	*	*	22·2	10	15·4	230	11·1	190	13·0	420
	45–64 ..	37·0	530	40·0	10	*	*	36·4	540	19·4	340	27·2	880
	65 & OVER	25·9	370	*	*	*	*	25·3	380	17·3	300	21·0	680
	ALL CLASSES AND AGES ..	100·0	1,440	100·0	20	100·0	30	100·0	1,490	100·0	1,750	100·0	3,230
ALL WOMEN	CLASS:												
	AB ..	17·2	700	8·1	10	15·0	30	17·0	730	12·3	510	14·7	1,250
	C	22·7	920	16·2	10	18·3	40	22·4	970	19·2	800	20·8	1,770
	DE ..	60·1	2,430	75·7	50	66·7	150	60·6	2,630	68·5	2,860	65·5	5,480
	AGE:												
	16–24 ..	6·3	260	21·6	10	5·8	10	6·6	280	19·8	830	13·1	1,110
	25–34 ..	17·6	710	16·2	10	16·7	40	17·5	760	20·1	840	18·8	1,600
	35–44 ..	22·8	920	16·2	10	39·2	90	23·5	1,020	21·0	870	22·2	1,890
	45–64 ..	39·4	1,590	35·2	20	32·5	70	39·0	1,690	28·2	1,180	33·7	2,860
	65 & OVER	13·9	560	10·8	10	5·8	10	13·4	580	10·9	460	12·2	1,040
	ALL CLASSES AND AGES ..	100·0	4,040	100·0	70	100·0	220	100·0	4,330	100·0	4,170	100·0	8,500

*=Either less than 0·5% or less than 10,000

NOTE: See note to *Table* 27

29 PROPORTIONS AND NUMBERS OF MEN AND WOMEN GAINFULLY EMPLOYED—1ST QUARTER, 1949

By social class and age

| | | WORKING | | | | | | NOT WORKING | | TOTAL | |
| | | FULL TIME | | PART TIME | | AT ALL | | | | | |
		%	'000	%	'000	%	'000	%	'000	%	'000
MEN	CLASS:										
	AB	91·3	1,790	*	*	91·3	1,790	8·7	170	100·0	1,970
	C	90·5	2,690	*	*	90·5	2,690	9·5	280	100·0	2,980
	DE	91·5	11,020	*	*	91·5	11,020	8·5	1,020	100·0	12,040
	AGE:										
	16–24 ..	92·6	2,190	*	*	92·6	2,190	7·4	180	100·0	2,370
	25–34 ..	97·5	3,390	*	*	97·5	3,390	2·5	90	100·0	3,480
	35–44 ..	97·8	3,620	*	*	97·8	3,620	2·2	80	100·0	3,710
	45–64 ..	95·3	5,020	*	*	95·3	5,020	4·7	250	100·0	5,270
	65 AND OVER	59·1	1,270	*	*	59·1	1,270	40·9	880	100·0	2,150
	ALL CLASSES AND AGES ..	91·3	15,500	*	*	91·3	15,500	8·7	1,470	100·0	16,980
WOMEN	CLASS:										
	AB	24·8	560	2·4	60	27·2	610	72·8	1,630	100·0	2,250
	C	35·4	1,230	3·0	100	38·4	1,340	61·6	2,140	100·0	3,480
	DE	35·2	4,960	5·6	790	40·8	5,750	59·2	8,350	100·0	14,100
	AGE:										
	16–24 ..	74·6	2,290	1·8	50	76·4	2,350	23·6	720	100·0	3,070
	25–34 ..	36·7	1,370	5·3	200	42·0	1,560	58·0	2,150	100·0	3,720
	35–44 ..	33·2	1,290	6·3	250	39·5	1,540	60·5	2,350	100·0	3,890
	45–64 ..	25·3	1,580	6·3	390	31·6	1,970	68·4	4,260	100·0	6,220
	65 AND OVER	7·8	230	1·9	60	9·7	280	90·3	2,640	100·0	2,920
	ALL CLASSES AND AGES ..	34·0	6,750	4·8	950	38·8	7,700	61·2	12,120	100·0	19,820
MEN AND WOMEN COMBINED	CLASS:										
	AB	55·8	2,350	1·3	50	57·1	2,410	42·9	1,810	100·0	4,210
	C	60·8	3,930	1·6	100	62·4	4,030	37·6	2,430	100·0	6,460
	DE	61·2	15,980	3·0	790	64·2	16,770	35·8	9,370	100·0	26,130
	AGE:										
	16–24 ..	82·4	4,480	1·0	50	83·4	4,540	16·6	900	100·0	5,440
	25–34 ..	66·1	4,760	2·7	200	68·8	4,960	31·2	2,240	100·0	7,200
	35–44 ..	64·7	4,910	3·2	250	67·9	5,160	32·1	2,430	100·0	7,590
	45–64 ..	57·4	6,600	3·4	390	60·8	6,990	39·2	4,500	100·0	11,490
	65 AND OVER	29·5	1,500	1·1	60	30·6	1,560	69·4	3,520	100·0	5,080
	ALL CLASSES AND AGES ..	60·5	22,260	2·6	950	63·1	23,200	36·9	13,600	100·0	36,800

*=Either less than 0·5% or less than 10,000

30 PROPORTIONS AND NUMBERS OF WOMEN GAINFULLY EMPLOYED —1ST QUARTER, 1949

By social class, age and marital status

| | | WORKING | | | | | | NOT WORKING | | TOTAL | |
| | | FULL TIME | | PART TIME | | AT ALL | | | | | |
	CLASS:	%	'000	%	'000	%	'000	%	'000	%	'000
	AB	11·3	160	3·1	40	14·4	200	85·6	1,220	100·0	1,420
	C	16·6	360	3·8	80	20·4	440	79·6	1,710	100·0	2,150
	DE	16·3	1,370	7·2	610	23·5	1,980	76·5	6,430	100·0	8,410
	AGE:										
MARRIED	16–24 ..	24·8	190	4·0	30	28·8	220	71·2	560	100·0	780
	25–34 ..	18·8	520	6·3	170	25·1	690	74·9	2,060	100·0	2,750
	35–44 ..	19·3	590	7·3	220	26·6	810	73·4	2,240	100·0	3,050
	45–64 ..	12·6	550	6·6	290	19·2	840	80·8	3,540	100·0	4,390
	65 AND OVER	3·9	40	1·8	20	5·7	60	94·3	970	100·0	1,020
	ALL CLASSES AND AGES ..	15·8	1,890	6·1	730	21·9	2,620	78·1	9,360	100·0	11,980
	CLASS:										
	AB	48·0	400	1·3	10	49·3	410	50·7	420	100·0	830
	C	65·6	870	1·7	20	67·6	900	32·4	430	100·0	1,330
UN-MARRIED	DE	63·1	3,590	3·2	180	66·3	3,770	33·7	1,920	100·0	5,690
	AGE:										
	16–24 ..	91·6	2,100	1·0	20	92·6	2,120	7·4	170	100·0	2,290
	25–34 ..	87·7	850	2·5	20	90·2	870	9·8	90	100·0	970
	35–44 ..	83·4	700	3·0	30	86·4	730	13·6	120	100·0	840
	45–64 ..	55·6	1,020	5·7	100	61·3	1,130	38·7	710	100·0	1,840
	65 AND OVER	9·8	190	2·0	40	11·8	220	88·2	1,670	100·0	1,900
	ALL CLASSES AND AGES ..	62·0	4,860	2·7	220	64·7	5,080	35·3	2,760	100·0	7,840

31 PROPORTIONS AND NUMBERS OF WOMEN GAINFULLY EMPLOYED —1ST QUARTER, 1949

By social class, age and domestic status

| | | WORKING | | | | | | NOT WORKING | | TOTAL | |
| | | FULL TIME | | PART TIME | | AT ALL | | | | | |
		%	'000	%	'000	%	'000	%	'000	%	'000
HOUSE-WIVES	CLASS:										
	AB	14·6	250	2·5	40	17·1	300	82·9	1,430	100·0	1,730
	C	21·1	560	3·5	90	24·6	650	75·4	1,980	100·0	2,630
	DE	19·9	2,070	6·8	700	26·7	2,780	73·3	7,630	100·0	10,400
	AGE:										
	16–24 ..	21·4	130	3·9	20	25·3	160	74·7	460	100·0	610
	25–34 ..	18·4	490	6·7	180	25·1	670	74·9	2,000	100·0	2,670
	35–44 ..	24·5	820	7·0	230	31·5	1,060	68·5	2,290	100·0	3,350
	45–64 ..	22·1	1,260	6·3	360	28·4	1,620	71·6	4,080	100·0	5,700
	65 AND OVER	7·2	180	1·8	40	9·1	220	90·9	2,200	100·0	2,420
	ALL CLASSES AND AGES ..	19·5	2,880	5·7	840	25·2	3,720	74·8	11,040	100·0	14,760
NON-HOUSE-WIVES	CLASS:										
	AB	58·8	300	2·1	10	60·9	320	39·1	200	100·0	520
	C	79·6	680	1·5	10	81·1	690	18·9	160	100·0	850
	DE	78·2	2,890	2·3	90	80·5	2,980	19·5	720	100·0	3,700
	AGE:										
	16–24 ..	87·9	2,160	1·3	30	89·2	2,190	10·8	270	100·0	2,460
	25–34 ..	83·7	870	1·9	20	85·6	890	14·4	150	100·0	1,040
	35–44 ..	87·1	470	2·4	10	89·5	480	10·5	60	100·0	540
	45–64 ..	60·5	320	6·6	30	67·1	350	32·9	170	100·0	520
	65 AND OVER	10·2	50	2·5	10	12·7	60	87·3	440	100·0	500
	ALL CLASSES AND AGES ..	76·4	3,870	2·2	110	78·6	3,980	21·4	1,080	100·0	5,060

32 PROPORTIONS AND NUMBERS OF THE ADULT POPULATION SPENDING HOLIDAYS AWAY FROM HOME—1948

By sex and social class

	MEN		WOMEN		TOTAL	
	%	'000	%	'000	%	'000
CLASS AB	76·9	1,510	78·0	1,750	77·5	3,260
C	68·0	2,020	71·8	2,500	70·0	4,520
DE	53·5	6,440	53·3	7,510	53·4	13,950
TOTAL ALL CLASSES	58·8	9,980	59·3	11,760	59·1	21,730

Source: *The Hulton Readership Survey 1949*
NOTE: These figures refer to holidays taken in 1948

33 PROPORTIONS AND NUMBERS OF HOLIDAY-MAKERS USING DIFFERENT FORMS OF TRANSPORT TO GET TO HOLIDAY RESORTS—1948

All classes and ages

	%	'000
TRAVELLING BY :		
RAIL AND/OR SHIP	58·1	12,630
PRIVATE OR HIRED CAR	17·2	3,740
MOTOR COACH	21·4	4,640
AIR	1·3	280
OTHER METHODS	2·0	450
TOTAL HOLIDAY-MAKERS	100·0	21,730

Source: *The Hulton Readership Survey 1949*
NOTE: These figures refer to holidays taken in 1948

34 PROPORTIONS AND NUMBERS OF THE ADULT POPULATION SPENDING HOLIDAYS AWAY FROM HOME—1947

By sex, social class and age

	ALL AGES		AGED 16–24		AGED 25–34		AGED 35–44		AGED 45–64		AGED 65 OR OVER	
	%	'000	%	'000	%	'000	%	'000	%	'000	%	'000
MEN:												
CLASS AB	76·1	1,400	66	160	80	150	62	350	76	610	71	130
C	64·9	1,860	58	210	69	360	71	460	65	620	54	200
DE	50·5	6,030	50	890	51	1,440	55	1,440	50	1,690	41	570
ALL MEN	55·8	9,290	53	1,270	55	1,950	61	2,250	57	2,920	46	900
WOMEN:												
CLASS AB	74·9	1,550	83	220	83	210	85	370	73	560	60	180
C	70·1	2,330	81	350	74	400	71	500	69	840	56	250
DE	51·1	7,140	60	1,440	54	1,530	50	1,350	52	2,170	37	690
ALL WOMEN	57·0	11,020	65	1,960	59	2,140	58	2,220	58	3,570	43	1,130
TOTAL MEN AND WOMEN	56·4	20,310	60	3,230	57	4,090	59	4,470	59	6,490	44	2,030

NOTE: The source of *Tables* 34—38 inclusive is *The Hulton Readership Survey 1948*, but the figures refer to holidays taken in 1947. A *detailed* investigation into holiday habits was not part of the 1949 Survey.

35 PROPORTIONS AND NUMBERS OF THE POPULATION SPENDING HOLIDAYS AWAY FROM HOME, AND TYPE OF RESORT WHERE HOLIDAY WAS SPENT—1947

By sex and domestic status

| | TOTAL "ADULT" POPULATION | | MEN | | | | WOMEN | | | |
| | | | HEADS OF HOUSEHOLDS | | OTHER MEN | | HOUSEWIVES | | OTHER WOMEN | |
	%	'000	%	'000	%	'000	%	'000	%	'000
Spending holidays in Great Britain:										
AT SEASIDE	34·8	12,530	36·0	4,190	30·0	1,510	33·7	4,830	39·9	1,990
IN COUNTRY	13·1	4,720	13·2	1,540	13·3	670	12·4	1,790	14·7	730
IN LONDON	2·6	940	2·2	250	3·2	160	2·6	370	3·3	160
IN OTHER CITIES AND TOWNS	2·5	920	2·7	320	2·7	140	2·3	320	2·8	140
TOTAL SPENDING HOLIDAYS IN GREAT BRITAIN	53·0	19,110	54·1	6,300	49·2	2,480	51·0	7,310	60·7	3,020
SPENDING HOLIDAYS ABROAD	3·3	1,200	2·4	280	4·8	240	3·0	440	4·9	240
Total taking holidays ..	56·3	20,310	56·5	6,580	54·0	2,710	54·0	7,750	65·6	3,270
TAKING NO HOLIDAYS ..	43·7	15,690	43·5	5,060	46·0	2,300	46·0	6,620	34·4	1,710
Total Population	100·0	36,000	100·0	11,640	100·0	5,010	100·0	14,370	100·0	4,980

NOTE: See note to *Table* 34

36 PROPORTIONS AND NUMBERS OF THE POPULATION SPENDING HOLIDAYS AWAY FROM HOME WHO STARTED THEM IN EACH MONTH—1947

(a) By social class

| | ALL CLASSES AND AGES | | CLASS AB | | CLASS C | | CLASS DE | |
	%	'000	%	'000	%	'000	%	'000
JANUARY–MARCH ..	0·9	180	1	20	1	40	1	120
APRIL	1·5	300	1	30	1	50	2	215
MAY	3·3	680	4	120	3	140	3	420
JUNE	13·4	2,720	15	440	14	570	13	1,710
JULY	28·9	5,860	21	620	28	1,180	31	4,070
AUGUST	30·9	6,280	34	1,000	30	1,240	30	4,040
SEPTEMBER	17·1	3,470	20	560	19	790	16	2,080
OCTOBER	2·4	480	2	70	2	100	2	310
NOVEMBER–DECEMBER	1·6	340	2	50	2	70	2	210
Total Holiday-makers	100·0	20,310	100	2,950	100	4,190	100	13,170

NOTE: See note to *Table* 34

37 NUMBERS OF POPULATION LIVING IN EACH REGION SPENDING HOLIDAYS IN DIFFERENT REGIONS OR ABROAD, OR NOT TAKING HOLIDAYS—1947

	POPULATION LIVING IN						
	ALL REGIONS	SOUTH-EAST	SOUTH-WEST AND WALES	MIDLANDS	NORTH-WEST	NORTH-EAST AND NORTH	SCOTLAND
Spending holidays in:	'000	'000	'000	'000	'000	'000	'000
SOUTH-EAST	7,180	4,440	800	880	330	500	230
SOUTH-WEST AND WALES ..	3,840	1,260	820	830	630	240	60
MIDLANDS	1,060	190	100	440	140	160	30
NORTH-WEST	2,550	200	120	510	930	660	130
NORTH-EAST AND NORTH ..	2,200	320	70	230	220	1,230	130
SCOTLAND	2,280	220	40	90	140	260	1,530
Total spending holidays in Great Britain	19,110	6,630	1,950	2,980	2,390	3,050	2,110
SPENDING HOLIDAYS ABROAD ..	1,200	600	100	120	160	80	140
Total taking holidays	20,310	7,230	2,050	3,100	2,550	3,130	2,250
TAKING NO HOLIDAYS	15,690	4,970	2,050	2,650	2,200	2,220	1,600
TOTAL POPULATION	36,000	12,200	4,100	5,750	4,750	5,350	3,850

NOTE: See note to *Table* 34

38 PROPORTIONS AND NUMBERS OF THE POPULATION SPENDING HOLIDAYS AWAY FROM HOME WHO TOOK HOLIDAYS OF DIFFERENT LENGTHS—1947

By sex

HOLIDAYS LASTING:	MEN %	MEN '000	WOMEN %	WOMEN '000	TOTAL %	TOTAL '000
UNDER 6 DAYS ..	3.6	330	3·7	410	3·7	740
6–10 DAYS	52·3	4,860	50·6	5,570	51·3	10,420
11–16 DAYS ..	38·2	3,550	35·3	3,900	36·7	7,450
17–22 DAYS ..	3·7	340	4·8	530	4·3	870
23–32 DAYS ..	1·4	130	3·8	420	2·7	540
33 DAYS AND OVER	0·8	70	1·8	200	1·3	270
TOTAL	100·0	9,290	100·0	11,020	100·0	20,310
AVERAGE LENGTH OF HOLIDAY AMONG PEOPLE WHO TOOK HOLIDAYS AWAY FROM HOME (DAYS)	11·1		11·8		11·5	
AVERAGE TIME SPENT ON HOLIDAYS AWAY FROM HOME PER HEAD OF TOTAL POPULATION (DAYS)	6·2		6·8		6·5	

NOTE: See note to *Table* 34

39 PROPORTIONS AND NUMBERS OF HOLIDAY-MAKERS USING DIFFERENT FORMS OF TRANSPORT TO GET TO HOLIDAY RESORTS—1947

By social class

Travelling by:	ALL CLASSES AND AGES		CLASS AB		CLASS C		CLASS DE	
	%	'000	%	'000	%	'000	%	'000
RAIL AND/OR SHIP	57·8	11,750	41	1,210	57	2,340	62	8,160
PRIVATE OR HIRED CAR ..	22·0	4,470	48	1,420	27	1,130	14	1,920
MOTOR COACH	15·7	3,190	6	160	12	510	19	2,520
MOTOR-CYCLE OR BICYCLE ..	1·8	370	1	30	1	50	2	290
AIR	1·1	220	3	100	1	40	1	80
OTHER METHODS	1·6	320	1	40	2	80	2	200
TOTAL HOLIDAY-MAKERS	100·0	20,310	100	2,950	100	4,190	100	13,170

(b) By age

Travelling by:	AGED 16–24		AGED 25–34		AGED 35–44		AGED 45–64		AGED 65 AND OVER	
	%	'000	%	'000	%	'000	%	'000	%	'000
RAIL AND/OR SHIP ..	64	2,050	62	2,520	54	2,410	56	3,650	55	1,110
PRIVATE OR HIRED CAR	12	390	19	800	27	1,200	24	1,560	26	520
MOTOR COACH	17	560	13	520	15	660	17	1,120	16	330
MOTOR CYCLE OR BICYCLE	4	120	3	120	2	100	1	20	*	*
AIR	1	40	1	60	1	40	1	60	1	20
OTHER METHODS ..	2	70	2	80	1	60	1	70	2	40
TOTAL HOLIDAY-MAKERS	100	3,230	100	4,090	100	4,470	100	6,490	100	2,030

NOTE: See note to *Table* 34

*=Either less than 0·5% or less than 10,000

40 PROPORTIONS AND NUMBERS OF POPULATION WITH ONE OR MORE CARS REGISTERED IN THEIR OWN NAME—1ST QUARTER, 1949

By sex, social class, age and domestic status

	ALL CLASSES AND AGES		CLASS					
			AB		C		DE	
	%	'000	%	'000	%	'000	%	'000
MEN OWNING, WHO ARE:								
Heads of households ..	15·7	1,890	53·6	820	24·5	540	6.4	530
Non-heads of households ..	6·7	340	23·0	100	11·4	90	4·0	150
ALL MEN OWNING	13·1	2,220	46·8	920	21·2	630	5·6	680
WOMEN OWNING, WHO ARE:								
Housewives	2·3	340	9·7	170	3·4	90	0·8	90
Non-housewives	1·6	80	5·6	30	2·4	20	0·9	30
ALL WOMEN OWNING	2·1	420	8·8	200	3·1	110	0·8	120
MEN AND WOMEN OWNING:								
1 only	7·0	2,590	25·5	1,070	11·3	730	3·0	790
2 or more	0·1	50	1·0	40	0·2	10	*	*
TOTAL OWNING ANY	7·2	2,650	26·5	1,120	11·5	740	3·0	790

	AGE									
	16–24		25–34		35–44		45–64		65 AND OVER	
	%	'000	%	'000	%	'000	%	'000	%	'000
MEN OWNING, WHO ARE:										
Heads of households	4·5	10	10·4	210	17·7	550	18·6	890	12·0	210
Non-heads of households ..	3·5	70	10·1	150	13·7	80	7·3	30	2·1	10
ALL MEN OWNING	3·5	80	10·3	360	17·0	630	17·6	930	10·4	220
WOMEN OWNING, WHO ARE:										
Housewives	*	*	1·4	40	2·7	90	2·9	170	2·0	50
Non-housewives	0·8	20	2·0	30	3·7	20	2·4	10	*	*
ALL WOMEN OWNING	0·7	20	1·7	60	2·8	110	2·9	180	1·7	50
MEN AND WOMEN OWNING:										
1 only	1·9	110	5·8	420	9·6	730	9·4	1,070	5·2	260
2 or more	*	*	*	*	0·2	10	0·2	30	0·2	10
TOTAL OWNING ANY	1·9	110	5·9	420	9·8	740	9·6	1,100	5·4	270

*=Either less than 0·5% or less than 10,000

NOTE:: The figures include persons with cars not currently licensed (some of which may not be roadworthy) and persons with commercially licensed vehicles considered and used by their owners partly as private cars.

41 PROPORTIONS OF MEN WITH ONE OR MORE MOTOR-CYCLES REGISTERED IN THEIR OWN NAME—1ST QUARTER, 1949

By social class and age

	PERCENTAGE OWNING ONE OR MORE MACHINES
ALL MEN	4·3
CLASS AB	3·5
C	4·7
DE	4·4
16–24	6·9
25–34	7·3
35–44	5·0
45–64	2·5
65 AND OVER	*

*=Either less than 0·5% or less than 10,000

42 PROPORTIONS AND NUMBERS OF POPULATION OWNING AND USING CYCLES—1ST QUARTER, 1949

By sex, social class and age

| | | TOTAL POPULATION | | USERS OF CYCLES | | | | | | OWNING BUT NOT USING | | TOTAL OWNING† | |
| | | | | WITH SOLE USE | | WITH SHARED USE | | TOTAL | | | | | |
		%	'000	%	'000	%	'000	%	'000	%	'000	%	'000
MEN	CLASS:												
	AB ..	100·0	1,970	24·8	490	2·1	40	26·9	530	3·3	70	29·2	570
	C ..	100·0	2,980	33·7	1,000	3·1	90	36·7	1,090	4·4	130	39·6	1,180
	DE ..	100·0	12,040	38·3	4,610	3·3	400	41·6	5,010	3·2	380	43·1	5,190
	AGE:												
	16–24 ..	100·0	2,370	58·3	1,380	5·9	140	64·2	1,520	5·6	130	66·9	1,580
	25–34 ..	100·0	3,480	42·0	1,460	4·1	140	46·1	1,610	3·8	130	47·9	1,670
	35–44 ..	100·0	3,710	38·3	1,420	2·8	100	41·1	1,520	3·2	120	42·9	1,590
	45–64 ..	100·0	5,270	30·6	1,610	2·6	140	33·2	1,750	2·8	150	34·7	1,830
	65 & OVER	100·0	2,150	10·7	230	*	*	10·9	240	2·0	40	12·8	280
	ALL CLASSES AND AGES	100·0	16,980	35·9	6,100	3·1	530	39·1	6,630	3·4	580	40·9	6,940
WOMEN	CLASS:												
	AB ..	100·0	2,250	21·7	490	2·8	60	24·5	550	4·8	110	27·9	630
	C ..	100·0	3,480	17·8	620	2·4	80	20·1	700	4·9	170	23·9	830
	DE ..	100·0	14,100	14·7	2,080	2·8	390	17·5	2,470	3·6	500	19·7	2,780
	AGE:												
	16–24 ..	100·0	3,070	34·9	1,070	6·4	200	41·2	1,270	9·6	300	47·7	1,470
	25–34 ..	100·0	3,720	23·1	860	3·9	140	27·0	1,000	5·9	220	31·0	1,150
	35–44 ..	100·0	3,890	17·2	670	2·3	90	19·5	760	3·6	140	21·9	850
	45–64 ..	100·0	6,220	8·9	560	1·6	100	10·5	660	1·9	120	11·6	720
	65 & OVER	100·0	2,920	0·9	30	*	*	1·3	40	*	*	1·5	40
	ALL CLASSES AND AGES	100·0	19,820	16·1	3,180	2·7	540	18·8	3,720	4·0	780	21·4	4,240
MEN AND WOMEN	CLASS:												
	AB ..	100·0	4,210	23·1	970	2·5	100	25·6	1,080	4·1	170	28·5	1,200
	C ..	100·0	6,460	25·1	1,620	2·7	170	27·8	1,790	4·7	300	31·1	2,010
	DE ..	100·0	26,130	25·6	6,690	3·0	790	28·6	7,480	3·4	880	30·5	7,970
	AGE:												
	16–24 ..	100·0	5,440	45·1	2,450	6·2	340	51·2	2,790	7·9	420	56·0	3,050
	25–34 ..	100·0	7,200	32·3	2,320	4·0	290	36·3	2,610	4·9	350	39·2	2,820
	35–44 ..	100·0	7,590	27·5	2,090	2·5	190	30·0	2,280	3·4	260	32·1	2,440
	45–64 ..	100·0	11,490	18·8	2,160	2·1	240	20·9	2,400	2·3	270	22·2	2,550
	65 & OVER	100·0	4,890	5·3	260	*	*	5·6	270	1·1	50	6·5	320
	ALL CLASSES AND AGES	100·0	36,800	25·2	9,290	2·9	1,070	28·1	10,360	3·7	1,360	30·4	11,180

*=Either less than 0·5% or less than 10,000

†NOTE: Owners of shared bicycles are counted at half-rate

43 FREQUENCY OF USE OF A CYCLE—1ST QUARTER, 1949

		TOTAL USERS		USING MORE THAN ONCE A WEEK		USING ONCE A WEEK OR LESS FREQUENTLY	
		%	'000	%	'000	%	'000
MEN	CLASS AB	100·0	530	44·8	240	55·2	290
	C	100·0	1,090	58·3	640	41·7	460
	DE	100·0	5,010	75·5	3,780	24·5	1,230
	AGE 16–24 ..	100·0	1,520	72·1	1,100	27·9	420
	25–34 ..	100·0	1,610	73·4	1,180	26·6	430
	35–44 ..	100·0	1,520	69·3	1,060	30·7	470
	45–64 ..	100·0	1,750	66·2	1,160	33·8	590
	65 AND OVER	100·0	240	71·3	170	28·7	70
	ALL CLASSES AND AGES	100·0	6,630	70·2	4,660	29·8	1,980
WOMEN	CLASS AB	100·0	550	49·5	270	50·5	280
	C	100·0	700	48·2	340	51·8	360
	DE	100·0	2,470	55·2	1,370	44·8	1,110
	AGE 16–24 ..	100·0	1,270	52·0	660	48·0	610
	25–34 ..	100·0	1,000	48·7	490	51·3	510
	35–44 ..	100·0	760	57·3	430	42·7	320
	45–64 ..	100·0	660	57·9	380	42·1	280
	65 AND OVER	100·0	40	33·3	10	66·7	30
	ALL CLASSES AND AGES ..	100·0	3,720	53·1	1,980	46·9	1,750
MEN AND WOMEN	CLASS AB	100·0	1,080	47·2	510	52·8	570
	C	100·0	1,790	54·3	970	45·7	820
	DE	100·0	7,480	68·8	5,150	31·2	2,330
	AGE 16–24 ..	100·0	2,790	63·0	1,760	37·0	1,030
	25–34 ..	100·0	2,610	63·9	1,670	36·1	940
	35–44 ..	100·0	2,280	65·3	1,490	34·7	790
	45–64 ..	100·0	2,400	64·0	1,540	36·0	870
	65 AND OVER	100·0	270	66·0	180	34·0	90
	ALL CLASSES AND AGES	100·0	10,360	64·1	6,630	35·9	3,720

44 PROPORTIONS AND NUMBERS OF THE ADULT POPULATION WHO ARE SMOKERS—1ST QUARTER, 1949

(a) By sex and social class

	ALL CLASSES		CLASS AB		CLASS C		CLASS DE	
Men:	%	'000	%	'000	%	'000	%	'000
SMOKING CIGARETTES ONLY ..	52·4	8,910	42·3	830	47·2	1,400	55·4	6,670
SMOKING CIGARETTES AND PIPE ..	15·0	2,550	23·8	470	16·9	500	13·1	1,580
SMOKING PIPE ONLY	11·7	1,980	11·9	230	12·4	370	11·4	1,380
TOTAL MEN SMOKERS	79·1	13,430	78·0	1,530	76·5	2,270	79·9	9,630
MEN SMOKING PIPES AT ALL	26·7	4,530	35·7	700	29·3	870	24·5	2,960
MEN SMOKING CIGARETTES AT ALL ..	67·4	11,460	66·1	1,300	64·1	1,900	68·5	8,250
Women:								
SMOKING CIGARETTES	37·7	7,470	38·9	910	36·4	1,270	37·6	5,290
MEN AND WOMEN SMOKERS	56·8	20,900	58·0	2,440	54·8	3,540	57·1	14,920

(b) By sex and age

	AGED 16–24		AGED 25–34		AGED 35–44		AGED 45–64		AGED 65 AND OVER	
Men:	%	'000	%	'000	%	'000	%	'000	%	'000
SMOKING CIGARETTES ONLY ..	56·2	1,330	58·2	2,030	59·6	2,210	52·6	2,770	26·5	570
SMOKING CIGARETTES AND PIPES ..	9·6	230	14·1	490	16·8	640	16·7	880	14·5	310
SMOKING PIPE ONLY	2·0	50	6·9	240	5·8	220	12·6	660	37·6	810
TOTAL MEN SMOKERS	67·8	1,610	79·2	2,760	82·5	3,060	81·9	4,320	78·6	1,690
MEN SMOKING PIPE AT ALL	11·6	270	21·0	730	22·6	860	29·3	1,540	52·1	1,120
MEN SMOKING CIGARETTES AT ALL ..	65·8	1,560	72·3	2,520	76·4	2,850	69·3	3,650	41·0	880
Women:										
SMOKING CIGARETTES	39·5	1,210	51·0	1,900	45·9	1,790	32·8	2,040	18·2	530
MEN AND WOMEN SMOKERS	51·8	2,820	64·7	4,660	63·8	4,850	55·3	6,360	43·8	2,220

45   PROPORTIONS AND NUMBERS OF CIGARETTE SMOKERS IN EACH SOCIAL CLASS AND AGE-GROUP—1ST QUARTER, 1949

(a) Among men

AGE-GROUP	ALL CLASSES		CLASS AB		CLASS C		CLASS DE	
	%	'000	%	'000	%	'000	%	'000
16–24	65·8	1,560	56·2	140	58·1	220	68·8	1,200
25–34	72·3	2,520	69·8	140	63·9	330	74·0	2,050
35–44	76·4	2,850	75·4	330	77·5	510	76·7	2,000
45–64	67·3	3,650	68·4	580	67·0	670	70·2	2,400
65 AND OVER ..	41·0	880	47·6	110	41·5	180	39·9	600
ALL AGE-GROUPS	67·4	11,460	66·1	1,300	64·1	1,900	68·5	8,250

(b) Among women

AGE-GROUP	ALL CLASSES		CLASS AB		CLASS C		CLASS DE	
	%	'000	%	'000	%	'000	%	'000
16–24	39·5	1,210	36·1	100	37·6	160	40·2	960
25–34	51·0	1,900	48·3	130	44·6	250	52·5	1,510
35–44	45·9	1,790	51·0	240	45·8	330	45·1	1,220
45–64	32·8	2,040	41·8	340	33·3	420	30·9	1,280
65 AND OVER ..	18·2	530	23·1	90	21·1	110	16·4	320
ALL AGE-GROUPS	37·7	7,470	38·9	910	36·4	1,270	37·6	5,290

46   PROPORTIONS AND NUMBERS OF PIPE SMOKERS IN EACH SOCIAL CLASS AND AGE-GROUP—1ST QUARTER, 1949

AGE-GROUP	ALL CLASSES		CLASS AB		CLASS C		CLASS DE	
	%	'000	%	'000	%	'000	%	'000
16–24	11·6	270	27·0	70	12·3	50	9·2	160
25–34	21·0	730	33·0	60	25·4	130	19·4	540
35–44	22·6	860	32·9	140	29·9	200	19·6	510
45–64	29·3	1,540	37·0	320	30·0	300	27·2	930
65 AND OVER ..	52·1	1,120	47·6	110	45·7	200	54·6	820
ALL AGE-GROUPS	26·7	4,530	35·7	700	29·3	870	24·5	2,960

47 NUMBER OF CIGARETTES AND QUANTITY OF PIPE TOBACCO SMOKED DAILY BY THE AVERAGE SMOKER—1ST QUARTER, 1949

By social class

	ALL CLASSES		CLASS AB		CLASS C		CLASS DE	
	CIGS. NO.	PIPE OZ.	CIGS. NO.	PIPE OZ.	CIGS. NO.	PIPE OZ.	CIGS. NO.	PIPE OZ.
Men:								
BY "CIGARETTE ONLY" SMOKERS ..	14·9		16·6		15·4		14·6	
BY "CIGARETTE AND PIPE" SMOKERS	11·9	0·33	14·3	0·31	12·6	0·32	11·0	0·33
BY "PIPE ONLY" SMOKERS		0·42		0·47		0·41		0·42
BY ALL MEN CIGARETTE SMOKERS ..	14·2		15·8		14·6		13·9	
BY ALL MEN PIPE SMOKERS.. ..		0·36		0·36		0·35		0·37
BY WOMEN CIGARETTE SMOKERS ..	6·5		8·3		6·5		6·2	
BY MEN AND WOMEN CIGARETTE SMOKERS	11·2		12·7		11·4		10·9	

48 AVERAGE NUMBER OF CIGARETTES SMOKED DAILY BY CIGARETTE SMOKERS—1ST QUARTER, 1949

By age within social class, either sex

Among all cigarette smokers

AGE	MEN				WOMEN			
	CLASS AB	CLASS C	CLASS DE	ALL CLASSES	CLASS AB	CLASS C	CLASS DE	ALL CLASSES
16–24 ..	12·0	10·1	12·1	11·8	7·0	5·5	5·3	5·5
25–34 ..	14·9	15·1	14·3	14·4	9·4	7·8	6·7	7·0
35–44 ..	18·1	15·4	15·0	15·5	9·0	7·3	7·0	7·3
45–64 ..	16·6	15·7	14·3	15·0	8·5	6·3	5·8	6·3
65 AND OVER	10·1	12·9	10·7	11·1	5·7	3·9	4·7	4·7
ALL AGES ..	15·8	14·6	13·9	14·2	8·3	6·5	6·2	6·5

49 AVERAGE AMOUNT (in ounces) OF TOBACCO SMOKED DAILY BY PIPE SMOKERS—1ST QUARTER, 1949

By social class

	ALL CLASSES	CLASS AB	CLASS C	CLASS DE
AGE 16–24	0·25	0·22	0·17	0·29
25–34	0·33	0·29	0·33	0·34
35–44	0·35	0·38	0·39	0·32
45–64	0·39	0·38	0·36	0·41
65 AND OVER	0·38	0·39	0·39	0·37
ALL AGES	0·36	0·36	0·35	0·37

50 INTENSITY OF CIGARETTE SMOKING—1ST QUARTER, 1949

By sex

	MEN		WOMEN		MEN AND WOMEN	
	%	’000	%	’000	%	’000
VERY HEAVY	*	*	*	*	*	*
HEAVY	7·8	1,330	0·7	130	4·0	1,460
AVERAGE	44·1	7,480	12·7	2,520	27·1	10,000
LIGHT	14·9	2,540	24·3	4,820	20·0	7,360
ALL CIGARETTE SMOKERS ..	67·4	11,460	37·7	7,470	51·4	18,930

*=Either less than 0·5% or less than 10,000

NOTE: The classification of smokers according to intensity is as follows:
Very heavy .. .. 44 or more cigarettes per day
Heavy .. .. 23–43 „ „ „
Average .. .. 8–22 „ „ „
Light .. .. Less than 8 „ „ „

51 DISTRIBUTION OF TOTAL TOBACCO SMOKED—1ST QUARTER, 1949

By social class

CLASS	PERCENTAGE OF POPULATION IN EACH CLASS	TOBACCO SMOKED WEEKLY (Thousands of Pounds)				
		IN CIGARETTES			IN PIPES	TOTAL
		BY MEN	BY WOMEN	TOTAL		
AB	11%	299	108	407	110	517 (14%)
C	17%	404	119	523	136	659 (17%)
DE	72%	1,677	477	2,154	477	2,631 (69%)
ALL CLASSES	100%	2,380	704	3,084	723	3,807 (100%)

52 BEER-DRINKING HABITS OF THE POPULATION—1ST QUARTER, 1949
(a) By sex and social class

	ALL CLASSES		CLASS AB		CLASS C		CLASS DE	
	%	'000	%	'000	%	'000	%	'000
Men:								
DRINKING EVERY DAY	13·6	2,300	20·1	390	13·1	390	12·6	1,520
DRINKING MORE THAN ONCE A WEEK BUT NOT EVERY DAY ..	20·5	3,480	18·9	370	19·3	580	21·0	2,530
TOTAL DRINKING REGULARLY ..	34·1	5,780	39·0	770	32·4	970	33·6	4,050
DRINKING ONCE A WEEK ..	16·1	2,730	10·8	210	13·1	390	17·7	2,130
DRINKING LESS THAN ONCE A WEEK	26·7	4,530	26·0	510	29·2	870	26·2	3,150
TOTAL DRINKING OCCASIONALLY	42·8	7,270	36·8	720	42·3	1,260	43·9	5,290
TOTAL DRINKING AT ALL ..	76·9	13,050	75·8	1,490	74·7	2,220	77·6	9,330
NEVER DRINKING BEER	23·1	3,930	24·2	480	25·3	750	22·4	2,700
All Men	100·0	16,980	100·0	1,970	100·0	2,980	100·0	12,030
Women:								
DRINKING EVERY DAY	2·2	430	3·7	80	2·6	90	1·8	260
DRINKING MORE THAN ONCE A WEEK BUT NOT EVERY DAY ..	3·8	760	3·2	70	3·3	110	4·1	580
TOTAL DRINKING REGULARLY ..	6·0	1,190	6·9	160	5·9	200	5·9	830
DRINKING ONCE A WEEK ..	7·2	1,430	4·9	110	6·4	220	7·8	1,100
DRINKING LESS THAN ONCE A WEEK	24·9	4,930	23·2	520	24·0	840	25·4	3,580
TOTAL DRINKING OCCASIONALLY	32·1	6,360	28·1	630	30·4	1,060	33·2	4,670
TOTAL DRINKING AT ALL ..	38·1	7,560	35·0	790	36·3	1,260	39·1	5,510
NEVER DRINKING BEER	61·9	12,270	65·0	1,460	63·7	2,210	60·9	8,590
All Women	100·0	19,820	100·0	2,250	100·0	3,480	100·0	14,100
Men and Women:								
DRINKING EVERY DAY	7·4	2,730	11·4	480	7·5	480	6·8	1,770
DRINKING MORE THAN ONCE A WEEK BUT NOT EVERY DAY ..	11·5	4,240	10·5	440	10·6	690	11·9	3,110
TOTAL DRINKING REGULARLY ..	18·9	6,970	21·9	920	18·1	1,170	18·7	4,880
DRINKING ONCE A WEEK ..	11·3	4,160	7·7	320	9·5	610	12·4	3,230
DRINKING LESS THAN ONCE A WEEK	25·7	9,470	24·5	1,030	26·4	1,710	25·7	6,730
TOTAL DRINKING OCCASIONALLY	37·0	13,630	32·2	1,350	35·9	2,320	38·1	9,960
TOTAL DRINKING AT ALL ..	56·0	20,600	54·1	2,280	54·0	3,490	56·8	14,840
NEVER DRINKING BEER	44·0	16,190	45·9	1,940	46·0	2,970	43·2	11,290
All Men and Women	100·0	36,800	100·0	4,210	100·0	6,450	100·0	26,130

*=Either less than 0·5% or less than 10,000

52 BEER-DRINKING HABITS OF THE POPULATION—1ST QUARTER, 1949
(b) By sex and age

	AGED 16–24		AGED 25–34		AGED 35–44		AGED 45–64		AGED 65 AND OVER	
	%	'000	%	'000	%	'000	%	'000	%	'000
Men:										
DRINKING EVERY DAY ..	5·2	120	7·9	270	11·8	440	18·9	1,000	21·9	470
DRINKING MORE THAN ONCE A WEEK BUT NOT EVERY DAY ..	17·1	400	23·9	830	23·5	870	19·7	1,040	15·3	330
TOTAL DRINKING REGULARLY	22·3	530	31·8	1,100	35·3	1,310	38·6	2,040	37·4	800
DRINKING ONCE A WEEK	17·1	410	20·4	710	18·2	670	13·7	720	10·6	230
DRINKING LESS THAN ONCE A WEEK ..	27·2	640	32·5	1,130	27·2	1,010	24·2	1,270	22·0	470
TOTAL DRINKING OCCASIONALLY ..	44·3	1,050	52·9	1,840	45·4	1,680	37·8	1,990	32·6	700
TOTAL DRINKING AT ALL	66·6	1,580	84·6	2,940	80·7	2,990	76·5	4,030	70·0	1,500
NEVER DRINKING BEER ..	33·4	790	15·4	530	19·3	720	23·5	1,240	30·0	650
All Men	100·0	2,370	100·0	3,480	100·0	3,710	100·0	5,270	100·0	2,150
Women:										
DRINKING EVERY DAY ..	*	*	1·1	40	1·4	50	2·8	170	5·2	150
DRINKING MORE THAN ONCE A WEEK BUT NOT EVERY DAY ..	2·3	70	4·0	150	5·0	190	4·0	250	3·4	100
TOTAL DRINKING REGULARLY	2·7	80	5·1	190	6·4	240	6·8	420	8·6	250
DRINKING ONCE A WEEK	4·0	120	10·5	390	9·8	380	6·7	420	4·1	120
DRINKING LESS THAN ONCE A WEEK ..	24·3	750	33·6	1,250	26·4	1,030	22·2	1,380	18·2	530
TOTAL DRINKING OCCASIONALLY ..	28·3	870	44·1	1,640	36·2	1,410	28·9	1,800	22·3	650
TOTAL DRINKING AT ALL	31·0	950	49·2	1,830	42·5	1,650	35·7	2,220	30·9	900
NEVER DRINKING BEER ..	69·0	2,120	50·8	1,890	57·5	2,240	64·3	4,000	69·1	2,020
All Women	100·0	3,070	100·0	3,720	100·0	3,890	100·0	6,220	100·0	2,920
Men and Women:										
DRINKING EVERY DAY ..	2·5	140	4·4	310	6·5	490	10·2	1,170	12·3	620
DRINKING MORE THAN ONCE A WEEK BUT NOT EVERY DAY ..	8·7	470	13·6	980	14·0	1,060	11·2	1,290	8·5	430
TOTAL DRINKING REGULARLY	11·2	610	18·0	1,290	20·5	1,550	21·4	2,460	20·8	1,050
DRINKING ONCE A WEEK	9·7	530	15·2	1,100	13·9	1,060	9·9	1,140	6·9	350
DRINKING LESS THAN ONCE A WEEK ..	25·5	1,390	33·1	2,380	26·8	2,030	23·1	2,650	19·8	1,010
TOTAL DRINKING OCCASIONALLY ..	35·2	1,920	48·3	3,480	40·7	3,090	33·0	3,790	26·7	1,360
TOTAL DRINKING AT ALL	46·5	2,530	66·3	4,770	61·2	4,640	54·4	6,250	47·5	2,410
NEVER DRINKING BEER ..	53·5	2,910	33·7	2,420	38·8	2,950	45·6	5,240	52·5	2,670
All Men and Women ..	100·0	5,440	100·0	7,200	100·0	7,590	100·0	11,490	100·0	5,080

*=Either less than 0·5% or less than 10,000

53 SPIRIT-DRINKING HABITS OF THE POPULATION—1ST QUARTER, 1949
(a) By sex and social class

	ALL CLASSES		CLASS AB		CLASS C		CLASS DE	
	%	'000	%	'000	%	'000	%	'000
Men:								
DRINKING EVERY DAY	1·5	260	5·3	100	1·8	50	0·8	100
DRINKING MORE THAN ONCE A WEEK BUT NOT EVERY DAY ..	3·4	570	10·1	200	4·7	140	1·9	230
TOTAL DRINKING REGULARLY ..	4·9	830	15·4	300	6·5	190	2·7	330
DRINKING ONCE A WEEK ..	4·4	740	9·6	190	5·7	170	3·2	380
DRINKING LESS THAN ONCE A WEEK	38·0	6,470	42·5	840	43·1	1,280	36·2	4,350
TOTAL DRINKING OCCASIONALLY	42·4	7,210	52·1	1,030	48·8	1,450	39·4	4,730
TOTAL DRINKING AT ALL ..	47·3	8,040	67·5	1,330	55·3	1,640	42·1	5,060
NEVER DRINKING SPIRITS ..	52·7	8,940	32·5	640	44·7	1,340	57·9	6,970
All Men	100·0	16,980	100·0	1,970	100·0	2,980	100·0	12,030
Women:								
DRINKING EVERY DAY	0·7	130	3·2	70	0·7	30	*	*
DRINKING MORE THAN ONCE A WEEK BUT NOT EVERY DAY ..	1·8	360	5·6	130	3·2	110	0·9	130
TOTAL DRINKING REGULARLY ..	2·5	490	8·8	200	3·9	140	1·1	160
DRINKING ONCE A WEEK ..	3·6	710	6·9	160	4·7	160	2·8	390
DRINKING LESS THAN ONCE A WEEK	36·6	7,260	43·7	980	42·3	1,470	34·1	4,800
TOTAL DRINKING OCCASIONALLY	40·2	7,970	50·6	1,140	47·0	1,630	36·9	5,190
TOTAL DRINKING AT ALL ..	42·7	8,460	59·4	1,340	50·9	1,770	38·0	5,350
NEVER DRINKING SPIRITS ..	57·3	11,360	40·6	910	49·1	1,710	62·0	8,750
All Women	100·0	19,820	100·0	2,250	100·0	3,480	100·0	14,100
Men and Women:								
DRINKING EVERY DAY	1·0	390	4·2	180	1·2	80	0·5	130
DRINKING MORE THAN ONCE A WEEK BUT NOT EVERY DAY ..	2·6	930	7·6	320	3·9	250	1·4	360
TOTAL DRINKING REGULARLY ..	3·5	1,320	11·8	500	5·1	330	1·9	490
DRINKING ONCE A WEEK ..	3·9	1,450	8·2	340	5·2	330	3·0	770
DRINKING LESS THAN ONCE A WEEK	37·3	13,720	43·2	1,820	42·7	2,750	35·0	9,150
TOTAL DRINKING OCCASIONALLY	41·2	15,170	51·4	2,160	47·9	3,080	38·0	9,920
TOTAL DRINKING AT ALL ..	44·8	16,490	63·2	2,660	53·0	3,410	39·9	10,410
NEVER DRINKING SPIRITS ..	55·2	20,310	36·8	1,550	47·0	3,040	60·1	15,720
All Men and Women	100·0	36,800	100·0	4,210	100·0	6,450	100·0	26,130

*=Either less than 0·5% or less than 10,000

53 SPIRIT-DRINKING HABITS OF THE POPULATION—1ST QUARTER, 1949
(b) By sex and age

	AGED 16–24		AGED 25–34		AGED 35–44		AGED 45–64		AGED 65 AND OVER	
Men:	%	'000	%	'000	%	'000	%	'000	%	'000
DRINKING EVERY DAY ..	*	*	0·6	20	0·9	30	2·2	120	3·7	80
DRINKING MORE THAN ONCE A WEEK BUT NOT EVERY DAY ..	2·2	50	2·7	90	3·9	150	4·1	220	2·9	60
TOTAL DRINKING REGULARLY	2·5	60	3·3	110	4·8	180	6·3	340	6·6	140
DRINKING ONCE A WEEK	3·2	80	5·0	170	4·3	160	4·8	250	3·6	80
DRINKING LESS THAN ONCE A WEEK ..	39·3	930	42·0	1,470	39·7	1,470	35·1	1,850	35·1	750
TOTAL DRINKING OCCASIONALLY ..	42·5	1,010	47·0	1,640	44·0	1,630	39·9	2,100	38·7	830
DRINKING AT ALL ..	45·0	1,070	50·3	1,750	48·8	1,810	46·2	2,440	45·3	970
NEVER DRINKING SPIRITS	55·0	1,300	49·7	1,730	51·2	1,900	53·8	2,830	54·7	1,180
All Men	100·0	2,370	100·0	3,480	100·0	3,710	100·0	5,270	100·0	2,150
Women:										
DRINKING EVERY DAY ..	*	*	*	*	0·7	30	0·9	60	1·0	30
DRINKING MORE THAN ONCE A WEEK BUT NOT EVERY DAY ..	1·5	50	2·4	90	2·9	110	1·4	90	1·1	30
TOTAL DRINKING REGULARLY	1·6	50	2·8	100	3·6	140	2·3	150	2·1	60
DRINKING ONCE A WEEK	3·0	90	4·9	180	5·1	200	3·0	180	1·8	50
DRINKING LESS THAN ONCE A WEEK ..	37·3	1,140	46·8	1,740	40·4	1,570	32·5	2,020	26·6	780
TOTAL DRINKING OCCASIONALLY ..	40·3	1,230	51·7	1,920	45·5	1,770	35·5	2,200	28·4	830
TOTAL DRINKING AT ALL	41·9	1,280	51·5	2,020	49·1	1,910	37·8	2,350	30·5	890
NEVER DRINKING SPIRITS	58·1	1,790	48·5	1,700	50·9	1,980	62·2	3,870	69·5	2,030
All Women	100·0	3,070	100·0	3,720	100·0	3,890	100·0	6,220	100·0	2,920
Men and Women:										
DRINKING EVERY DAY ..	*	*	0·5	30	0·8	60	*	*	2·1	110
DRINKING MORE THAN ONCE A WEEK BUT NOT EVERY DAY ..	1·9	100	2·5	180	3·4	260	2·6	300	1·8	90
TOTAL DRINKING REGULARLY	2·0	110	3·0	210	4·2	320	4·1	480	3·9	200
DRINKING ONCE A WEEK	3·1	170	4·9	350	4·7	360	3·8	440	2·6	130
DRINKING LESS THAN ONCE A WEEK ..	38·1	2,070	44·5	3,210	40·0	3,040	33·7	3,870	30·2	1,530
TOTAL DRINKING OCCASIONALLY ..	42·1	2,240	49·4	3,560	44·7	3,400	37·5	4,310	32·8	1,660
DRINKING AT ALL ..	43·2	2,350	52·4	3,770	48·9	3,720	41·6	4,790	36·7	1,860
NEVER DRINKING SPIRITS	56·8	3,090	47·6	3,430	51·1	3,870	58·4	6,700	63·3	3,220
All Men and Women ..	100·0	5,440	100·0	7,200	100·0	7,590	100·0	11,490	100·0	5,080

*=Either less than 0·5% or less than 10,000

54 WINE-DRINKING HABITS OF THE POPULATION—1ST QUARTER, 1949
By sex and social class

	ALL CLASSES		CLASS AB		CLASS C		CLASS DE	
Men:	%	'000	%	'000	%	'000	%	'000
DRINKING MORE THAN ONCE A WEEK	1·9	320	6·8	130	2·3	70	1·0	120
DRINKING ONCE A WEEK OR LESS FREQUENTLY	39·3	6,670	55·3	1,090	46·9	1,390	34·8	4,190
TOTAL DRINKING WINE	41·2	6,990	62·1	1,220	49·2	1,460	35·8	4,310
NEVER DRINKING WINE	58·8	9,980	37·9	750	50·8	1,510	64·2	7,730
All Men	100·0	16,970	100·0	1,970	100·0	2,970	100·0	12,040
Women:								
DRINKING MORE THAN ONCE A WEEK	1·6	320	7·0	160	2·1	70	0·6	90
DRINKING ONCE A WEEK OR LESS FREQUENTLY	46·5	9,220	59·8	1,340	54·1	1,880	42·5	5,990
TOTAL DRINKING WINE	48·1	9,540	66·8	1,500	56·2	1,950	43·1	6,080
NEVER DRINKING WINE	51·9	10,280	33·2	750	43·8	1,520	56·9	8,020
All Women	100·0	19,820	100·0	2,250	100·0	3,470	100·0	14,100
Men and Women:								
DRINKING MORE THAN ONCE A WEEK	1·7	640	6·9	290	2·2	140	0·8	210
DRINKING ONCE A WEEK OR LESS FREQUENTLY	43·2	15,890	57·7	2,430	50·8	3,280	39·0	10,180
TOTAL DRINKING WINE	44·9	16,530	64·6	2,720	53·0	3,420	39·8	10,390
NEVER DRINKING WINE	55·1	20,270	35·4	1,490	47·0	3,030	60·2	15,740
All Men and Women	100·0	36,800	100·0	4,210	100·0	6,450	100·0	26,130

54   WINE-DRINKING HABITS OF THE POPULATION—1ST QUARTER, 1949

(b) By sex and age

	AGED 16–24		AGED 25–34		AGED 35–44		AGED 45–64		AGED 65 AND OVER	
Men:	%	'000	%	'000	%	'000	%	'000	%	'000
DRINKING MORE THAN ONCE A WEEK ..	0·8	20	1·7	60	1·7	60	2·7	140	1·9	40
DRINKING ONCE A WEEK OR LESS FREQUENTLY	42·6	1,010	43·9	1,530	40·7	1,510	36·6	1,930	32·5	700
TOTAL DRINKING WINE..	43·4	1,030	45·6	1,590	42·4	1,570	39·3	2,070	34·4	740
NEVER DRINKING WINE	56·6	1,340	54·4	1,890	57·6	2,130	60·7	3,200	65·6	1,410
All Men	100·0	2,370	100·0	3,480	100·0	3,700	100·0	5,270	100·0	2,150
Women:										
DRINKING MORE THAN ONCE A WEEK ..	0·8	30	1·3	50	2·2	90	1·9	120	1·4	40
DRINKING ONCE A WEEK OR LESS FREQUENTLY	47·6	1,460	57·5	2,140	50·3	1,950	42·8	2,660	34·3	1,000
TOTAL DRINKING WINE..	48·4	1,490	58·8	2,190	52·5	2,040	44·7	2,780	35·7	1,040
NEVER DRINKING WINE	51·6	1,580	41·2	1,530	47·5	1,850	55·3	3,440	64·3	1,880
All Women	100·0	3,070	100·0	3,720	100·0	3,890	100·0	6,220	100·0	2,920
Men and Women:										
DRINKING MORE THAN ONCE A WEEK ..	0·8	40	1·5	110	2·0	150	2·2	260	1·6	80
DRINKING ONCE A WEEK OR LESS FREQUENTLY	45·4	2,470	50·9	3,660	45·6	3,460	40·0	4,590	33·5	1,700
TOTAL DRINKING WINE..	46·2	2,510	52·4	3,770	47·6	3,610	42·2	4,850	35·1	1,780
NEVER DRINKING WINE	53·8	2,930	47·6	3,430	52·4	3,980	57·8	6,640	64·9	3,290
All Men and Women ..	100·0	5,440	100·0	7,200	100·0	7,590	100·0	11,490	100·0	5,070

NOTE: "Wine" includes port and sherry, but excludes non-alcoholic and tonic wines

55 PROPORTION AND NUMBER OF NON-DRINKERS—1ST QUARTER, 1949

By social class and age

	MEN		WOMEN		MEN AND WOMEN	
	%	'000	%	'000	%	'000
ALL CLASSES AND AGES	18·1	3,070	36·3	7,200	27·9	10,270
CLASS AB	14·6	290	25·2	570	20·2	850
C	17·8	530	32·3	1,120	25·6	1,650
DE	18·7	2,250	39·1	5,510	29·7	7,760
AGE 16–24	25·3	600	40·7	1,250	34·0	1,850
25–34	12·6	440	24·5	910	18·8	1,350
35–44	14·6	540	32·5	1,270	23·8	1,810
45–64	18·6	980	38·9	2,420	29·6	3,400
65 AND OVER ..	23·3	500	46·4	1,360	36·6	1,860

NOTE: These people are those who never drink any form of alcohol, but they are not necessarily teetotal "on principle"

56 USE OF COSMETICS—1ST QUARTER, 1949
By domestic status, social class and age

| | ALL CLASSES AND AGES | | CLASS | | | | | |
			AB		C		DE	
All Women	%	'000	%	'000	%	'000	%	'000
USING: FACE POWDER	68·4	13,560	82·0	1,840	76·8	2,670	64·2	9,050
LIPSTICK	53·7	10,640	65·1	1,460	58·8	2,050	50·6	7,130
CLEANSING PREPARATIONS	28·4	5,640	43·0	970	34·9	1,220	24·5	3,460
ROUGE	22·8	4,510	30·1	680	25·4	890	21·0	2,950
NAIL VARNISH	12·5	2,470	23·9	540	16·3	570	9·7	1,370
MASCARA	4·2	830	8·4	190	5·4	190	3·2	450
NONE OF ABOVE	28·8	5,720	15·9	360	20·8	720	32·9	4,640
Non-Housewives								
USING: FACE POWDER	81·6	4,130	87·3	450	86·5	740	79·6	2,940
LIPSTICK	74·4	3,770	77·8	400	75·8	640	73·6	2,720
CLEANSING PREPARATIONS	40·8	2,068	49·6	260	46·8	400	38·1	1,410
ROUGE	30·0	1,520	27·1	140	30·0	260	30·3	1,120
NAIL VARNISH	24·0	1,220	34·2	180	29·6	250	21·3	790
MASCARA	7·1	360	12·0	60	9·9	80	5·7	210
NONE OF ABOVE	15·1	770	10·2	50	11·8	100	16·6	610
Housewives								
USING: FACE POWDER	63·9	9,430	80·4	1,390	73·7	1,940	58·7	6,110
LIPSTICK	46·6	6,870	61·3	1,060	53·3	1,400	42·4	4,410
CLEANSING PREPARATIONS	24·2	3,570	41·0	710	31·1	820	19·7	2,050
ROUGE	20·3	3,000	31·0	530	24·0	630	17·6	1,830
NAIL VARNISH	8·5	1,250	20·8	360	12·0	320	5·5	580
MASCARA	3·2	470	7·3	130	4·0	100	2·3	240
NONE OF ABOVE	33·5	4,950	17·7	300	23·7	620	38·7	4,020

| | AGE | | | | | | | | | |
	16–24		25–34		35–44		45–64		65 AND OVER	
All Women	%	'000	%	'000	%	'000	%	'000	%	'000
USING: FACE POWDER	91·9	2,820	86·7	3,220	78·6	3,060	58·8	3,660	27·3	800
LIPSTICK	90·7	2,790	81·8	3,040	66·7	2,590	33·0	2,060	5·6	160
CLEANSING PREPARATIONS	43·7	1,340	39·6	1,470	34·6	1,350	20·7	1,290	6·6	190
ROUGE	30·3	930	38·2	1,420	29·3	1,140	14·7	910	3·8	110
NAIL VARNISH	28·3	870	16·2	600	14·0	550	6·7	420	1·3	40
MASCARA	8·9	270	7·1	260	4·3	170	1·8	120	*	*
NONE OF ABOVE	4·8	150	10·8	400	18·1	700	38·5	2,400	70·9	2,070
Non-Housewives										
USING: FACE POWDER	92·2	2,270	90·4	940	84·4	450	65·0	340	25·5	130
LIPSTICK	91·5	2,250	87·4	910	71·9	390	39·5	210	2·9	10
CLEANSING PREPARATIONS	46·5	1,140	49·4	510	45·4	240	27·3	140	4·0	20
ROUGE	30·7	760	42·2	440	36·9	200	19·6	100	4·0	20
NAIL VARNISH	32·1	790	26·1	270	18·0	100	10·1	50	1·1	10
MASCARA	9·4	230	8·6	90	4·4	20	2·4	10	*	*
NONE OF ABOVE	3·9	90	6·7	70	11·5	60	33·6	180	72·7	370
Housewives										
USING: FACE POWDER	90·8	560	85·3	2,280	77·7	2,600	58·3	3,320	27·6	670
LIPSTICK	87·5	540	79·6	2,130	65·9	2,210	32·4	1,850	6·2	150
CLEANSING PREPARATIONS	32·4	200	35·8	960	32·9	1,100	20·0	1,140	7·2	170
ROUGE	28·6	180	36·6	980	28·1	940	14·2	810	3·8	90
NAIL VARNISH	12·8	80	12·3	330	13·4	450	6·4	360	1·4	30
MASCARA	6·5	40	6·6	180	4·3	140	1·8	100	*	*
NONE OF ABOVE	8·3	50	12·4	330	19·2	640	39·0	2,220	70·5	1,710

*=Either less than 0·5% or less than 10,000

NOTE: Informants were asked about their use of cosmetics in the 7 days preceding interview. The figures, therefore, are estimates of the numbers of women using the listed cosmetics in any one week.

57 THE "BEAUTY-CONSCIOUS" WOMAN—1ST QUARTER, 1949

Proportions and numbers of women using some or all of the following:

Cleansing Preparations, Rouge, Nail Varnish, Mascara

By domestic status, social class and age

	ALL CLASSES AND AGES		CLASS					
			AB		C		DE	
	%	'000	%	'000	%	'000	%	'000
All Women								
USING: ALL FOUR	1·4	280	3·4	80	2·2	70	0·9	130
3 OR MORE	6·5	1,290	14·5	330	8·4	290	4·8	680
2 OR MORE	18·5	3,660	30·9	700	23·1	800	15·3	2,170
1 OR MORE	41·4	8,210	56·6	1,250	48·5	1,690	37·2	5,260
NONE OF FOUR ..	58·6	11,610	43·4	970	51·5	1,790	62·8	8,850
Non-Housewives								
USING: ALL FOUR	2·4	120	3·9	20	4·1	30	1·8	70
3 OR MORE	11·6	590	18·0	90	14·0	110	10·2	380
2 OR MORE	29·4	1,490	35·6	180	34·2	280	27·5	1,020
1 OR MORE	58·4	2,960	65·5	340	64·2	540	56·1	2,080
NONE OF FOUR ..	41·6	2,110	34·5	180	35·8	300	43·9	3,700
Housewives								
USING: ALL FOUR	1·1	160	3·3	60	1·5	40	0·6	60
3 OR MORE	4·8	700	13·4	240	6·5	170	2·9	300
2 OR MORE	14·7	2,170	29·5	520	19·5	510	11·0	1,150
1 OR MORE	35·6	5,250	53·9	940	43·5	1,140	30·5	3,180
NONE OF FOUR ..	64·4	9,510	46·1	800	56·5	1,490	69·5	7,230

	AGE									
	16–24		25–34		35–44		45–64		65 AND OVER	
	%	'000	%	'000	%	'000	%	'000	%	'000
All Women										
USING: ALL FOUR	2·6	80	2·3	90	1·7	70	0·9	50	*	*
3 OR MORE	11·5	350	9·5	360	9·0	350	3·6	230	0·6	20
2 OR MORE	31·2	950	29·2	1,090	23·0	890	10·4	650	2·7	80
1 OR MORE	68·8	2,010	60·0	2,230	48·4	1,880	29·3	1,830	8·7	260
NONE OF FOUR ..	34·2	1,050	40·0	1,490	51·6	2,010	70·7	4,400	91·3	2,670
Non-Housewives										
USING: ALL FOUR	2·9	70	3·2	30	2·0	10	1·1	10	*	*
3 OR MORE	12·8	310	15·6	160	13·2	70	7·1	40	*	*
2 OR MORE	34·2	840	38·5	400	29·1	160	15·1	80	2·1	10
1 OR MORE	68·8	1,690	69·0	720	60·3	330	36·4	190	6·5	30
NONE OF FOUR ..	31·2	770	31·0	320	39·7	210	63·6	330	93·5	470
Housewives										
USING: ALL FOUR	1·5	10	2·0	50	1·7	60	0·8	40	*	*
3 OR MORE	6·3	40	7·2	190	8·4	280	3·2	180	0·6	10
2 OR MORE	19·1	120	25·6	680	22·1	740	9·9	560	2·8	60
1 OR MORE	53·6	330	56·5	1,510	46·5	1,560	28·6	1,630	9·1	210
NONE OF FOUR ..	46·4	280	43·5	1,160	53·5	1,790	71·4	4,070	90·9	2,200

*=Either less than 0·5% or less than 10,000

NOTE: The term "beauty-conscious" has been coined to describe women who appreciate the value of cosmetics as aids to beauty. The use of powder and lipstick is not regarded as a criterion, as their use is becoming a commonplace of modern society, but women using one or more of the cosmetics listed in the heading to this table *are* defined as "beauty-conscious".

58 THE "BEAUTY-CONSCIOUS" WOMAN—1ST QUARTER, 1949

By age-groups within social class

	ALL CLASSES	CLASS AB	CLASS C	CLASS DE
AGE:	%	%	%	%
16–24	66	77	72	63
25–34	60	74	72	56
35–44	49	72	59	41
45–64	29	53	38	22
65 AND OVER ..	9	21	14	5
ALL AGES	41	57	49	37

NOTE: For definition of the term "beauty-conscious", see footnote to *Table* 57

59 NUMBERS AND PROPORTIONS OF WOMEN HAVING HAD PERMANENT WAVES DURING THE FOUR MONTHS PREVIOUS TO DATE OF ENQUIRY —1ST QUARTER, 1949

By domestic status, occupation, social class and age

	ESTIMATED POPULATION	PERMS IN LAST FOUR MONTHS					
		HAIRDRESSER		HOME		TOTAL	
		NO.	%	NO.	%	NO.	%
All Women	19,820,000	2,460,000	12·4	470,000	2·4	2,930,000	14·8
BY DOMESTIC STATUS:							
HOUSEWIVES—NON-WORKING	11,040,000	1,120,000	10·2	210,000	1·9	1,330,000	12·1
HOUSEWIVES—WORKING ..	3,720,000	600,000	16·0	80,000	2·3	680,000	18·3
OTHER WOMEN	5,070,000	740,000	14·6	180,000	3·5	920,000	18·1
BY CLASS:							
A	730,000	170,000	23·2	22,000	3·0	190,000	26·2
B	1,510,000	280,000	18·7	40,000	2·5	320,000	21·2
C	3,480,000	580,000	16·7	100,000	3·0	680,000	19·7
D	12,380,000	1,280,000	10·3	290,000	2·3	1,570,000	12·6
E	1,720,000	150,000	8·9	20,000	1·1	170,000	10·0
BY AGE:							
16–24	3,070,000	450,000	14·7	120,000	4·0	570,000	18·7
25–34	3,720,000	510,000	13·8	140,000	3·8	650,000	17·6
35–44	3,890,000	580,000	14·8	100,000	2·5	680,000	17·3
45–64	6,220,000	750,000	12·1	100,000	1·6	850,000	13·7
65 AND OVER	2,920,000	170,000	5·7	10,000	0·5	180,000	6·2

NOTE: In this and subsequent tables on permanent waves, working is defined as gainfully employed, whole or part time, as in *Table* 29

60 NUMBERS AND PROPORTIONS OF WOMEN WHO HAVE PERMANENT WAVES AT ALL, AND NUMBERS AND PROPORTIONS DOING SO IN ANY ONE MONTH—1ST QUARTER, 1949

By domestic status, occupation, social class and age

	ESTIMATED POPULATION	HAVING PERMS AT ALL		HAVING A PERM IN ANY ONE MONTH		
		NO.	AS % OF ALL INFORMANTS	NO.	AS % OF ALL "HAVING PERMS AT ALL"	AS % OF ALL INFORMANTS
All Women	19,820,000	9,620,000	**48·5**	870,000	**9·0**	**4·4**
BY DOMESTIC STATUS:						
HOUSEWIVES—NON-WORKING	11,040,000	4,900,000	**44·5**	430,000	**8·7**	**3·9**
HOUSEWIVES—WORKING ..	3,720,000	2,060,000	**55·4**	180,000	**8·9**	**5·0**
OTHER WOMEN	5,070,000	2,660,000	**52·4**	260,000	**9·8**	**5·1**
BY CLASS:						
A	730,000	400,000	**54·6**	50,000	**12·8**	**7·0**
B	1,510,000	850,000	**56·0**	140,000	**15·9**	**8·9**
C	3,480,000	1,950,000	**56·0**	180,000	**9·0**	**5·0**
D	12,380,000	5,820,000	**47·0**	460,000	**8·2**	**3·7**
E	1,720,000	600,000	**34·8**	40,000	**7·3**	**2·5**
BY AGE:						
16–24	3,070,000	1,680,000	**54·6**	170,000	**10·3**	**5·6**
25–34	3,720,000	2,150,000	**57·8**	160,000	**7·4**	**4·3**
35–44	3,890,000	2,250,000	**58·0**	180,000	**7·8**	**4·5**
45–64	6,220,000	2,930,000	**47·1**	300,000	**10·2**	**4·8**
65 AND OVER	2,920,000	610,000	**20·6**	60,000	**10·3**	**2·1**

61 NUMBERS OF WOMEN HAVING A PERMANENT WAVE IN ANY ONE MONTH, AT A HAIRDRESSER'S OR AT HOME—1ST QUARTER, 1949

By domestic status, occupation, social class and age

| | TOTAL FEMALE POPULATION | | HAVING A PERM IN ANY ONE MONTH | | | | | |
| | | | AT HAIRDRESSER | | AT HOME | | TOTAL | |
	ESTIMATED NUMBER	% OF TOTAL IN EACH GROUP	ESTIMA-TED NUMBER	% OF TOTAL IN EACH GROUP	ESTIMA-TED NUMBER	% OF TOTAL IN EACH GROUP	ESTIMA-TED NUMBER	% OF TOTAL IN EACH GROUP
All Women	19,820,000	**100**	730,000	**100**	140,000	**100**	870,000	**100**
BY DOMESTIC STATUS:								
HOUSEWIVES—NON-WORKING	11,040,000	**56**	360,000	**49**	70,000	**48**	430,000	**49**
HOUSEWIVES—WORKING ..	3,720,000	**19**	160,000	**22**	20,000	**16**	180,000	**21**
OTHER WOMEN	5,070,000	**25**	210,000	**29**	50,000	**36**	260,000	**30**
BY CLASS:								
A	730,000	**4**	40,000	**6**	5,000	**4**	45,000	**6**
B	1,510,000	**8**	120,000	**17**	20,000	**12**	140,000	**16**
C	3,480,000	**17**	150,000	**20**	30,000	**19**	180,000	**20**
D	12,380,000	**62**	380,000	**52**	80,000	**61**	460,000	**53**
E	1,720,000	**9**	40,000	**5**	5,000	**4**	45,000	**5**
BY AGE:								
16–24	3,070,000	**16**	140,000	**19**	40,000	**26**	180,000	**20**
25–34	3,720,000	**19**	120,000	**17**	30,000	**25**	150,000	**18**
35–44	3,890,000	**20**	150,000	**20**	30,000	**19**	180,000	**20**
45–64	6,220,000	**30**	260,000	**36**	35,000	**26**	295,000	**35**
65 AND OVER	2,920,000	**15**	60,000	**8**	5,000	**4**	65,000	**7**

62 NUMBERS OF WOMEN HAVING PERMS IN ANY ONE MONTH
SHOWING THE NUMBER AND PROPORTION
OF THEM WHO HAD HOME PERMANENT WAVES
—1ST QUARTER, 1949

By domestic status, occupation, social class and age

| | HAVING PERMS IN ANY ONE MONTH | | |
| | | HOME PERMS | |
	ALL PERMS	NO.	% OF "ALL PERMS"
All Women	870,000	140,000	**16**
BY DOMESTIC STATUS:			
HOUSEWIVES—NON-WORKING	430,000	70,000	**16**
HOUSEWIVES—WORKING ..	180,000	20,000	**12**
OTHER WOMEN	260,000	50,000	**20**
BY CLASS:			
A	45,000	5,000	**11**
B	140,000	20,000	**12**
C	180,000	30,000	**16**
D	460,000	80,000	**18**
E	45,000	5,000	**13**
BY AGE:			
16–24	180,000	40,000	**21**
25–34	150,000	30,000	**22**
35–44	180,000	30,000	**16**
45–64	295,000	35,000	**12**
65 AND OVER	65,000	5,000	**9**

63 THE CINEMA-GOING HABITS OF POPULATION—1ST QUARTER, 1949

Men and Women

(a) By social class

Going to Cinema:		ALL CLASSES		CLASS AB		CLASS C		CLASS DE	
		%	'000	%	'000	%	'000	%	'000
TWICE A WEEK OR MORE	..	16·6	6,100	7·6	320	12·5	810	19·0	4,970
ONCE A WEEK	.. ..	23·9	8,790	20·2	850	24·3	1,570	24·4	6,370
GOING REGULARLY ..	..	40·5	14,890	27·8	1,170	36·8	2,380	43·4	11,340
ONCE A FORTNIGHT ..	..	6·8	2,490	9·7	410	8·2	530	6·0	1,560
ONCE A MONTH	.. ..	8·9	3,280	13·9	580	10·0	650	7·8	2,040
LESS OFTEN	..	26·4	9,720	33·6	1,420	30·6	1,970	24·2	6,330
GOING OCCASIONALLY	..	42·1	15,490	57·2	2,410	48·8	3,150	38·0	9,930
NEVER	..	17·4	6,420	15·0	630	14·4	930	18·6	4,860
All Men and Women ..	..	100·0	36,800	100·0	4,210	100·0	6,460	100·0	26,130

(b) By age

Going to Cinema:	AGED 16–24		AGED 25–34		AGED 35–44		AGED 45–64		AGED 65 AND OVER	
	%	'000	%	'000	%	'000	%	'000	%	'000
TWICE A WEEK OR MORE	40·0	2,180	18·3	1,320	14·5	1,100	11·2	1,290	4·3	220
ONCE A WEEK	32·2	1,750	31·6	2,270	24·7	1,870	20·3	2,330	11·0	560
GOING REGULARLY ..	72·2	3,930	49·9	3,590	39·2	2,970	31·5	3,620	15·3	780
ONCE A FORTNIGHT ..	8·3	450	9·5	680	7·1	540	5·9	680	2·8	140
ONCE A MONTH	7·1	390	9·5	690	10·3	780	9·3	1,070	7·0	350
LESS OFTEN	9·4	510	22·4	1,620	29·9	2,270	32·2	3,700	32·0	1,620
GOING OCCASIONALLY ..	24·8	1,350	41·4	2,980	47·3	3,590	47·4	5,440	41·8	2,120
NEVER	3·0	160	8·7	630	13·5	1,030	21·1	2,430	42·9	2,180
All Men and Women ..	100·0	5,440	100·0	7,200	100·0	7,590	100·0	11,490	100·0	5,080

64 PROPORTIONS AND NUMBERS OF "ADULT" POPULATION ATTENDING GREYHOUND RACE MEETINGS, BY FREQUENCY OF ATTENDANCE —1ST QUARTER, 1948

(a) By sex and social class

	ALL CLASSES AND AGES		CLASS AB		CLASS C		CLASS DE	
Men:	%	'000	%	'000	%	'000	%	'000
ATTENDING REGULARLY ..	2·8	460	1·5	30	2·1	60	3·1	370
ATTENDING OCCASIONALLY ..	5·2	870	3·5	60	4·3	120	5·7	680
NEVER GO NOW	92·0	15,320	95·0	1,750	93·6	2,680	91·2	10,900
All Men	100·0	16,650	100·0	1,840	100·0	2,860	100·0	11,950
Women:								
ATTENDING REGULARLY ..	0·5	100	0·5	10	0·5	20	0·5	70
ATTENDING OCCASIONALLY ..	1·8	350	1·4	30	2·0	70	1·8	260
NEVER GO NOW	97·7	18,900	98·1	1,990	97·5	3,240	97·7	13,660
All Women	100·0	19,350	100·0	2,030	100·0	3,330	100·0	13,990
Men and Women Combined:								
ATTENDING REGULARLY ..	1·5	560	1·0	40	1·3	80	1·7	440
ATTENDING OCCASIONALLY ..	3·4	1,210	2·4	90	3·0	190	3·6	930
NEVER GO NOW	95·1	34,230	96·6	3,740	95·7	5,920	94·7	24,570
All Men and Women	100·0	36,000	100·0	3,870	100·0	6,190	100·0	25,940

64 PROPORTIONS AND NUMBERS OF "ADULT" POPULATION ATTENDING GREYHOUND RACE MEETINGS, BY FREQUENCY OF ATTENDANCE —1ST QUARTER, 1948

(b) By sex and age

	AGED 16–24		AGED 25–34		AGED 35–44		AGED 45–64		AGED 65 AND OVER	
Men:	%	'000	%	'000	%	'000	%	'000	%	'000
ATTENDING REGULARLY	1·2	30	4·1	140	3·9	140	2·5	130	0·9	20
ATTENDING OCCASIONALLY	4·4	100	6·3	230	5·6	200	5·3	270	3·2	60
NEVER GO NOW	94·4	2,250	89·6	3,160	90·5	3,340	92·2	4,710	95·9	1,870
All Men	100·0	2,380	100·0	3,530	100·0	3,680	100·0	5,110	100·0	1,950
Women:										
ATTENDING REGULARLY	0·7	20	0·8	30	0·6	20	*	*	*	*
ATTENDING OCCASIONALLY	2·1	60	2·3	80	2·6	100	1·4	90	0·5	10
NEVER GO NOW	97·2	2,970	96·9	3,530	96·8	3,730	98·2	6,080	99·4	2,600
All Women	100·0	3,050	100·0	3,640	100·0	3,850	100·0	6,190	100·0	2,620
Men & Women Combined:										
ATTENDING REGULARLY	0·9	50	2·4	170	2·2	170	1·3	150	0·5	20
ATTENDING OCCASIONALLY	3·1	170	4·3	310	4·0	300	3·2	360	1·6	70
NEVER GO NOW	96·0	5,210	93·3	6,690	93·8	7,060	95·5	10,790	97·9	4,480
All Men and Women ..	100·0	5,430	100·0	7,170	100·0	7,530	100·0	11,300	100·0	4,570

*=Either less than 0·5% or less than 10,000

Source: *The Hulton Readership Survey 1948*

NOTE : Questions relating to attendance at greyhound race meetings were not asked in the 1949 Survey

65 PROPORTIONS AND NUMBERS OF THE POPULATION AGED 21 AND OVER PARTICIPATING IN FOOTBALL POOLS—1ST QUARTER, 1949

(a) By sex and social class

	ALL CLASSES		CLASS A		CLASS B		CLASS C		CLASS D		CLASS E	
	%	'000	%	'000	%	'000	%	'000	%	'000	%	'000
MEN	49·5	7,850	22·5	140	34·5	420	42·8	1,200	55·3	5,480	46·1	610
WOMEN ..	18·8	3,400	8·6	60	14·4	200	17·0	550	20·3	2,400	11·9	190
MEN AND WOMEN	33·1	11,250	15·1	200	23·7	620	28·9	1,750	37·3	7,880	28·0	800

(b) By age and sex

	AGED 21–24		AGED 25–34		AGED 35–44		AGED 45–64		AGED 65 AND OVER	
	%	'000	%	'000	%	'000	%	'000	%	'000
MEN	60·6	760	56·6	1,970	53·7	1,990	47·2	2,490	29·3	630
WOMEN	24·2	330	23·6	880	22·5	880	18·1	1,130	6·6	190
MEN AND WOMEN	41·6	1,090	39·5	2,850	37·7	2,870	31·4	3,620	16·2	820

NOTE: Informants were asked if they had sent in a football pool coupon within the seven days preceding the interview. The figures are, therefore, estimates of the weekly proportions and numbers of participants.

66 DISTRIBUTION OF THE TOTAL AMOUNT SPENT WEEKLY BETWEEN PARTICIPANTS IN EACH CATEGORY OF INTENSITY—1ST QUARTER, 1949

STAKE	PERCENTAGE IN EACH CATEGORY		TOTAL AMOUNT SPENT WEEKLY			PERCEN-TAGE SPENT WEEKLY IN EACH CATEGORY
	% OF THE TOTAL POPULATION (AGED 21 AND OVER)	% OF ALL PARTI-CIPANTS	BY MEN £	BY WOMEN £	BY MEN AND WOMEN £	
10/- OR MORE	1·2	3·6	292,000	14,000	306,000	16·9
5/- AND LESS THAN 10/- ..	5·1	15·3	460,000	44,000	504,000	27·8
2/6 AND LESS THAN 5/- ..	12·5	38·0	522,000	129,000	651,000	35·7
1/- AND LESS THAN 2/6 ..	12·8	38·6	203,000	140,000	343,000	18·9
LESS THAN 1/-	1·5	4·5	2,000	10,000	12,000	0·7
TOTAL	33·1	100·0	1,479,000	337,000	1,816,000	100·0

67 PERCENTAGE OF PARTICIPANTS IN EACH CATEGORY OF INTENSITY—1ST QUARTER, 1949

(a) By sex

STAKE	MEN	WOMEN	MEN AND WOMEN
10/- OR MORE	4·8	0·6	3·6
5/- AND LESS THAN 10/- ..	19·9	4·5	15·3
2/6 AND LESS THAN 5/-	43·3	26·0	38·0
1/- AND LESS THAN 2/6	30·8	56·9	38·6
LESS THAN 1/-	1·2	12·0	4·5

(b) By age

STAKE	MEN AND WOMEN COMBINED				
	AGED 21–24	AGED 25–34	AGED 35–44	AGED 45–64	AGED 65 AND OVER
10/- OR MORE	3·0	3·5	4·1	3·4	3·1
5/- AND LESS THAN 10/-	14·4	16·4	16·5	13·9	14·4
2/6 AND LESS THAN 5/-	34·0	40·2	38·4	39·3	28·4
1/- AND LESS THAN 2/6	39·5	37·0	36·3	39·4	48·8
LESS THAN 1/-	9·1	2·9	4·7	4·1	5·3

68 AVERAGE AMOUNT SPENT WEEKLY (in shillings) PER PARTICIPANT —1ST QUARTER, 1949

By sex and social class

	ALL CLASSES	CLASS A	CLASS B	CLASS C	CLASS D	CLASS E
MEN	3·8	7·6	4·5	4·0	3·6	3·3
WOMEN	2·0	2·1	2·0	2·0	2·0	1·7
MEN AND WOMEN ..	3·2	6·0	3·7	3·3	3·1	2·9

(b) By sex and age

	AGED 21–24	AGED 25–34	AGED 35–44	AGED 45–64	AGED 65 AND OVER
MEN	3·5	3·9	3·9	3·7	3·2
WOMEN	1·6	2·0	1·9	2·1	1·5
MEN AND WOMEN ..	2·9	3·3	3·3	3·2	2·3

SUMMARY INDEX OF TABLES